Serving Urban Teens

Recent Titles in
Libraries Unlimited Professional Guides for Young Adult Librarians
C. Allen Nichols and Mary Anne Nichols, Series Editors

Serving Older Teens
Sheila B. Anderson

Thinking Outside the Book: Alternatives for Today's Teen Library Collection
C. Allen Nichols

Serving Homeschooled Teens and Their Parents
Maureen T. Lerch and Janet Welch

Reaching Out to Religious Youth: A Guide to Services, Programs, and Collections
L. Kay Carman

Classic Connections: Turning Teens on to Great Literature
Holly Koelling

Digital Inclusion, Teens, and Your Library: Exploring the Issues
and Acting on Them
Lesley S. J. Farmer

Extreme Teens: Library Services to Nontraditional Young Adults
Sheila B. Anderson

A Passion for Print: Promoting Reading and Books to Teens
Kristine Mahood

The Teen-Centered Book Club: Readers into Leaders
Bonnie Kunzel and Constance Hardesty

Teen Programs with Punch: A Month-by-Month Guide
Valerie A. Ott

Serving Young Teens and 'Tweens
Sheila B. Anderson, editor

The Guy-Friendly Teen Library: Serving Male Teens
Rollie Welch

SERVING URBAN TEENS

Paula Brehm-Heeger

Libraries Unlimited Professional Guides for Young Adult
Librarians Series
C. Allen Nichols and Mary Anne Nichols, Series Editors

A Member of the Greenwood Publishing Group

Westport, Connecticut • London

Library of Congress Cataloging-in-Publication Data

Brehm-Heeger, Paula.
  Serving urban teens / Paula Brehm-Heeger.
     p. cm. — (Libraries Unlimited professional guides for young adult
  librarians series, ISSN 1532–5571)
  Includes bibliographical references and index.
  ISBN 978–1–59158–377–6 (alk. paper)
  1. Young adults' libraries—United States. 2. Libraries and teenagers—
United States. 3. Libraries and metropolitan areas—United States. I. Title.
Z718.5.B74 2008
027.62'6—dc22   2007045415

British Library Cataloguing in Publication Data is available.

Library of Congress Catalog Card Number: 200745415
ISBN: 978–1–59158–377–6
ISSN: 1532–5571

First published in 2008

Libraries Unlimited, 88 Post Road West, Westport, CT 06881
A Member of the Greenwood Publishing Group, Inc.
www.lu.com

Printed in the United States of America

The paper used in this book complies with the
Permanent Paper Standard issued by the National
Information Standards Organization (Z39.48-1984).

10 9 8 7 6 5 4 3 2 1

For Isabella

CONTENTS

SERIES FOREWORD

We firmly believe that teens should be provided equal access to library services, as well as an equal level of services as those provided to other library customers. We are proud of our association with Libraries Unlimited. It continues to prove itself as the premier publisher of books to help library staff serve teens. This series has succeeded because our authors know the needs of those library employees working with young adults. Without exception, they have written useful and practical handbooks for library staff. In this volume, we're especially proud to add Paula Brehm-Heeger's name to that list of authors.

Often in urban settings, library services can play an important role in teens' lives. Her contribution will help urban libraries and their employees meet the unique needs of teens living in their cities. Paula's efforts in Cincinnati have helped her local library, and we are sure her advice and research will help yours as well.

We hope this series is useful to you, providing you with helpful ideas to serve teens, and that Paula's work will further inspire you to do great things to make teens at home in your library.

Mary Anne Nichols
C. Allen Nichols
Series Editors

ACKNOWLEDGMENTS

I would like to offer my deepest thanks and gratitude to Tricia Suellentrop, Michele Gorman, Sarah Cornish Debraski, Janet Buttenweiser, Marin Younker, and Rollie Welch for teaching me what it truly means to be an advocate for teens; Sandy Bolek, Rick Ryan, Therese Bigelow and all of the Cancun "West Side" librarians for their continued personal support; my mom and dad for making public libraries a part of my life; and my husband Ned—where would I (and many of my commas) be without you?

INTRODUCTION

Growing up during the 1980s in an area roughly fifteen minutes, or just a short car ride, from the heart of the city of Cincinnati, Ohio, I spent a lot of time at the public library, particularly as a middle school student. I was a part-time latchkey kid, and it was just five minutes from my junior high to the local library. After school, the library was often where I went. I wish I could report that I spent my afternoons roaming the library's stacks discovering the great literature of the world. I did enjoy my time at the library, but I was *not* busy finding great works of literature. Instead, my friends and I tromped through the library, loudly stopping by the drinking fountain, the pay phone, the restroom, and the tables full of other teens to talk, flirt, and socialize. Although it is likely the library staff members were hoping we would sit quietly and read or study, my friends and I were generally interested in doing just about anything besides sitting quietly. We did not have anywhere else to be, and no one was at home waiting for us. The library was a relatively safe option for something to do and someplace to go after school. We were there to take advantage of a great local resource, whether or not the library was ready for us.

Anyone visiting today the library branch of my teenage years would see a good example of a growing trend in libraries across the United States. My library was built originally to serve a suburban population perhaps based on the concept that families—parents and children—would visit the library together, use or check out library material, and leave. Probably from the outset, the library of my childhood served urban teens, and surely my use of the library was as an urban teen in that it often did not involve visiting the library with parents or family members and frequently revolved around interacting with other teenagers rather than using or checking out library resources. These kinds of characteristics of library use that have been traditionally associated with urban locations are increasingly being found throughout large metropolitan areas, and my library is no different—it is increasingly serving urban teens. Library branches in so-called inner-ring suburbs, the older, first ring of suburbs that are "adjacent to or located in close proximity to major cities" (Michigan Suburbs Alliance, *Why Inner Ring*), and in smaller cities are increasingly sharing urban experiences similar to those of traditional inner-city or downtown libraries. These smaller cities and inner-ring suburbs are increasingly serving a diverse population living in areas with more concentrated poverty and deteriorating infrastructure (Michigan Suburbs Alliance, *Why Inner Ring*). A visitor to my own library would still find teens using the library in so-called traditional ways: studying, doing research, and working on homework alone or with a group of friends. But they would also find an increasing number of teens using the library in more typically urban ways, much the way my friends and I utilized the library, as a place to hang out, especially during the after-school hours for teens who would certainly identify more with the term *urban* than the term *suburban*. Working in Kansas City and Independence, Missouri; Anderson, Indiana; and Cincinnati, Ohio, as a professional librarian, I have seen these same trends in teen library use repeated again and again, and during each year of my professional experience I have heard librarians talking about the adjustments they are (hopefully) making to better serve their urban teens. This usage has become a significant and important part of the very services that the library offers to teen customers in many areas. The question is, are libraries truly recognizing this trend and adapting to it?

This trend is not merely a figment of the imaginations of librarians talking at conferences or systemwide meetings in large metropolitan library systems. This demographic shift is demonstrated in part by a change in the very definitions used by the U.S. Census Bureau, which in 2003 changed its definitions of *urban* to ensure a more accurate count of who lives in urban settings. Tellingly, the U.S. Census Bureau's definitions of two types of urban areas, *urbanized areas* and *urban clusters* were changed (United States Department of Agriculture, Measuring Reality: New Definitions), and the Census Bureau now classifies as urban "all territory, population, and housing units located within an urbanized area or urban cluster," which is generally defined as areas that have "a population density of at least 1,000 people per square mile" and surrounding areas that have an overall density of "at least 500 people per square mile" (United States Census Bureau, Geographic Changes for Census 2000 and Glossary). These densely settled urban areas do not necessarily include any a large city (currently, more than 150 urbanized areas do not), though urban cities and large metropolitan areas do continue to be at the core of what is considered urban. For example, Atlanta, Georgia, and San Diego, California, both appear on the Census Bureau's list of urbanized areas as one might expect. But this list also includes Missoula, Montana, and Muskegon, Michigan (United States Census Bureau, Alphabetically Sorted List of Urban Areas). Likewise, the Census Bureau's list of urban clusters contains several areas that many would not associate with being urban in any sense, including Jackson, Wyoming, and Princeton, Indiana (United States Census Bureau, Alphabetically Sorted List of Urban Clusters). The changes in the Census Bureau's definitions reflect a widespread demographic shift, "a decade of urban growth and restructuring" (United States Department of Agriculture, Measuring Rurality: New Definitions) in which the population density and socioeconomic characteristics typically associated with urban are now found not just in inner-city or downtown areas but in many areas within metropolitan areas and in smaller cities outside of metropolitan areas. The traditional boundaries of what was considered urban (and which were frequently followed when thinking about library services) are increasingly becoming less clear, less concentrated, more diffuse, and more widespread. As the U.S. Census Bureau describes, "Many places are now split between urban and rural components," and, notably, after updating their definitions to adequately describe this new reality, an additional 3 percent of the total United States population (approximately 5 million people) were newly classified as urban due to this recognition that areas can be both partly urban and partly rural (United States Census Bureau, Measuring Rurality: What is Rural?), with 68 percent of Americans living in areas they describe as urban (United States Department of Agriculture 2007).

What does this mean for libraries? The Census Bureau definitions likely reflect the reality that more and more people in the United States are living in increasingly urban environments. Many public libraries that, even ten years ago, served primarily suburban or even rural areas now serve communities considered urban in some way. No longer is it solely the charge of older libraries or a downtown or main library located in the inner city to serve urban teens. As urbanization has spread in communities across the United States, so has the need for libraries to adjust their resources and services to meet the needs of today's young people living in these new urban environments.

How do teens in these urban areas differ from teens in rural or truly suburban areas? Urban areas are home to large numbers of teens. Like all teens, urban teens like to travel in groups, and because these teens live in heavily populated areas, there are more of them. Teens living in urban areas tend to be a less homogenous group than in suburban and rural environments, coming from a wide array of cultural, ethnic, economic, and religious backgrounds. This diversity makes librarians' jobs more exciting but also requires thoughtful consideration for ensuring that services and programs emphasize inclusion, celebrate diversity, and provide opportunities for all teens to be involved. Additionally, although librarians working in urban environments will confirm that large groups of teens visit and hang out at libraries after school, these same librarians sometimes face the issue that teens in urban areas have access to more facilities and institutions that provide programming and activities specifically designed to attract teenagers. Libraries in urban environments face competition for teens' valuable time when it comes to programming and activities in a way that libraries in suburban and rural areas do not experience. Urban teens also tend to be relatively sophisticated, likely having had firsthand experiences (not just through watching things on TV or on the Internet) that produce a more worldly perspective than their rural and suburban peers. I can recall visiting a library located in a rural area and watching a teen talent show. Although the teens involved were clearly having a great time, the urban teens I knew would have had very different expectations for song selections, talents, and audience members. The teens I worked with would surely have been more likely to sing pop singles, present a dance routine, and invite their friends to attend, whereas the teens at the rural library were singing classic country and well-known hymns, playing the piano, and inviting their parents to the show.

This guide is intended to offer practical and effective models for creating and enhancing public library service to teens, giving special consideration to both the opportunities and challenges discussed previously that are presented by urban settings. It is a resource for those working in public libraries in areas accustomed to serving urban teens as well as those working in increasingly urban environments who may have less experience serving the large volume of diverse and sophisticated teens visiting the library every day. Novice and experienced teen librarians, generalists as well as reference librarians, frontline library staff, managers, administrators, and other library decision makers will find a wealth of information to help build better services to address the needs of urban teens.

In chapter 1, those working in libraries serving urban areas will find historical context for their service. Chapter 2 examines common organizational structures for teen services in urban settings, methods for supporting teen services through better communication, key competencies needed by staff serving teens, and the valuable role teens can play as both paid staff and regular volunteers. A framework for making staff training in serving teens a reality, including how to effectively gain administrative and management support and the steps to take in designing and implementing teen services training, can be found in chapter 3. Chapter 4 discusses why libraries serving urban areas need to create and maintain spaces dedicated specifically to teens, ideas for addressing staff concerns about creating and expanding these teen areas, the concept of the library as a so-called third place for teens in the community, technology, security, marketing considerations, and concrete tips for making teen areas a reality. In chapter 5, you will find an overview of some of the most popular genres and titles frequently recommended for and requested by teens in urban areas, ideas on how to ensure your organization's collection development process supports the creation of high-interest, high-demand teen collections, tips for involving teens in the collection development process, and suggestions on how to evaluate your collection. Chapter 6 offers options for the beginning teen programmer looking for ideas on generating support, finding funding, and planning regular teen programs and includes tips for experienced programmers looking for new ideas along with suggestions for effectively sharing program resources in multibranch library systems. Finally, chapter 7 discusses unique factors affecting partnerships in urban library settings and offers examples of outstanding services for teens in urban areas developed through effective outreach and partnerships.

Defining who is an urban teen or what exactly qualifies as an urban area is an increasing complex task, and generalizations will never adequately address the needs of the wide variety of teens living in urban areas. This guide, however, does offer public libraries serving both traditional urban and increasingly urban areas suggestions to more fully understand and recognize the demands, challenges, and opportunities presented by the changes in their communities and the needs of their teen customers in order to continue to succeed in the years to come.

WORKS CITED

Michigan Suburbs Alliance. *Why Inner Ring?* Accessed July 5, 2007, available at http://www.michigansuburbsalliance.org/about_us/why_inner_ring.php.

United States Census Bureau. *Geographic Changes for Census 2000 + Glossary,* "Urban and Rural." Accessed March 31, 2007, available at http://www.census.gov/geo/www/tiger/glossary.html#urbanandrural.

United States Census Bureau. Alphabetically sorted list of Urban Areas. Accessed July 6, 2007, available at http://www.census.gov/geo/www/ua/ua2k.txt.

United States Census Bureau. Alphabetically sorted list of Urban Clusters. Accessed July 6, 2007, available at http://www.census.gov/geo/www/ua/uc2k.txt.

United States Department of Agriculture, Economic Research Service. *Measuring Rurality: New Definitions in 2003.* Accessed March 31, 2007, available at http://www.ers.usda.gov/Briefing/Rurality/NewDefinitions/.

United States Department of Agriculture, Economic Research Service. *Measuring Rurality: What Is Rural?* Accessed March 31, 2007, available at http://www.ers.usda.gov/Briefing/Rurality/WhatIsRural/.

1

◇ ◇ ◇

HIGHLIGHTS IN THE HISTORY OF SERVING URBAN TEENS

It is difficult to imagine an urban area in the United States without a public library. Most cities have multiple library branches, sometimes even multiple library systems, within a few miles of one another. But public libraries have not always been part of the urban landscape. Not long ago, many people living in urban areas depended on informal sources for borrowing and renting books. These early libraries usually involved loaning private book collections out to fee-paying members, and many had one thing in common: They were not for young people. School district libraries that did serve children and teenagers concentrated their resources on supporting formal education. Many young people in urban areas had little access to noneducational or noncurriculum material.

It is hard for librarians working with teens today to understand how radical the concept of developing public library services specifically designed for youth, particularly older children and teenagers, may have seemed during the nineteenth and early part of the twentieth centuries. Older children and teenagers had jobs and financial responsibilities. They were often treated more like adults than kids. People between the ages of 10 and 15 made up 13.6 percent of the labor force in 1870, and by 1900 this percentage had increased to 18.25 percent. Forty percent of these young people worked in industry, a major component of many urban areas (Braverman 1979). But even in the early nineteenth century, there was pressure on employers not to treat young people just as they would adults. By the 1830s, many states had passed laws making it illegal to employ young children in industrial settings (Indiana Department of Labor 2007). The idea that young people should be required to attend school also began to take hold, as evidenced by the passage of a compulsory school attendance law by the state of Massachusetts, the first of law of its kind, in 1852 (Bernier et al. 2006). Around this time, many public libraries in urban industrial areas were founded and began to design and expand services. Young people were almost always an afterthought for these early libraries, if they were considered at all.

Advocates for library service to teenagers did exist at these early urban libraries, however. These early leaders formulated clear philosophies of service; pioneered unique programming, partnerships, and outreach activities; served as informal mentors to new librarians enthusiastic and passionate about serving teens; and laid the foundation for services libraries offer to young adults in urban areas today.

Urban libraries have enjoyed several benefits that have helped make these the places where service to teens developed and flourished. Unlike their rural counterparts, urban libraries have had the benefit of being located in communities with large numbers of teens in a concentrated area. And, unlike in many rural communities, in urban areas it has always been easier for teens to travel to library locations. Additionally, libraries in urban areas frequently employed more staff members, making it easier for early pioneers to successfully argue for employing specialists dedicated to serving teenagers, to educate new librarians in the need for providing service to teens, and to pass along vital knowledge and core philosophies about serving teens. Rural libraries employing fewer people did not necessarily have the same opportunities to dedicate staff and resources specifically to serving teens, nor was it as easy to pass institutional knowledge from one generation of librarians serving teens to the next.

This chapter is intended to give librarians working in urban areas historical context for their service by touching briefly on dedicated individuals, innovative public libraries, unique programs, and significant events that have impacted the evolution of library service to teens in urban areas. The "Further Reading" section at the end of this chapter offers suggestions for those looking to read more.

ORIGINS OF YOUNG ADULT SERVICES

It is difficult to identify a single beginning moment as the so-called starting point for young adult service in urban areas. Children and teenagers, especially younger teenagers, were often historically referred to collectively as *young people.* For libraries, the concept of adolescence or the teenage years being separate from childhood or adulthood is relatively new. The 1823 opening of the Brooklyn Youth Library, which was sponsored by the Apprentice Library Association of Brooklyn (Stone 1977), is a starting point for thinking about the evolution of services to for youth. A unique feature of this library was the provision that it could actually be used by teenagers. Although other libraries may have had age restrictions in place that prevented use of material by children and younger teens, the Brooklyn Youth Library was open to boys older than 12. Girls older than 12 were allowed to access this library for one hour a week (Vandergrift 1996). Such age restrictions and the focus on excluding young people from service were commonplace in urban libraries of the nineteenth century.

Calls for reexamination of libraries' view of young people and possible change were heard as early as 1876, when William I. Fletcher of the Watkinson Library in Hartford, Connecticut, discussed in a report for the U.S. Bureau of Education that public libraries should discontinue the practice of restricting children's access to library material (Stone 1977) and should also work with schools to provide service to young people (Vandergrift 1996).

Around the same time, other libraries and library administrators began to acknowledge the importance of collections and services for young people and children. One such librarian/administrator was William Brett, who was appointed the librarian of the Cleveland Public Library in 1884. During his tenure, he encouraged the development of facilities and services that were designed for children (Stone 1977). The Cleveland Public Library continued to offer greater access to its collection to larger segments of the population, and in 1890 Cleveland became the first large urban public library to allow "unrestricted access of all persons, to all books, at all times" (Stone 1977, 178). Allowing patrons' access to open shelves was one part of the Cleveland Public Library's remarkable new policy. The statement also meant that age restrictions that limited who could use library material were eliminated. Cleveland's new rules were a significant departure from library traditions that ignored young people or specifically disallowed or discouraged their use of materials.

A NEW ERA FOR YOUTH SERVICES
New York Public Library

In 1906, youth services in urban areas entered a new era when Anne Carroll Moore left her position as the head of the Children's Library at the Pratt Institute in Brooklyn to take a job with the New York Public Library

(Braverman 1979). Moore explored ways to serve the city's young people. She helped build service to youth at the New York Public Library through her own work and also by hiring high school librarian Mabel Williams. As "supervisor of Work with Schools" Williams was instrumental in expanding services to teens, making more than 2,000 school visits in 1921 (Braverman 1979). Mabel Williams helped lead the New York Public Library to the forefront of the emerging field of young adult services. She trained and mentored staff to work with teenagers and worked to change what she felt were the negative attitudes many library staff had toward teenagers. Retraining staff was just one part of the equation for success for Williams, who also prioritized hiring new librarians who believed in her philosophy of providing extensive and individualized services to teenagers. Importantly, she also worked to create physical spaces, areas within library locations, and collections specifically geared toward teens and their browsing and reading interests. Under her leadership, teens were offered new types of activities, including clubs based on their hobbies and interests. Notably, Williams worked directly with teenagers, involving them in a wide variety of activities, not dissimilar from many programs offered at urban public libraries today (Atkinson 1986).

Williams was not alone in her commitment to serve young people. The New York Public Library was at the forefront nationally in exploring the options for serving older youth. Early outreach services were being offered through activities like those led by Amelia Munson, who in 1926 developed services for students in "continuation schools." Although continuation schools eventually disappeared and were replaced by institutions similar to today's vocational high schools, Munson's work is an early example of an urban library intentionally designing services for nontraditional or alternative schools (Braverman 1979).

Service to teenagers continued to expand throughout the New York Public Library system. In 1930, the system hired the first assistant trained in and charged with specifically serving teenage library users for the Chatham Square Branch. By 1939, there were 69 "school and reference assistants" in the various branches of the New York Public Library (Braverman 1979).

The commitment to serving young people and teenagers reached a noteworthy high point with the opening of the New York Public Library's Nathan Straus Branch in 1941, which was designed and dedicated specifically to serve people younger than 21 (Bernier et al. 2006). Under the direction of Margaret Scoggin, the Nathan Straus Branch offered young people a chance to use a variety of new technologies of the time, including a printing press, a Victrola and record collection, a radio, and a movie projector. Young people were also given the opportunity to develop and participate in the creation of programs and publications. The branch hosted an active teen book reviewers group, and excerpts from reviews by teens were included in the *Books for Young People* booklist (Atkinson 1986). This list that would later become the well-known *Books for the Teen Age,* which has been produced annually by New York Public Library for more than 75 years.

Cleveland Public Library

In 1926, the Cleveland Public Library opened the Stevenson Room under the direction of Jean Carolyn Roos. Designed for people ages 14 to 21, the Stevenson Room included staff dedicated to and trained in serving teenagers and included a collection of books that was likely to appeal to teens (Braverman 1979). Cleveland continued to support serving teenagers and eventually created an independent Office for Service to Youth, later renamed the Youth Department in 1943 (Atkinson 1986). As the head of this office, Jean Carolyn Roos worked to provide training for all librarians in working with young adults.

The Cleveland Public Library was another urban library that experimented with the model of creating a branch specifically designed for young people, much like New York Public Library's Nathan Straus Branch. In 1943, the Alta Branch of the Cleveland Public Library opened (Atkinson 1986). Although the idea of a branch specifically for young people was eventually abandoned by the Cleveland Public Library, it seems clear that the origins of service to teens in public libraries can be found in these innovative and daring ideas tried out by libraries in large urban areas.

Enoch Pratt Free Library

The Enoch Pratt Free Library, another library serving an urban area, also played a major role in laying the foundations of young adult service. When a new Central Library was opened in 1933, it included a separate area designed for use by teenagers. Margaret Alexander Edwards was appointed the young people's assistant and initially worked in the new area a few hours a day, and by 1937 she had become a full-time staff member working in the Young People's Corner of the Enoch Pratt's Central Library (Atkinson 1986).

Edwards helped make Enoch Pratt a national leader in young adult library services for libraries in urban and nonurban areas alike. By the

1940s, she was holding monthly meetings with the staff focused on serving teenagers, and by 1945 every branch of the Enoch Pratt Free Library had a staff member designated to work with young adults (Atkinson 1986).

Typical of her innovative and outreach-minded approach to library services, Edwards did not limit her activity to what was happening in the library. She initiated the Pratt Library's Book Wagon. During summers from 1942 to 1944, Edwards took a horse-drawn wagon full of books up and down the streets of some of the poorest areas of Baltimore, visiting both predominately white and predominately African American neighborhoods. She concentrated on areas with very low library use and in the first summer registered more than 450 new library users (Atkinson 1986).

END OF AN ERA

Eventually, however, what seems to have been the first golden age of young adult services in libraries serving urban areas began to fade. The post–World War II era produced fewer resources for teen services and an overall decrease in support for services to young adults. In 1946, the New York Public Library created a new reference department, and although this new department was charged with overseeing reference services in the branches, notably absent was any specific responsibility for service to young adults (Atkinson 1986). In 1939, the branch libraries boosted 60 young adult–focused assistants. By 1946, this number had been cut significantly. In 1953, the young adult–focused Nathan Straus Branch was closed, and the collection and related services were moved (Braverman 1979). And in 1956, cost cutting resulted in the possibility of combining children's and young adult services at the New York Public Library. Mabel Williams and Margaret Scoggin successfully argued against this combination (Atkinson 1986). But the impulse to group teens and children together would continue and can still be seen in libraries serving urban areas today.

MORE RECENT HISTORY

The emphasis on reference and effective use of new technologies continued to be a focus in public libraries, especially in the 1970s. This meant that positions previously dedicated to specialized service groups, like young adults, were often replaced with generalist (Public Libraries as Partners in Youth Development, *The Wallace Foundation*). Although rural libraries with smaller numbers of staff likely always relied heavily on generalists to provide service to teenagers, this was a shift for urban libraries that had previously led the charge to dedicate both staff and space specifically to serve teens.

Los Angeles Public Library

That is not to say that innovative programs and services disappeared in urban libraries during the latter part of the twentieth century. The Los Angeles Public Library's 1976 Science Fiction and the Media program is a great example of how service to teens continued to grow and thrive in some urban areas. Open to all ages but designed with the goal of attracting teenagers, this program featured a UFO expert, makeup specialist, animator, and panel discussion with well-known science fiction authors Larry Niven, Jerry Pournelle, Alan Dean Foster, and George Clayton Johnson. Three hundred and fifty people, more than half of whom were from Southern California, attended the event (Holmes and Baldwin 1978). In 1977, the Los Angeles Public Library built on this success by hosting a second major event for teenagers, the Comic and Cartooning Festival, with an impressive list of presenters, included including Don Rico, Sergio Aragones from *MadMagazine,* Dan Glut from Marvel Comics, and Jack Kirby, creator of *The All American Boy.* More than 600 people attended, and two-thirds of them were teenagers (Holmes and Baldwin 1978).

The 1990s

By the 1990s, many libraries in large urban areas saw a need to provide not only services but also physical space at the library for teenagers. The Los Angeles Public Library again played a leadership role in young adult services and in 1994 opened TeenS'cape, a space specifically designed for teens and featuring teen-friendly furniture and staff (Bernier et al. 2006). Los Angeles continued to focus on serving teens and in 2001 reinstated their young adult coordinator position and changed several part-time young adult librarian positions to full-time young adult librarian positions (Bernier et al. 2006).

A number of libraries in urban areas initiated new services in the 1990s. Programs were often designed to attract previously underserved groups and involved cooperation and partnership with community agencies. Houston Public Library, for example, started After School Programs Inspire Reading Enrichment (ASPIRE). Resources and support for ASPIRE were supplied not only by the library but also by the city of Houston and were piloted at two branches in 1996. The centers were supported by Houston's mayor and city council and were located in mainly

Hispanic and African American neighborhoods. The centers were staffed with volunteers who provided one-on-one tutoring and also served as role models (Chelton 2000).

In the late 1990s, the Young Adult Library Services Association saw the need to address the unique issues and concerns specifically of young adult librarians working in large urban areas and created the YA-Urban and initiated a Serving Young Adults in Large Urban Populations discussion group. In 1996, the Search Institute's Healthy Communities, Healthy Youth initiative, based on the framework of a list of critical developmental assets, helped launch a new era of teen services for public libraries in urban areas. This initiative offered community leaders, including librarians, a new perspective on issues related to creating successful communities through supporting the development of competent, caring young people.

In 1999, the DeWitt Wallace Reader's Digest Fund Public Libraries as Partners in Youth Development initiative offered nine urban libraries funding and support to explore new ways of providing service to teens in urban areas. Participating libraries included the Brooklyn Public Library (New York), Enoch Pratt Free Library (Maryland), Fort Bend County Libraries (Texas), Free Library of Philadelphia (Pennsylvania), King County Library System (Washington), Oakland Public Library (California), Public Library of Charlotte and Mecklenburg County (North Carolina), Tucson-Pima Public Library (Arizona), and the Washoe County Library System (Nevada). This extensive initiative also involved a substantial amount of research and produced published evaluations and reports. Using funds and resources provided through the Public Libraries as Partners in Youth Development project, the Brooklyn Public Library began converting generalist positions to positions specializing in children's and young adult services (Public Libraries as Partners in Youth Development, *The Wallace Foundation*).

In the late 1990s and early 2000s, several urban libraries received the Urban Libraries Council Highsmith Award in recognition of programs specifically designed for teenagers. The award "recognizes library programs or initiatives that exemplify the principles of positive youth development" (Urban Libraries Council, *Highsmith Award of Excellence Guidelines*). These programs include:

- Denver Public Library's After School Program. This program provides young people with a place to go in the after-school hours when there is less adult supervision and dangerous and risky behavior is more likely to occur. Teens work as program assistants and are trained in leadership and teamwork skills by library staff. Staff also evaluate and mentor teens throughout the program.

- The Dallas Public Library's Teen Wise Centers. These centers focus on urban teens ages 12 to 18 likely to engage in at-risk activities and offer access to technology, games, tutoring, and guest speakers.

- The Free Library of Philadelphia's Teen Leadership Assistants Program. More than 200 teen leadership assistants work with adult after-school leaders to provide homework and computer help to younger children. Teen associate leaders, alumni of the Teen Leadership Program who are college students, work as mentors and trainers for the Teen Leadership Assistants Program.

- The Orange County Library System's Teen Library Corp. Teens ages 13 to 18 are offered hands-on community service experience. The program led to the creation of a teen program aid position, which gives teens a chance to be involved directly with projects and programs presented by the library's Children's and Young Adult Department.

The twenty-first century has continued to be a time of expansion of teen services in many urban libraries. The Phoenix Public Library set a new standard for spaces designed specifically for teenagers with Teen Central, which opened in 2001. This space, designed by and for teens, was opened to much acclaim from youth services professionals across the country, community members, and teens. Consciously deciding to involve teens in the planning process from the start, the library invited teens to focus groups at which they were able to discuss ideas and suggestions with the librarians and those physically designing the new space. Teens helped the Teen Central space, including layout, collections, and the kinds of services that would be offered (Kendall 2003). Teen Central was awarded the Urban Libraries Council Highsmith Award in 2003.

The New York Public Library, long a leader in serving teens in large urban areas, returned to its roots when, in 2004, it completed a $275,000 renovation of the Nathan Straus Young Adult Center. Like its 1940s predecessor, the new Nathan Straus Center featured the latest technology, including Wi-Fi access, music, and teen-friendly furniture and staff. These renovations were based on polls that asked teens to envision their dream library (New York Public Library Press Release, *Books and Beyonce!*).

One of the most recent additions to the new round of innovative teen spaces located in large urban areas is the Public Library of Charlotte and Mecklenburg County's Imaginon, the Joe and Joan Martin Center. This new facility, which opened in 2005, is a partnership between the library and the Children's Theater of Charlotte. Housed in the Children's Theater are both the library's space for children and the Loft, the Library's separate space for teens. The Loft includes technology designed to allow teens to explore animation and filmmaking (Imaginon, *About Imaginon*).

PUTTING IT IN PERSPECTIVE

The history of library service to young adults in urban areas clearly demonstrates that issues faced by today's teen librarians are surprisingly similar to those faced by early advocates like Mabel Williams and Margaret Alexander Edwards. For example, the goal of employing staff dedicated specifically to serving teens is one many teen advocates work toward today. It was also an idea supported by both Williams and Edwards. Then, as now, similar barriers existed, such as resources not being available and a lack of consistent institutional support for service to young adults. Negative staff attitude toward teens has also been a persistent issue in the history of teen services in libraries serving urban areas. In her book *The Fair Garden and the Swarm of Beasts* (1994, reprint), originally published more than thirty years ago, Margaret Alexander Edwards expressed her belief that many staff think libraries will be ruined if they open their doors and embrace teenagers. Many present-day young adult librarians in urban areas struggle with similar negative attitudes by staff about teens.

Recent award-winning programs and services developed by libraries in urban areas offer hope to those advocating for increased service to teens and also demonstrate a renewed understanding of the importance of serving young adults. Tools like the Search Institute's 40 Developmental Assets are valuable resources for educating staff, communities, and decision makers about the community-wide implications for serving, or not serving, teenagers. Establishing and maintaining service to teens in the wide variety of urban areas across the country has never been a simple or easy task, yet these are just the places in which public library service to teens originated. Today's advocates for teen services have a great opportunity to build on the knowledge gained from past librarians and the service models, programs, and training they designed and implemented.

WORKS CITED

Atkinson, Joan. 1986. "Pioneers in Public Library Service to Young Adults." *Top of the News* 43 (Fall): 27–44.

Bernier, Anthony, Mary K. Chelton, Christine A. Jenkins, and Jennifer Burke Pierce, comps. 2006. *Two Hundred Years of Young Adult Library Services History.* Accessed January 30, 2006, available at http://www.voya.com/whatsin voya/web_only_articles/Chronology_200506.shtml.

Braverman, Miriam. 1979. *Youth, Society, and the Public Library.* Chicago: American Library Association.

Chelton, Mary K. 2000. *Excellence in Library Services to Young Adults: The Nation's Top Programs, 3rd Edition.* Chicago: American Library Association.

Holmes, Fontayne, and Carol Baldwin. 1978. "Steps to Cooperative YA Programming." *School Library Journal* 24 (May): 28

Imaginon. *About Imaginon.* Accessed August 28, 2007, available at http://www.imaginon.org/about_imaginon/default.asp.

Indiana Department of Labor. History: Child Labor in America. Accessed March 22, 2007, available at http://web.archive.org/web/20070306233529/http://www.in.gov/labor/childlabor/history.html.

Kendall, Karl. 2003. "Safe, Structured, and Teen-Friendly." *Voice of Youth Advocates* 26 (December): 380–81.

New York Public Library Press Release. *Books and Beyonce!* Accessed March 21, 2007, available at http://www.nypl.org/press/2004/teencentral.cfm.

Public Libraries as Partners in Youth Development. *The Wallace Foundation.* Accessed March 30, 2006, available at http://www.wallacefoundation.org/WF/KnowledgeCenter/KnowledgeTopics/Libraries/PLPYD.htm

Stone, Elizabeth W. 1977. *American Library Development, 1600–1899.* New York: H. W. Wilson.

Urban Libraries Council. *ULC/Highsmith Award of Excellence.* Accessed April 6, 2006, available at http://www.urbanlibraries.org/highsmithaward.html.

Vandergrift, Kay E. 1996. "Female Advocacy and Harmonious Voices: A History of Public Library Services and Publishing for Children in the United States—Imagination and Scholarship: The Contributions of Women to American Youth Services and Literature." *Library Trends* 44 (Spring): 1–47.

FURTHER READING

Chelton, Mary K. 1994. *Excellence in Library Services to Young Adults: The Nation's Top Programs, 1st Edition.* Chicago: American Library Association.

Chelton, Mary K. 1997. *Excellence in Library Services to Young Adults: The Nation's Top Programs, 2nd Edition.* Chicago: American Library Association.

Edwards, Margaret A. 1994. *The Fair Garden and the Swarm of Beasts: The Library and the Young Adult.* Chicago: American Library Association.

Vaillancourt, Renee. 2004. *Excellence in Library Services to Young Adults: The Nation's Top Programs, 4th Edition.* Chicago: American Library Association.

2

◇ ◇ ◇

STAFF AND VOLUNTEERS

"Can I have my senior pictures taken at the library?" This was a question I received not too long ago from a teen advisory board (TAB) member. She had been an active TAB member at the central library, located in an urban downtown area, for five years. After carefully considering all of her options for her senior photograph backdrop, this teen came to the conclusion that her involvement with the library was something she always wanted to remember because it had been such a positive part of her high school experience. How did this teen and the library arrive at such a significant moment? In a word: relationships. My TAB member's positive feelings about the library have everything to do with her positive feelings about the people who work with her and help her while she is there.

Perhaps no element in serving teens in an urban area is as important as the staff who are serving them. A library with staff at all levels who are enthusiastic and well versed in the unique needs of teens can help make the goal of enhancing and expanding service to teens a reality. This chapter will examine common organizational structures for teen services in urban settings, methods for supporting teen services through better communication, key competencies needed by staff serving teens, and the valuable role teens can play as both paid staff and regular volunteers. This chapter is meant to serve as a starting point for those libraries serving urban areas that are just beginning to establish teen services and as a resource for libraries with established teen services and programs looking for new ideas.

ALL STAFF SERVE TEENS

In her article "The Coolness Factor: Ten Libraries Listen to Youth," Elaine Meyers reported on the results of interviews she conducted with teens in urban libraries. Among the findings were that teens did not find library staff helpful or friendly and that teens often think librarians are mean and simply do not like kids (Meyers 1999). These results highlight the challenge of bridging the gap between staff and teens in urban settings. When staff are not prepared and willing to enthusiastically serve teens, it is likely those attitudes will be reflected in teens forming a negative opinion about the library.

It is important to recognize that in urban areas, many teen customers may not in fact use the library for traditional purposes like quiet reading, studying, or researching. Instead, teens may use the library, either by choice or because it is their only option, as their home away from home, spending long hours after school and on weekends at their local branch. They may use it as a spot to hang out with friends, socialize, and talk. This kind of use presents a unique challenge for urban libraries, many of which are small facilities with limited staffing and space. But meeting these kinds of unique needs is a crucial part of serving teens in urban areas. If teens are not utilizing the library space strictly for traditional purposes, library staff need to reexamine their own ideas about teens' use of the library and the role library staff members play in teens' lives.

The Search Institute, an independent nonprofit organization whose mission is to provide leadership, knowledge, and resources to promote healthy children, youth, and communities, has created a list of 40 Developmental Assets that they consider to be the important "building blocks of healthy development that help young people grow up healthy, caring and responsible" (Search Institute, *40 Developmental Assets*). Introducing the asset-based approach to serving teens is a vital step in deepening staff understanding of their role in providing library service to teens in urban communities. Staff with an understanding of these developmental assets are much more likely to appreciate why it is essential to maintain positive attitudes and relationships with teens. One question to ask when increasing teen services competency is whether staff actually feel it is their professional responsibility to be interested and engaged in healthy youth development. In fact, such relationships, and a true understanding of how to build those relationships, is crucial for laying the foundation for teen services and leads to stronger libraries and stronger communities.

In many urban settings, this information may need to be communicated to many different staff members at various levels and locations. Keeping the information simple is vital to helping staff embrace and understand their role. Hoping that every staff member will be transformed into a teen advocate may not be realistic, but clear and consistent communication about serving teens and addressing their unique developmental needs is the first step for creating an organizational culture that does more than simply tolerate teens but, in fact, embraces and even welcomes them.

What to Communicate to All Staff

- Success depends on the active involvement of all staff, not just those people with a specialization in teen or youth services.
- Helping teens build their developmental assets does not require a master's degree in library science (MLS).
- The future of the library depends on creating healthy, happy community members. The more developmental assets teens have, the more likely they are to grow into lifelong library users who support and value all community institutions, including the library.
- Building strong relationships between teens and library staff is at the core of helping teens build developmental assets.
- Teens in urban areas come from a variety of backgrounds and may have very few positive adult role models in their lives. Library staff members may be the only positive adult role models with whom some urban teens have daily contact.

Building Developmental Assets

All staff can engage in simple, everyday actions that help teens build the 40 Developmental Assets identified by the Search Institute. Following are several assets followed by specific examples of how library staff can support teens in each area.

Asset: Other Adult Relationships

Any staff member can be involved in offering teens support in this important area. Often in urban settings, library staff are the nonparent

Figure 2.1.

The 40 Developmental Assets for Adolescents

EXTERNAL ASSETS

SUPPORT

Family support	Family life provides high levels of love and support.
Positive family communication	Young person and her or his parent(s) communicate positively, and young person is willing to seek advice and counsel from parent(s).
Other adult relationships	Young person receives support from three or more nonparent adults.
Caring neighborhood	Young person experiences caring neighbors.
Caring school climate	School provides a caring, encouraging environment.
Parent involvement in schooling	Parent(s) are actively involved in helping young person succeed in school.

EMPOWERMENT

Community values youth	Young person perceives that adults in the community value youth.
Youth as resources	Young people are given useful roles in the community.
Service to others	Young person serves in the community one hour or more per week.
Safety	Young person feels safe at home, at school, and in the neighborhood.

BOUNDARIES AND EXPECTATIONS

Family boundaries	Family has clear rules and consequences and monitors the young person's whereabouts.
School boundaries	School provides clear rules and consequences.
Neighborhood boundaries	Neighbors take responsibility for monitoring young people's behavior.
Adult role models	Parent(s) and other adults model positive, responsible behavior.
Positive peer influence	Young person's best friends model responsible behavior.
High expectations	Both parent(s) and teachers encourage the young person to do well.

CONSTRUCTIVE USE OF TIME

Creative activities	Young person spends three or more hours per week in lessons or practice in music, theater, or other arts.
Youth programs	Young person spends three or more hours per week in sports, clubs, or organizations at school and/or in community organizations.
Religious community	Young person spends one hour or more per week in activities in a religious institution.
Time at home	Young person is out with friends "with nothing special to do" two or fewer nights per week.

INTERNAL ASSETS
COMMITMENT TO LEARNING

Achievement motivation	Young person is motivated to do well in school.
School engagement	Young person is actively engaged in learning.
Homework	Young person reports doing at least one hour of homework every school day.
Bonding to school	Young person cares about her or his school.
Reading for pleasure	Young person reads for pleasure three or more hours per week.

POSITIVE VALUES

Caring	Young person places high value on helping other people.
Equality and social justice	Young person places high value on promoting equality and reducing hunger and poverty.
Integrity	Young person acts on convictions and stands up for her or his beliefs.
Honesty	Young person "tells the truth even when it is not easy."
Responsibility	Young person accepts and takes personal responsibility.
Restraint	Young person believes it is important not to be sexually active or to use alcohol or other drugs.

(continued)

Figure 2.1. (*Continued*)

SOCIAL COMPETENCIES

Planning and decision making	Young person knows how to plan ahead and make choices.
Interpersonal competence	Young person has empathy, sensitivity, and friendship skills.
Cultural competence	Young person has knowledge of and comfort with people of different cultural/racial/ethnic backgrounds.
Resistance skills	Young person can resist negative peer pressure and dangerous situations.
Peaceful conflict resolution	Young person seeks to resolve conflict nonviolently.

POSITIVE IDENTITY

Personal power	Young person feels he or she has control over "things that happen to me."
Self-esteem	Young person reports having a high self-esteem.
Sense of purpose	Young person reports that "my life has a purpose."
Positive view of personal future	Young person is optimistic about her or his personal future.

This list is an educational tool. It is not intended to be nor is it appropriate as a scientific measure of the developmental assets of individuals.

The list of 40 Developmental Assets® is reprinted with permission from Search Institute®. Copyright © 1997, 2006 Search Institute, 615 First Avenue NE, Minneapolis, MN 55413; 800-888-7828 www.search-institute.org. All Rights Reserved.

adults with whom teens spend much of their out-of-school time. To support teens in this area, staff should:

- Know teens' names. The simple act of individual acknowledgement helps communicate caring and support. It does not take much to find out a teen's name, and this effort can make a big difference when it comes to a young person's perception of the library, especially for a teen living in an urban area where it is easy to get lost in the shuffle. It can also help teens develop a positive view of themselves in the community as someone worth knowing and respecting.

- Greet teens when they come into the library. Library staff can set a positive and welcoming tone with a simple smile and hello when the after-school crowd shows up. It is a great way to break down the perception that teens are only noticed at the library when they are doing something negative or wrong. Ask them how their day has been, how school was, what happened during their day. This can have a particularly positive impact on teens in urban areas who may be accustomed to being treated and seen only as a member of a group rather than acknowledged as an individual.

- Celebrate accomplishments teens may wish to share with staff members. Many teens may be looking for someone to tell about a good grade or an adult to whom they can recount the details of a winning basketball game. Encouraging teens to take pride in their accomplishments can be as simple as offering a sincere "Great job!" and will go a long way to building goodwill for the library and helping teens feel positive about themselves. Of course, sometimes the things that happen in teens' lives are negative. For teens living in urban areas where it is not uncommon to live in poverty, negative events unfortunately can be a regular part of life. Staff members should be open to listening when teens talk about what happened that was bad or confusing and should be prepared to refer teens to organizations that can provide further assistance, such as shelters and clinics offering free counseling.

- When teens make efforts to follow guidelines and moderate behavior, especially in response to staff requests to do so, staff should acknowledge these efforts and thank teens for their assistance in making the library a great place to be. Because urban areas are home to a diverse group of teenagers, it is important to realize that not all teens have the same experience in following rules or meeting behavior expectations. Consistently and clearly articulating reasonable expectations for behavior can be a challenge for staff working in urban libraries, and meeting these expectations can be equally challenging for teenagers. When teens make a concerted effort to do so, staff should provide affirmative and positive feedback.

Asset: Adult Role Models

Unlike small rural communities where adults may personally know virtually every teenager in town, in urban areas many teenagers may go through an entire day and not interact with a single adult who knows them by name. Whether staff working in urban libraries realize it, many of them serve as role models for teens, perhaps the only or most important real-life adult role models. This is a heavy responsibility. Do staff recognize this? They should. All staff can be positive adult role models. Staff can:

- Treat teens with respect. Teens deserve the same respect as any other library customer. In treating their teen customers with dignity, no matter how difficult a situation may be, staff can communicate an important level of respect for teens as well as model how to treat others in the community, regardless of how frustrating or difficult the circumstances may be.

- Provide clear expectations for teen behavior. Engage in clear, consistent enforcement of expectations to break down the perception that librarians just do not like teens. If teens spend a lot of time at the library, as is often the case in urban areas, library staff have the opportunity to model positive behaviors by responding in a consistent, reasonable way when confronted with challenges or problems.

- Make a point to keep the library property clean. In some urban communities, the library is one of the cleanest, neatest places on the block. As Rollie Welch, young adult librarian for the Cleveland Public library, commented in 2005 on the YA-Urban listserv, a discussion list for library staff serving teens in urban settings, "[T]hey [branch libraries] are kind of like an oasis in some of our rougher neighborhoods.... [I]t is not uncommon to see boarded up stores and homes and trash next to a branch with the small lawn trimmed, windows cleaned and parking lot paved." Picking up trash and making visible efforts to maintain the library's clean appearance are important in communicating the library's commitment to the community and also important in communicating to teens that everyone is responsible for keeping things clean, even in a big city where people often do not know one another or an urban area where many people are living in poverty. By picking up trash in and around the library building, staff members send a message about taking responsibility for making the community an inviting place.

Asset: Control and Independence

All staff can play a role in ensuring teens feel a level of control and independence, another important asset. Staff can:

- Treat teens as individuals, rather than as a group, particularly when addressing issues related to behavior. This is particularly important in urban areas where teens are sometimes viewed by many—both inside and outside the library—as one large, anonymous group rather than as individuals. Broadly categorizing teens often leads to enforcing rules or suspensions for a whole class of users without taking into account if they actually participated in an event or are aware of an issue. Teens put in this situation feel a lack of control, and in an urban area you can bet this is not an uncommon experience for many teenagers. Libraries have the opportunity to play a unique role in this area of teens' lives and are often the first place in the community to offer young people an element of independence and control in the form of a library card. The library has a tradition of recognizing young people's rights to have a separate account from their parents. This gesture sets the stage for the library to continue throughout the span of the teen years to serve as an organization in the community that recognizes and appreciates teens' right to have control over their lives.

- Take the time to explain to teens exactly how to find information when conducting a reference interview or providing reader's advisory. Use follow-up questions to be certain teens not only get the information they need but also have a clear understanding of how that information was found. For teens living in busy urban areas and attending schools with many students, the opportunities to receive individual instruction may be limited. Librarians offering this one-on-one attention clearly not only help teens understand how best to use library resources but also reinforce to teens that they have the right to be empowered to make individual choices by being informed about how systems work and about the variety of choices available to them.

- Offer teens choices of activities by providing independent access to board games and craft or drawing supplies. Although these supplies may be located close to a service point for convenience, allowing teens to use these resources on their own terms permits them to maintain control over this important aspect of their library use. For teens in urban areas living in poverty or with many siblings or extended family members in one house, having the chance to choose a board game independently without having to negotiate with brothers, sisters, or other family members may be an especially treasured aspect of visiting the library and asserting independence and control.

- Another useful tool for communicating with staff about the role they play in supporting healthy youth development is the Forum for Youth Investment's "Libraries as Positive Developmental Settings" chart. This chart provides concrete examples of how libraries can act either as a "Benefit Zone" for teens or as a "Danger Zone."

Figure 2.2.

	Libraries as Positive Developmental Settings	
BENEFITS ZONE	**FEATURES**	**DANGER ZONE**
Physical space is safe; youth feel comfortable and welcome; building is open weekends and evenings.	*Physical and Psychological Safety*	Physical hazards are present; youth feel unwelcome; building hours are inconsistent.
Some spaces and activities are designed with teens' needs in mind; activities managed consistently with mutual respect for youth and adults.	*Appropriate Structure*	Spaces and activities are too restrictive (e.g., not allowing for groups to meet, talk); activities are inconsistent, unclear, or change unexpectedly.
Designated areas are available for youth to interact with peers; youth feel supported by staff.	*Supportive Relationships*	Youth do not have opportunities to interact with peers; youth feel ignored or not supported by staff.
Youth are encouraged to join groups and activities; programs, activities and materials reflect youth interests.	*Opportunities to Belong*	Youth are excluded from activities; programs, activities, and materials do not reflect youth interests.
Library staff have high expectations of youth and encourage and model positive behaviors.	*Positive Social Norms*	Library staff allow negative behaviors to go unaddressed or make some teens feel unwelcome, rather than helping them understand expectations.
Youth-focused programs and activities are challenging and based on youth input; youth are encouraged to take active roles in the overall functioning of the library.	*Support for Efficacy and Mattering*	Youth input is not considered; activities are not challenging; youth are not offered leadership roles.
Staff help youth identify interests and opportunities to develop and practice skills in the library and the community.	*Opportunities for Skill Building*	Youth do not have opportunities to develop and practice skills in areas of interest.
Library offers opportunities for families; homework help is available; space is available for youth and community meetings and activities; library works with schools and maintains information on local resources.	*Integration of Family, School, Library, and Community Efforts*	Library does not offer opportunities for family activities; homework help is not available; library does not partner with schools and community organizations; no information on local resources available.
Library offers information on health and social service resources, helps assess options, may make referrals; transportation, snacks, small stipends are available for special programs.	*Basic Care and Services*	Library is not equipped to make social service referrals; snacks, transportation are never available.

Reprinted with permission from The Forum for Youth Investment, Washington, DC.

Is Your Library in the Benefit Zone?

Compare your library with the Forum for Youth Investment chart. Observe all public service staff and reflect on these simple questions to find out where your library fits:

- Are staff smiling and greeting teens?
- Are staff going out of their way to be friendly to all teens, not just to those walking up to a desk?
- Do all staff members, including security guards, enforce rules in the same way for teens and adults?
- Are staff walking to the shelves whenever possible with teens?
- Do staff give teens their undivided attention when teens are asking a question or needing assistance?
- Do staff clearly explain what they are doing and what resources they are using as they search for information or answer questions for teens?
- If a teen needs additional help in a different section of the library, do staff walk them to the appropriate desk and introduce them to a staff person who will be able to help before completing the interaction?
- Do staff spend as much time on a question from a teen as on a question from an adult?

DEDICATING STAFF SPECIFICALLY TO SERVING TEENS

Ensuring that all staff are educated, informed, and enthusiastic about serving teens can be an invaluable asset for successfully serving the many teens visiting an urban library. Having staff positions dedicated specifically to teen services, however, is likely to produce higher levels of engagement and positive feelings of ownership among teen customers. In *New Directions for library Service to Young Adults* (2002), Patrick Jones lists 12 goals that "represent what libraries do to make the vision of services to young adults a reality." In the second of his goals, he argues that employing young adult specialists creates building blocks of success in serving young adults. In libraries working to meet the unique needs of teen customers in urban areas, it is imperative for libraries to seriously consider making the commitment to employing at least one staff member per location dedicated specifically to teen services.

A critical factor in creating successful service to teens in any library setting is whether teen services–dedicated staff have an MLS. Recent research suggests "an increase in teen services to a greater degree in libraries where a dedicated full- or part-time librarian engineered those services" (Alessio and Buron 2006, 48). This research did show that libraries that dedicate staff to serving young people in general—for example, dedicating librarians to serving everyone younger than age 18—had some success in generating teen participation but that this success was less than that realized by libraries that dedicate staff specifically to teen services. Libraries in which a full- or part-time non-MLS staff member designed services for teens reported some increase in teen participation. Once again, however, these increases were lower than those libraries that use staff members with an MLS to design teen services regardless of if the MLS staff were specifically dedicated to teen services or dedicated to serving youth generally (Alessio and Buron 2006). In other words, the greatest impact in serving teens was realized when libraries dedicated an MLS staff member to specifically serve teens, followed by libraries that dedicate an MLS staff member to serve youth in general and, last, by libraries that dedicate non-MLS staff to specifically serve teens.

An informal survey conducted of members of the Urban Libraries Council, an organization that includes "urban public libraries serving the cities of 100,000 or more individuals in a Standard Metropolitan Statistical Area" (Urban Libraries Council, *Membership Eligibility*), found that a broad range of staffing models are currently being employed to provide teen services. The survey instrument can be found in the appendix of this book. Not all libraries may be in a position to immediately dedicate staff specifically to teen services. Even libraries participating in the grant-funded Public Libraries as Partners in Youth Development project, in which several large metropolitan and urban libraries received additional funding for projects designed to enhance services to teens, commented that building staff capacity for teen services takes time, no matter the circumstances. It does not happen overnight, particularly in large library systems in which resources are in short supply and several layers of decision makers need to be convinced of the necessity for dedicating staff specifically to serving teens.

The following are typical models for how teen services are currently being provided in libraries serving urban areas. All reflect a commitment to expanding services to teens. It must be acknowledged, however, that some models clearly offer more resources, flexibility, and commitment than others. Included are ideas for taking each model closer to the Young Adult Library Services Association's "desired future" for teen services in which "there will be a young adult librarian in every public and secondary school library" (Young Adult Library Services Association 2005).

RTL: Regional Teen Librarians

In this model, dedicated staff are assigned to provide teen services at more than one branch or location. Their job title specifically includes the words *young adult* or *teen* librarian, and job duties clearly indicate this is a service area on which the position will focus. These positions may or may not require an MLS. Regional teen librarians frequently operate under the direction of a teen or youth services manager or coordinator.

The RTL approach demonstrates a clear organizational commitment to serving teens. There are several ways staff can work to enhance the RTL model:

- Have regularly scheduled meetings for all teen librarians.
- Invite key decision makers to attend teen librarian meetings.
- Include a variety of teen librarians in planning meeting agendas and long-term projects in the area of teen services.
- Raise the profile of teen librarians. Encourage them to participate on committees or task forces throughout the organization, making sure to spread information about the importance of serving teens and advocating for teens whenever they can.
- Encourage teen librarians to work regionally to promote and plan services, including teen volunteer opportunities.

TST: Teen Services Team

In this model, staff are assigned or volunteer to work with a team or committee that plans, implements, and presents teen services for an entire library system. Some library systems include only MLS staff members on these teams, whereas other libraries open up membership to anyone with an interest in serving teens regardless of education level or experience. The TST usually meets on a regular basis, perhaps monthly or bimonthly. The focus of this model tends toward planning large, systemwide events like teen summer reading programs and Teen Read Week activities. In multibranch systems, branches supplement activities by providing programs and services on a location-by-location basis.

This model clearly takes advantage of one of the major resources for many libraries serving urban areas: the size of their staff. Bringing together staff members with experience and enthusiasm for serving teens provides opportunities for enhancing teen services not available to individuals working independently in a single location. Depending on the circumstances, this model usually indicates a level of support from administrators and decision makers. Libraries using this approach report some significant successes and clearly expect that the library be actively engaged in serving teens. Membership on the TST is not usually part of a job title and may or may not be listed as a required job duty.

There are several ways staff can work to enhance the TST model:

- Make the TST a self-directed work team. This will help staff build leadership skills while working to provide teen services.
- Create a formalized, rotating leadership structure for the TST. This will engage all members and create a sense of ownership and responsibility for the outcomes of teen services.
- Invite key decision makers to attend meetings. This will keep them informed about what services for teens are being planned as well as introduce high-level staff to important issues and concepts related to teen services work.
- Assign a member of the team to communicate successes to all staff. Use staff updates and year-end reports to highlight the dynamic services the TST is providing and to emphasize the importance of serving teens.
- Explore the possibility of including a formal administrative sponsor in the TST structure. Find out if there is someone on the executive or administrative council with whom the TST can communicate regularly about activities and upcoming events.
- Broaden the scope of the TST to include not only planning hands- on activities but also long-term planning for sustainable teen services.
- Develop a formal mission and goals statement that can be easily communicated to all staff.
- Examine how the TST can enhance outreach activities. In libraries that have an outreach services department, make sure a member of the outreach staff has been invited to participate on the TST. If teen services are not a current part of the outreach department, explore ideas for how the TST might provide expanded outreach activities.

YS: Youth Services

Some libraries surveyed report that all services to teens and children are categorized as YS. In this model, every library location has at least one full-time youth librarian who devotes a portion of his or her time to teen services. The job title and duties reflect the expectation that certain positions plan and develop services for the entire age range, 0 to 18. This model may include one or two positions centered at a central library that are specifically designated as teen services. A youth services coordinator or manager position is often part of this model and is charged with planning and implementing all services for children and teens. Organizations employing this model clearly have a commitment to serving teens, but due to limited resources they may be unable to dedicate staff strictly to teen services.

There are several ways staff can work to enhance the YS model.

- Consider scheduling separate meetings and creating distinct avenues of communication about teen services issues. This will help identify the different needs of each service and highlight success in serving teens.
- Support the inclusion of the YS coordinator or manager as a member of an executive or administrative council or decision-making group.
- Investigate opportunities for the YS coordinator to provide feedback on the hiring and evaluation of staff focusing on teen services.
- Work with human resources to ensure that teen services job duties are clearly stated in job postings and job descriptions.
- Work with human resources or managers to be sure that interviews for YS jobs include questions specifically about service to teens.
- Identify opportunities for YS staff who demonstrate enthusiasm for serving teens to advance to positions of leadership.

CL: Children's Librarians as Teen Services Providers

Many libraries serving urban areas have a rich tradition of offering dynamic and innovative children's services. Most have long-standing summer reading programs for children and have at least one staff member dedicated to serving children at every location. Nearly every location or branch library hosts weekly programs for children. Libraries using the children's librarians as teen services providers model utilize children's librarians to provide services to everyone younger than age 18, from babies to teenagers. In this model, children's librarians may or may not be encouraged to expand programming and services to the young people older than 12. This can be extremely difficult for staff members already planning and presenting heavily attended weekly preschool, toddler, and baby story times. Children's librarians have a full schedule of outreach duties in addition to daily public service duties, including reference and circulation responsibilities. Job titles and duties use the broader term *youth* instead of *teen* when describing duties.

There are several ways staff can work to enhance the children's librarian as teen services provider model:

- Explore the option of having one or two children's librarians concentrate efforts on the 12 to 18 age range. Well-planned, quality teen events and programs open the door for staff and administration to see new opportunities in services specifically geared toward teens.
- Look for resources outside of children's services to dedicate to teens. Unfortunately, this model often puts children and teen advocates in competition for resources. Making the case that service to teens is very different and distinct from service to children is an important part of asking for resources to be realigned.
- Ask an expert, perhaps from the psychology or education department of a local university, in the area of teen development to speak at a children's services meeting or staff training day. Providing an expert from outside the library profession to speak to the developmental differences between teens and children is a great way to help staff understand the real differences between effectively serving the two groups. One of the benefits of working in an urban area is that such an expert is not difficult to find.

Ad Hoc Model

In the ad hoc model, the library has acknowledged that serving teens is something worth doing and may even require that service is provided but has dedicated little or no staff resources to providing that service. Frequently in this model, teen services falls to whoever is willing to volunteer, sees a need, or simply enjoys working with teens. If no willing volunteer is available, someone with little or not interest in specifically serving teens may be required to participate. Some libraries require this staff member have an MLS, but many do not. Children's librarians, branch managers, outreach, and general reference librarians are all likely default providers of service to teens in this model. Serving teens does not appear in any job title or job description.

There are several ways staff can enhance the ad hoc model:

- Advocate for consistency. Is there any position at all locations in which teen services responsibility could be officially incorporated?

- Seek opportunities to advocate for why teens deserve the same attention as does service to children and adults and why dedicated staff are an essential part of providing this important level of service.

- In this model, it may be important to remember the motto "nothing succeeds like success." Some decision makers may not be aware of the real potential of serving teens in urban settings. Building the case takes action from dedicated staff who have a vision of helping the library reach a higher level in which staff resources are dedicated to teen services. Examine the other options listed in this chapter that are being used by libraries serving urban areas. Is it possible to build capacity in order to move to any of these models, even if reaching the ideal of having a teen librarian at every location remains a long-term goal?

Impact of Master's of Library/Information Science Staff

In all of the models used by libraries serving teens in urban settings, positions are populated to varying degrees by both MLS and non-MLS staff. As noted earlier, current research indicates that non-MLS staff can be successful in creating and maintaining successful programs and services when they are the sole providers of service to teens, but libraries dedicating MLS staff to serving teens often report higher levels of success. Whether all staff serving teens should be required to have an MLS degree will depend on a number of factors for each individual library system. Some considerations may include:

- Are children's and reference librarians required to hold an MLS? If so, should the same educational requirement be included when searching for staff to serve teens?

- Are there staff involved in directing service to teens on an organizational or systemwide level? For example, staff members may be going beyond planning programs and providing outreach directly to teens. They may be developing partnerships with teen service agencies in the community, working to create a comprehensive, long-term strategy for the library in the area of teen services, and training other staff in how to work with and serve teens. Do staff directing service in these ways hold an MLS? Are positions directing service in other areas required to hold an MLS? If so, the same educational requirement should be included for teen services.

Clearly, staff working in libraries serving urban areas face unique challenges in serving teens. There are large numbers of diverse teens often using the library in nontraditional ways for which the library facility was probably not originally designed. Teens' understanding about behavior expectations, their willingness to moderate behavior, and staff's willingness to be reasonable and consistent in enforcing those expectations are frequently areas that require intense work and effort to improve. And teens have a variety of choices about how to spend their time when it comes to attending programs and events. Asking non-MLS staff to meet these challenges can produce some positive results, but these results are often not as positive as when MLS staff are charged with developing teen services. In urban areas where the environment is challenging, having MLS staff dedicated specifically to serving teens is the most likely way to produce long-term success.

Teen Librarian Job Descriptions

Creating a job description that specifically includes teen services as the primary focus of the job duties for a position is a great opportunity to ensure that service to teens becomes part of the organizational culture of the library. Essential elements to be considered in a formal teen librarian job description may include: strong support of intellectual freedom for teen users; developing and maintaining relationships with schools and community organizations; expertise and experience in serving young adults; passion, enthusiasm, and commitment for serving teens; and knowledge of an asset-based approach to service.

Possible Interview Questions for a Teen Services Librarian

- Why are you interested in serving teens?
- What parts of your past or current jobs have prepared you for a job serving teens?
- What are the most important elements to being a good teen librarian? Give examples of how you have demonstrated these.
- What does it mean to be an advocate for a particular group of library users? Give an example of when you have been an advocate in the library for a particular group. Describe the effect of your advocacy on staff or customers. Have you ever demonstrated this kind of advocacy on behalf of teenagers, inside or outside of the library?
- Give specific examples of what you would prioritize when enhancing or building a teen area, particularly when working with limited or no funding.

- Give an example of a successful reader's advisory interaction you have had with a teen. How did you know it was successful?
- What are the essential elements in providing quality outreach service to teens?
- Why is outreach to teens important? If possible, give an example of when you have provided quality outreach to a teen audience or observed another library staff member providing quality outreach to teens.
- Describe the essential elements of a quality program for teens.
- Give a specific example of a program for teens with which you have been involved or describe a specific idea for a teen program.
- Give an example of a program you have created, helped plan, or observed that involved teen participation. How did significant teen participation result in a more successful program?
- What is the value of having teens involved as volunteers at the library and in planning and presenting programs and services for other teens?
- Every day at 2:45, a large group of teenagers invades your branch, talking loudly, laughing, using all the computers, and eating or drinking in the library. The staff is becoming frustrated by this daily routine. As a teen librarian and advocate, what is your role in handling the situation? What specific steps would you take to work through this issue?

Sample Elements to Include in a Teen Librarian's Job Duties

- Delivers excellent customer service that is friendly, positive, and enthusiastic.
- Provides reader's advisory and reference services that are accurate and thorough.
- Is approachable and friendly.
- Has experience working with diverse groups of people.
- Understands the benefits of walking to resources with teen customers and of following up whenever possible to ensure complete service.
- Serves as a role model for other staff by modeling excellent service, particularly in serving teenagers.
- Helps develop and define library service levels, especially in the area of teen services.
- Emphasizes excellence in public service to all customers but especially in the role of being a resource for teens, their parents, caregivers, and teachers.
- Takes every available opportunity to make a positive impact on teens' lives.

(continued)

(*Continued*)

- Is a leader in maintaining a positive, enthusiastic, and professional attitude, particularly in serving teens.
- Communicates openly and effectively about library situations, including any security situation involving teens.
- Works with all staff positively and effectively, delegating and empowering when appropriate and working as a team to accomplish goals, particularly in the area of teen services.
- Works to maintain appropriate size, currency, organization, accessibility, and appeal of the library's teen collections.
- Weeds the teen collection continuously.
- Markets teen materials through effective displays.
- Creates and maintains a high-circulation, high-turnover collection.
- Plans, develops, and delivers enthusiastic, innovative, and enriching teen programs, utilizing a variety of media and components, that serve fundamentally as an enriching and entertaining community resource supporting teens' development as healthy, caring young people.
- Continuously develops skills and experience in developing and delivering enthusiastic, exciting, developmentally appropriate, and fun programs.
- Visits local schools and community agencies to promote library resources and literacy.
- Attends training opportunities in the area of teen services.
- Emphasizes being an advocate for teen services excellence.

SECURITY STAFF

Many libraries in urban settings have a security guard on duty during all or part of the library's open hours. In libraries in urban areas, this guard may be employed directly by the library or may be a contract worker employed by a security firm or service working on-site at the library. Some libraries handle security by working directly with police officers. Regardless of the specific employment circumstances, security staff often have more interaction with teenagers than almost any other library staff member. It is vital that all staff working at the library as security guards be aware of and sensitive to the same important considerations as regular library staff when working with teen customers. Because security officers are often the first responders when the noise level begins to inch up in a building or when groups of teens start to come in and out of the library or gather at entrances after school, they play a significant role in setting the tone for library-teen interactions.

Security guards can be an invaluable asset when working with teens and can build friendly and positive relationships with regular teen customers. They can also inadvertently create issues and generate negative responses from teens. Security staff, like all library staff, should approach situations in a consistent manner and deliver the same messages to teens about using the library. Be sure to communicate regularly with security guards, not just discuss problems as they arise. Do not leave communication as a one-way transaction, though. Give security officers opportunities to initiate discussions and offer their input. Remember, they often spend more time out on the floor than other library staff members, and they may offer a different and valuable perspective on how to handle situations.

When training and working with a new security guard, be sure to find out what the guard knows about teens and teen experiences. Ask if the guard has any previous experience working with teens, particularly in urban areas, and if he or she has experience working with diverse groups of people. Many times guards have had some volunteer experiences at other youth-serving organizations, such as their church or a local boys' or girls' club. They also may have worked security for other youth-serving organizations in urban areas. Talk about these experiences, drawing on the positives and redirecting and coaching guards in any areas that do not fit with the library's mission and values. Security guards need to take a firm stance with teens at the library, but they should also understand that seeking to develop positive, productive relationships with teens is part of their job, too.

One final point to consider is the issue of having guards in uniform. Being able to quickly identify security staff is important; however, it may be worth considering ways to soften your library security guard uniforms. Many teens who exhibit challenging behavior are likely to have had previous, sometimes negative experiences with people in uniforms, particularly teens in urban areas where brushes with security guards and police officers are not uncommon for young people. Uniformed library security guards may therefore produce unprovoked negative reactions. Teens may be more defensive and difficult with a uniformed guard than if they were dealing with an out-of-uniform adult telling them the same thing.

In some instances, you will need the assistance of the police. Persistent, illegal activity sometimes occurs in the library or on the library's property, particularly in libraries located in urban communities with concentrated poverty and high crime statistics. For example, there may be obvious drug dealing going on in the parking lot. One phone call or visit from a police officer may not be enough to resolve an issue, and the problem may not go away simply because the police have intervened and addressed it once or twice. When crime and illegal activity begin to permeate the library and surrounding area, you must respond proactively. After legitimately determining that there is a real problem and discussing the issue with on-site security and community police officers, contact administration and community leaders. Viable, long-term solutions are needed. The library has a role to play in helping formulate and being a part of the community's response. One of the first steps you can take is asking police officers to do walk-throughs of the building. This sends a message that the illegal activity is unacceptable and will not be tolerated in or around the library.

Guidelines for Security Guards on Effective Ways to Work with Teens

- Know names.
- Focus on the behavior, not the person.
- Pose alternatives, not threats.
- Establish clear rules and enforce them respectfully and consistently. For example, determine up front how many people will be permitted per computer and stick with this guideline.
- Include parents in finding solutions, if necessary and possible.
- Separate annoying behaviors from disorderly or possibly criminal behaviors, such as verbal and physical abuse, and respond accordingly.

TEENS AS STAFF AND VOLUNTEERS
Teens as Paid Staff

When libraries serving urban areas consider the role teens can play in providing and enhancing services, employing teens as paid staff should be at the top of the list. Reasons to consider this approach include:

- When it comes to the perception of the library, teen employees help alter the image of the library as a stuffy, "Shhh!" environment to something more youthful and lively. Good teen employees can be excellent, energetic staff people. Their presence sends the immediate message to other teen customers that libraries are not just for adults or young children. Perhaps most important, teen employees can be excellent, energetic staff in their own right.
- Employing teens in paid positions increases the likelihood that the library can recruit staff members from the immediate community

in which the library is located. Library positions such as shelvers and student assistants often pay better and have more reasonable hours that other job options for teenagers, particularly in neighborhoods with high poverty rates and few local businesses. Frequently, teens in urban areas are looking for an after-school job in their neighborhood that is a short distance from their home or school, but unlike rural or truly suburban communities, the local job prospects for teens in some urban areas are slim. Many teens do not own a car or have easy access to transportation, limiting where and when they can work. This makes for a great recruiting situation for the library. And when teens from the local community work for the library, they and their peers see themselves reflected in the library in a new way.

- Many librarians started their careers as high school or college students working part-time library jobs. They report that this experience influenced their decision to pursue a career in the field. Libraries should prioritize creating job opportunities for students from a variety of neighborhoods and communities. Staff diversity can be increased by offering a variety of teens the chance to start a career in libraries while they are in high school.

- As an added benefit, teen employees can serve as a great resource for ideas on how to serve their peers. They can offer opinions and input about planning and creating services to all teens, and their input is particularly valuable and practical because they have the ability to discuss issues as both a teenager and as a library employee. They can also offer library staff members an edge in planning unique and high-demand programs, an important thing to keep in mind for libraries in urban areas that compete with many other organizations for teens' time. Teen employees are likely to have a better grasp of what is already being offered in the area for teens and what activities and programs teens *wish* were being offered.

- Employing teens in a large library system often means multiple library staff members will have the opportunity to work directly with teens, hiring, supervising, or evaluating teen employees. Quality teen employees are great public relations for teen services and can have a very positive influence on staff members who previously may have been negative about or resistant to carving out a place for teen services.

- Employing teens is a great way for the library to continue to engage teens as they reach their older high school years. In many urban settings, once teenagers are old enough to get a job, the extra time they once spent at the library is now spent working. Besides making it possible for the library to recruit enthusiastic young people as staff members, offering teenagers much-needed employment opportunities is a great way to keep older teens engaged and active with library activities throughout their teen years.

Teens as Volunteers

Teen volunteer programs are an excellent way to help teens build their developmental assets, a key element in serving teens in urban areas. These programs provide teens a chance to build self-confidence, an avenue for teen achievement and recognition of that achievement, and a chance to gain skills that will help teens when they begin their search for paying jobs—all skills teens living in urban areas desperately need but may not have many opportunities to develop. When I asked Marin Younker, teen services librarian at the Seattle Public Library, to follow up her library's survey response with more details about why they supported a teen volunteer program, she replied, "Teen volunteers bring an enthusiasm and fresh perspective to the job, offering that elusive teen input that we all seek and a chance for us to learn together while assisting with essential library tasks."

On a practical level, many teens living in urban areas are required to fulfill service hours for their school or church. These requirements offer a great opportunity for the library to enhance service to teens while making sure the library continues to be viewed by teens as relevant to their lives throughout their adolescent years. Libraries looking to support teens in growing into healthy, contributing members of their communities should assist teens in achieving volunteer requirements. Plus, these requirements make it easy to recruit willing teen volunteers.

A volunteer program that provides teens meaningful activities can also help promote a feeling of ownership and responsibility toward the library. This sense of ownership often plays an important part in maintaining a positive environment in urban libraries working with large after-school crowds. In libraries without a teen volunteer program, the first step to initiating one may be to simply and sincerely ask "Why not?" Here are a number of reasons an organization may be resistant to establishing a teen volunteer program, along with possible solutions for addressing these concerns:

- Problem: We have tried it before, and it did not work.
- Possible solution: Investigate the reasons why the program was stopped. Larger library systems may have long institutional memories, so start out by addressing concerns about what happened the

last time a teen volunteer program was started. Try to alleviate those fears by listening patiently and thoroughly explaining your plan.

- Problem: We do not have anyone to be in charge of the program.
- Possible solution: Go in with a plan for consistency at all locations. Work with human resources and staff to establish clear ownership of the program on an administrative level. Create documents that are easy for staff to utilize when recruiting and orienting teen volunteers and for scheduling and tracking teen volunteer hours.
- Problem: We already have adult volunteers. We do not need teen volunteers, too.
- Possible solution: Explain that teen volunteers add a new dimension to a volunteer program. Plus, teens may be able to volunteer at times that are not as convenient for adults, including evenings, weekends, and during summer.
- Problem: They will do things staff get paid to do.
- Possible solution: If this is a concern, work closely with your human resources department to establish clear dos and don'ts for teen volunteer activities and communicate these guidelines to all staff working with teen volunteers.
- Problem: I cannot possibly use all the teens that will want to volunteer, or I do not have time to come up with work for all the teens who will volunteer
- Possible solution: Establish guidelines for recommended numbers of teen volunteers and create a process for teens to apply for open volunteer positions. Empower staff to communicate to teens that there are times when all volunteer positions are filled but that teens can apply for later consideration.
- Problem: I keep receiving requests to use court-assigned volunteers.
- Possible solution: Address up front whether the library will accept teens looking for a place to do court-assigned community service hours. Communicate this decision and the reasons to all staff and do not let this issue derail implementation of a general teen volunteer program.

Evaluating the success of a teen volunteer program involves following up with staff to be sure the program is working for them. Simple questions to ask staff as part of this evaluation process include:

- Did your branch participate in the teen volunteer program? If not, why not?

- What types of activities did your teens do? (Please be specific if possible.)
- What worked?
- What did not work?
- What changes would you recommend to the teen volunteer program?

Sample Volunteer Agreement

Thank you for joining the _____ Library Teen Volunteer Team! Volunteering is a great way to help the library achieve our mission of (state your mission), and we appreciate your support.

You will learn a lot as a teen volunteer. Your experiences may even lead to a future career as a librarian. Plus, volunteer work is also an excellent reference for college and future jobs.

The library will:

Offer a safe work environment.

Provide a library staff member to answer your questions and provide feedback about your work.

Recognize how important your volunteer work is to the success of the library.

As a teen volunteer, you will:

Be on time and let staff know when you arrive.

Wear a badge or nametag that identifies you as a library volunteer.

Let the library manager know if you cannot make it to work.

Let the library manager know if you will not be able to continue volunteering.

Dress appropriately.

Act respectfully to customers and employees.

Not talk about any customer by name.

The parent of a teen volunteer will:

Support quality work habits and dependability.

Help the teen get to work on time.

Make sure the teen has a way home if needed within 15 minutes of the end of his/her work shift.

Discuss with the teen the responsibility of agreeing to volunteer.

Examples of typical duties:

Signing up kids and teens for the library's Summer Reading Program.

Setting up for programs.

Crowd control, offering help to parents with many small children, and taking attendance at children's programs.

Creating displays.

Helping with story times.

Setting a good example for other library customers.

Teens as Teachers

Teens reading to kids—what could be better? Many libraries in urban settings work with large groups of both teens and children on a daily basis. A program in which teens read one-on-one or in small groups to kids is a great addition to any volunteer program, offering a meaningful experience to teens while also supporting literacy skills for kids. As the Youth Activism Project, explains, "It is no secret that kids listen to kids. Teenagers . . . can be excellent teachers, credible messengers, and effective recruiters. Many believe the real benefit is that peer educators practice what they preach and avoid risky behaviors" (Youth Activism Project, *Adults Only*).

As with any new program, it is a good idea to start with a needs assessment. Find out if there is any other group or organization offering a similar program. Conduct a survey of staff to find out if customers and parents often contact the library looking for reading and literacy tutoring or help for children. Talk to teens and measure their response when asked about participating in such a program. Ask teachers or representatives of area school districts what they think. There may also be organizations such as AmeriCorps in your community willing and able to help train teen volunteers for a specific volunteer program that involves teens reading to or with young children.

Once you have established a need for and interest in what is often referred to as a book buddies program in which teens and younger children read together, decide when you would like to offer the program and how it will be structured. This kind of program can be an excellent fit for summer months and can even be offered in connection with a summer reading program in which participating teens and kids receive credit for the time spent reading together as book buddies. Schedule training sessions for teens, perhaps one- or two-hour sessions during which expectations are clearly discussed, including the need for teens to be reliable in keeping their schedule and positive in interacting with kids. Sessions can focus entirely on the younger child reading aloud to the teenager or can combine this with the teenager also reading aloud to their younger partners.

After an initial group of teens has been trained, spread the word to the community about this great new resource available at the library designed for young people struggling with reading skills. Set an age limit for children to participate in the program, such as "open to kids age 6 to 11." If your marketing efforts are successful, be prepared for a significant response, because many young people in urban areas need additional help in learning and practicing their reading skills but their families are often not able to afford private tutoring help.

Set a time limit on the book buddies session and make it clear to parents that the sessions are for a specific purpose—developing reading skills—and are not designed to function as a long-term activity. Teen volunteers should never be in a position of serving as ad hoc babysitters or feel pressure to entertain a child for long amounts of time. Advertising book buddy sessions as "lasting 20 minutes" will help communicate the finite time limit on the activity. Ask teens to sign up for shifts of one or two hours (three to five sessions), and work with staff to schedule interested children during each teen's shift.

The sessions should be carried out in the public space, perhaps in a quieter corner or area of the library. Avoid putting book buddy pairs in closed areas or meeting rooms. Be sure teen volunteers have a staff contact in case any needs or issues come up while they are hosting a book buddy session.

Establish desired outcomes and a concrete action plan. Outcomes might include strengthening the library's teen volunteer program, engaging a wider variety of teens in library activities, and helping enhance literacy for young people in the community. If your library's mission statement mentions literacy, be sure to highlight the clear connection to the teen reader program. Once the outcomes are established, approach key decision makers with an action plan and clear ideas for what resources will be needed, how the program will be managed, and specifics about the training that will be provided for participating teens. Talk to children's services and human resource staff to establish the necessary internal partnerships needed to make the program a success. Be creative in recruiting teens, making sure to look outside any existing teen volunteer group to find interested teens. Many teens like to work with children, and they may not immediately think of the library as a place that might offer this kind of great opportunity.

Be sure to include an evaluation of the program in your plan. This evaluation should be targeted to participating teens, children, parents, and library staff members. If you decide to conduct a book buddy program during the entire year and not just during summer months, be sure to build in regular evaluation of the program.

This suggested book buddies program not only offers teens a valuable experience to teach and model positive behavior for younger children, such a program also inherently includes both structure and focus. Urban libraries participating in the Public Libraries as Partners in Youth Development project reported that these two elements—structure and focus—were essential in designing and developing successful programs for teens. Volunteer programs set up with this in mind will likely produce quality results for both the library and teenagers, and libraries should consider additional opportunities that build on teens' interests, such as volunteer opportunities similar in design and training to the book buddies program but with a different focus, such as technology.

Teens Teaching Technology Awareness

For many urban libraries, it may be more difficult to design a large-scale volunteer program based on teens helping with technology because these libraries may not have multiple workstations. Consider adapting the steps in the book buddies training and set up steps for a small group of teen tech helpers. Like teens in the book buddies programs, teen tech helpers would be offered specific training and given a specific schedule. Unlike the book buddy teens who were paired with a particular child, however, teen tech helpers might work a two-hour shift during which they act as a resource for any and all library computer users. During their shift, teens might help format word processing documents, help customers sign up for an e-mail account, or help customers understand how to fill out a job application online. In addition to the steps outlined for establishing a book buddies program, a teen tech helpers program might include finding funding to provide teens with T-shirts that identify them as such.

Training staff in the area of emerging technology is another area in which teens can function as great teachers. The Young Adult Library Services Association (YALSA) has recently established Teen Tech Week, an annual event held during March. Celebrating this new national initiative can serve as a great incentive for hosting a technology-related event designed to recruit teens for a teen tech helper volunteer program. Consider taking YALSA's advice and host a teen tech fair. Ask teens to bring in their favorite piece of technology to share with librarians. Many teens have access to a variety of highly portable technologies that they use on a daily basis but is something of a mystery to many librarians. A two-hour technology fair is a great chance for librarians to receive hands-on training in the latest technologies and for teens to have the opportunity to showcase their knowledge about a subject many find engaging and interesting. Host the technology event on a Saturday or during summer. If possible, make it a morning event and invite the teens to stay and have lunch afterward with librarians. Offering lunch will serve as an incentive for teens to participate and also provide a chance for positive interactions between teens and library staff.

Additional Considerations for Teen Volunteer Programs

When considering a teen volunteer program, keep in mind that children and tweens often respond positively to teens. For libraries in urban settings, helping to promote programs and signing kids up for summer reading clubs are regular tasks assigned to teen volunteers. Although staffing a reading club table for several hours on a summer afternoon is not be a task many libraries have the resources to assign to paid staff, a teen volunteer working in this capacity can generate a lot of interest among younger children and can offer a meaningful way for teens to contribute to the library and to their community.

If you do establish a teen volunteer program, it is likely that you will be asked by teens and other members of the community if teenagers needing to fulfill court-ordered service hours will be accepted as volunteers. The Queens Borough Public Library is an example of a library in an urban area that embraced this opportunity with amazing results. Their Teen Empowerment Project, selected by the Young Adult Library Services Association as one of the top five programs in the fourth round of Excellence in Library Service to Young Adults in 2003, involves the library working with the Second Chance Program of the Queens District Attorney's Office. Teens who are first-time offenders are offered the chance to complete a 12-week program at the library. They attend courses on computer skills and career options instead of facing possible conviction. If teens complete this program, they receive a certificate and the district attorney recommends that all charges be dropped (Gips 2000).

No matter the final structure or focus, teen volunteer programs are clearly an integral part of serving teens in an urban setting. As Michele Gorman, manager of ImaginOn, the innovative teen space at the Public Library of Charlotte and Mecklenburg County, says, "When it's done a right, a teen volunteer program that allows for meaningful participation is win-win for everyone in the public library because teens have a chance to develop ownership and adults have an opportunity for valuable feedback."

PARTNERSHIPS BETWEEN LIBRARY DIVISIONS AND DEPARTMENTS

Chapter 7 will discuss community partnerships at length. And though the first place many teen services librarians look for partners is in the greater community, do not forget to look in your own backyard, too. There are often excellent collaborative partnership options available within many large urban library systems. Although teen advocates or dedicated teen services staff are the primary staff concerned with delivering excellent library service to teens, other library departments and divisions may have resources and staff that can support this goal. Keeping in mind the idea that collaborative partnerships involve coming together to create new goals, here are some ideas for cross-department and division partnerships for enhancing services to teens:

Partner with technical services to increase volunteer and internship options for teens. Often, large technical services divisions have work that is well suited for teens. Tasks such as labeling, unpacking, and moving materials are easily explained and monitored. Teen services staff in urban settings understand the importance of offering teens meaningful opportunities for contributing their skills to enhance library services. Possible job opportunities within the library are also vital for urban teens. Technical services staff are often under pressure to decrease turnaround time for getting material onto the shelves without additional resources to accomplish this task. The issues may seem unrelated, but if the two divisions start a dialogue and are willing to collaborate and create new goals, partnering will greatly benefit both divisions. Additional benefits for such a partnership include enhancing teens' understanding of library operations and budgets, expanding technical services staff awareness of the skills and talents of teens, increasing options for positive teen-staff interactions beyond public services staff, and offering technical services staff the opportunity to discuss and better understand the place nontraditional material formats, such as graphic novels and manga, have in serving teens.

Other public service departments offer partnership possibilities, too. Creative thinking and open dialogue can help staff realize that material and programs from some seemingly unlikely areas can play a part in serving teens and enhancing and expanding the reach of these areas. Many public libraries in urban areas have developed small-business resources and staff specializing in this in-demand area. Partnership options include programming on copyright, patents, and careers for teens. Programming on songwriting or becoming a professional musician can be greatly enhanced by collaborating with experts from multiple areas. Although a program developed exclusively by a teen services department on poetry might have the sole goal of offering teens an opportunity for creative expression, a program developed in collaboration with other subject experts may offer additional opportunities for teens, including a chance to understand more fully their options for getting into the music business, understanding how to copyright their material, and realizing the importance of practical matters like contracts.

CONCLUSION

Staff and volunteers play a vital and unique role in urban libraries. Both are essential in creating a positive, productive environment at the library.

For urban locations, this can be a challenging task. Many urban libraries are faced with serving hundreds of teen visitors from diverse backgrounds every day. These library facilities are often small, older, and not equipped to handle the space or technology needs of the many regular teen users. But a well-trained staff working with committed teen volunteers can, regardless of facility and technology constraints, make a huge difference in the lives of urban teen library users.

WORKS CITED

Alessio, Amy, and Nick Buron. 2006. "Measuring the Impact of Dedicated Teen Service in the Public Library." *Young Adult Library Services* 4 (3) (Spring): 47–49.

Gips, Michael A. 2000. *News and Trends.* Security Management Online. Accessed July 15, 2007, available at http://www.securitymanagement.com/library/000915.html.

Jones, Patrick. 2002. *New Directions for Library Service to Young Adults.* Chicago: American Library Association.

Meyers, Elaine. 1999. "The Coolness Factor: Ten Libraries Listen to Youth." *American Libraries* 30 (November): 42.

Search Institute. *40 Developmental Assets.* Accessed April 26, 2006, available at http://www.search-institute.org/assets/forty.html.

Urban Libraries Council. *Membership Eligibility.* Accessed March 21, 2007, available at http://www.urbanlibraries.org/join/eligibility.html.

Young Adult Library Services Association. 2005. *Strategic Plan.* Accessed March 21, 2007, available at http://www.ala.org/ala/yalsa/aboutyalsab/strategic-plan2005.pdf

Youth Activism Project. *Adults Only.* Accessed March 22, 2007, available at http://www.youthactivism.com/Adults_Only.php.

FURTHER READING

Adkins, D. 2004. "Changes in Public Library Youth Services: A Content Analysis of Youth Services Job Advertisements." *Public Library Quarterly* 23 (3/4): 59–73.

Alternative Teen Services. Accessed March 21, 2007, available at http://yalibrarian.com/.

Capozzoli, T. 2002. "How to Succeed with Self-Directed Work Teams." *Supervision* 63: 25.

Cart, Michael. 1998. "Young Adult Library Service Redux?: Some Preliminary Findings." *Journal of Youth Services in Libraries* 11 (4) (Summer): 391–95.

Chelton, Mary K. 2005. "Perspectives on YA Practice: Common YA Models of Service in Public Libraries: Advantages and Disadvantages." *Young Adult library Services* 3 (4) (Summer): 4–6, 11.

Erez, A., J. A. Lepine, and H. Elms. 2002. "Effects of Rotated Leadership and Peer Evaluation on the Functioning and Effectiveness of Self-Managed Teams: A Quasi-Experiment." *Personnel Psychology* 55: 929.

Gnehm, Kurstin Finch. 2002. *Youth Development and Public Libraries: Tools for Success*. Evanston, IL: Urban Libraries Council.

Higgins, Susan E. 2005. "Should Public Libraries Hire Young Adult Specialists?" *Journal of Youth Services* 7 (4) (March): 382–91.

Holmes, F. 1987. "Why YA Coordinators Disappear: A Rebuttal." *Voice of Youth Advocates* 10 (June): 66–67.

Isacco, J. M. 1985. "Why YA Coordinator Positions Are Eliminated: An Administrator's Viewpoint." *Voice of Youth Advocates* 8 (June): 110–11.

Jones, Patrick. 1995. "Young and Restless in the Library." *American Libraries* 26 (November): 1038–40.

Jones, Patrick. 2001. "Why We Are Kids' Best Assets." *School Library Journal* 47 (November): 44–47.

Kendall, Karl, 2003. "Teen Central: Safe, Structured, and Teen-Friendly." *Voice of Youth Advocates* 26 (5) (December): 380–81.

McLaughlin, Milbrey, W. 2000. *Community Counts: How Youth Organizations Matter for Youth Development*. Washington, DC: Public Education Network.

O'Dell, Katie. 2002. *Library Materials and Services for Teen Girls*. Greenwood Village, CO: Libraries Unlimited.

Phelps, J. 2005. "Ten Steps to Deploying Self-Directed Teams." *Cost Engineering* 47: 36.

Public Libraries as Partners in Youth Development. 1999. *The Wallace Foundation*. Accessed March 22, 2007, available at http://www.wallacefoundation.org/WF/KnowledgeCenter/KnowledgeTopics/Libraries/PLPYD.htm.

Rosenzweig, Susan. 1995. "Leading by Example." *School Library Journal* 41 (October): 58.

Rutherford, Dawn. 2004. "What Does Professionalism Mean for Young Adult Librarians?" *Young Adult Library Services* 3 (1) (Fall): 13–15.

Shoemaker, K. 1998. "Top Ten Myths and Realities for Working with Teen Volunteers." *Voice of Youth Advocates* 21 (1) (April): 24–27.

Spielberger, Julie, Carol Horton, and Lisa Michels. 2004. *New on the Shelf: Teens in the Library: Summary of Key Findings from the Evaluation of Public Libraries as Partners in Youth Development, A Wallace Foundation Initiative*. Accessed July 15, 2007, available at http://www.wallacefoundation.org/KnowledgeCenter/KnowledgeTopics/Libraries/NewontheShelf.htm.

Tata, J., and S. Prasad. 2004. "Team Self-Management, Organizational Structure, and Judgments of Team Effectiveness." *Journal of Managerial Issues* 16 (2): 248.

Tuccillo, Diane. 2001. "Positive Youth Development: A Positive Move for Libraries." *The Unabashed Librarian* (119): 21–23.

Urban Libraries Council. *Survey Results*. Accessed April 28, 2006, available at http://www.urbanlibraries.org/showcase/plypd_results.html.

Yohalem, Nicole, and Karen Pittman. 2003. *Public Libraries as Partners in Youth Development: Lessons and Voices from the Field*. The Forum for Youth Investment. Accessed July 15, 2007, available at http://www.urbanlibraries.org/files/PLPYDreport_FINAL.pdf.

Young Adult Library Services Association. *Young Adults Deserve the Best: Competencies for Librarians Serving Young Adults*. Accessed March 26, 2006, available at http://www.ala.org/ala/yalsa/profdev/youngadultsdeserve.cfm.

3

◇ ◇ ◇

TEEN SERVICES TRAINING

Subsequent chapters focus on many essential elements for expanding and enhancing service to teens in urban settings. But the benefits of inviting physical spaces, high-interest collections of materials, dynamic programming, and effective community partnerships amount to little if not combined with library staff members who understand the vital role they play in positively serving teens. These staff may or may not be specialists trained specifically in serving teens, but they must be well trained, enthusiastic, and committed to serving the age group. If your library is looking to improve service to teens, one part of the equation for achieving excellence must be training staff to positively and effectively respond to the needs of teen customers.

In many libraries that serve teens in urban areas, a wide variety of staff interact with teens every day. When it comes to working with teens, what kinds of skills do these staff members bring to the job? Do they understand that their daily interactions with teens can make or break the library's efforts to engage this age group? Do all library staff realize that their actions have a significant and perhaps long-lasting effect on teens' perceptions about the library? This chapter will discuss the benefits of providing staff with training on how to serve teens. To truly make a difference in how teens are served in your library, teen services training cannot be an elective opportunity for the highly motivated or merely curious, nor can it be a one-time or occasional opportunity. To truly make an impact on how teens are served, all staff should receive training on how to serve teens, and this training should be incorporated as a standard component of your library's ongoing orientation and training program.

This chapter provides a framework for making this training a reality, including how to effectively gain administrative and management support and the steps to take in designing and implementing a formal training plan. Any large urban library system seeking to create a long-term change in staff attitudes and behaviors toward teens through staff training must have administrative support in order to succeed. Important training topics such as special considerations for effective teen services training (e.g., building awareness of teens' adolescent developmental needs) are included. Please note that training for teen services–designated staff is *not* included in this chapter. That is not to say that training for these staff should not be an emphasis in your library. Tips for selecting well-trained and highly motivated teen services staff are included in chapter 2, as are suggestions for effective ongoing professional development for teen services staff, including effective communication and information sharing, evaluating performance, and self-evaluations of performance, mentoring, and more. In this chapter, the focus is on something bigger: Is the staff at your library equipped to make a difference in their teen customers' daily lives?

WHY TRAIN STAFF TO SERVE TEENS

Simply put, a well-trained staff can make a tremendously positive impact on teens' use of the library, and this is especially true in urban areas. While working in a large branch library in an urban area, a librarian I know was surprised to hear that when one of his young teen customers was asked to write an essay on a hero, the teen wrote about his librarian. This teen's mother informed my friend that her son was new to the area and that the one place he had felt immediately accepted was at the library. This was, she said, because my library friend had made such a point to be friendly to her son, asking how his day went and making sure to invite him to any upcoming programs and events. These simple, positive interactions with a library staff member had a far-reaching, positive, and significant impact on this teenager's life. What if all of your library staff members made it a priority to interact positively with teens? How might this positively affect teens' behavior inside and outside the library building, particularly in the lives of teens who live in busy, crowded areas where their needs and interests are often ignored?

Keep in mind that many library staff members bring to their jobs little or no experience working with or talking to teenagers. For most libraries, knowledge of adolescent development and a desire to help teens are not standard elements of job postings. In many cases, staff members' backgrounds can be very different from those of the teen customers they serve, and they may not realize that the things they say and do can have a big impact on whether teens continue to use the library and its services. For example, when challenging situations involving teens arise, the first reaction many public librarians have is to institute policies and guidelines designed to alter or correct teen behavior. Of course, behavior guidelines are helpful and necessary tools for public libraries. When it comes to teens, however, behavior guidelines are only a part of the answer and may "fix" the problem merely by driving away what should be a significant and important customer group. A more successful solution is to help staff reflect on their perceptions and expectations about the library and teens as users of the library. Lead staff to better understand the reasons why teens act they way they do and to involve staff in finding ways to make the library more teen-friendly and a more productive experience for both staff and teens.

Some libraries serving urban populations have reported very positive results after instituting systemwide routine training for all their staff. Examples include the Multnomah Public Library, New York Public Library, Queens Public Library, and Brooklyn Public Library, all of which train staff using a similar Everyone Serves Youth curriculum (originally designed by the Multnomah Public Library and available at http://brooklyn publiclibrary.info/youth/). For New York, Queens, and Brooklyn, this resulted in more then 4,000 staff members at all levels receiving training aimed to "develop the understanding, attitudes and skills needed to provide excellent service to children and teens" (Urban Libraries Council 2006). Any library that truly wants to see a return on its investment in teen services and that truly wants to make a positive impact on the service it provides to teens should follow these libraries' leads and make teen services training a part of the ongoing orientation and training program for all staff.

Empowering and motivating staff to effectively and positively serve teens require committing to implementing a formal, systematic training program in which all staff receive the information they need to better understand and care about their teen customers and develop the skills they need to serve them better. Such a training structure is a sign that a library is recognizing the unique needs of teen customers. Unfortunately, training staff to work effectively with teens is sometimes undertaken by libraries not as a first step but as a last resort in response to a perceived "teen problem." A library may suddenly be motivated to train staff on teen-related topics because a chronic situation has boiled over into a violent incident, complaints have sharply increased from adult customers, a media report about troublesome teens at the library has received attention, or staff frustrations have reached a breaking point. These libraries may have the best intentions when deciding to initiate one-time training. But sporadic training such as this is not likely to produce real change or lasting results—or actually address the problems. Moving your staff's teen services perspective from "nuisance" and "crowd control" to high levels of satisfaction and involvement takes a serious, ongoing commitment, not something that can be forgotten once a problem has gone away or been accepted as part of the landscape.

Arguments in Favor of Training Staff to Serve Teens

Addressing the need for increased staff training should happen before problems arise. A great way to get started is to build a list of reasons why your library needs to offer the training similar to the following list. Money and resources for staff training are often limited, and a compelling list of reasons will help support your case when requesting resources. Even though the case may be a bit more complicated to build without a looming crisis, proactively pursuing all-staff training ultimately produces the best results.

Keep your list of reasons ready why everyone in the library must serve teens. This list can be helpful when seeking funding for training from both internal and external sources. It can also act as a great training tool for helping staff members talk about specific ways in which the library is proactively addressing teen needs and working to be sure that all staff are equipped in maintaining a quality library environment for everyone.

Why All Staff Must Be Trained in Serving Teens

Why 1: Teens make up a significant portion of the library's customer base, and the number will continue to grow.

Details: At 81 million strong, people born between 1982 and 2002 make up the second largest population group in the United States (Abram and Luther 2004). Many teens are choosing to spend their out-of-school time at the library. In order to capitalize on this, staff must be offered a chance to gain the necessary skills to handle the large influx of teen customers. Not supporting staff to develop the necessary skills in this area does a disservice to both teens and staff. Use census numbers from your local community to reinforce the large number of teens that need service.

Why 2: Whether the community or the library wants to admit it, there is no escaping the reality that *every* staff member serves teens. It is just a question of how *well* they serve them and what the outcomes will be.

Details: Each individual staff person should understand that serving teens is his or her responsibility. In the same way everyone understands it is his or her job to serve seniors or businesspeople, all staff need to fully embrace their role in serving teens and in understanding that teens deserve and require the same level of service as every other customer group.

Why 3: Increased knowledge leads to better understanding and more effective communication, and library staff have an important role to play in helping teens find their place in the library community.

Details: Once staff have a greater understanding of the developmental realities of the teenage years, they will be in a better position to set realistic expectations for teens. This increased understanding will help staff effectively and positively communicate expectations in a way teens can understand and appreciate. This in turn increases the chance that teens will respond to requests to moderate their behavior when necessary. Supplement this reason with real-life experiences from staff members who have changed their approach to teens and witnessed positive results.

Why 4: Resources dedicated to building teen services are wasted if frontline staff members regularly respond negatively to teenagers.

Details: Although it is important to have a specialist on hand to focus on developing services specifically for teens, there is little doubt that many teens' first or only experience with the library may come through interactions with nonteen librarians. If frontline staff members are negative in their interactions with teens, this can ultimately sabotage other enhancements to teen services. Teen survey results may be especially effective in driving home this point.

Why 5: Other professionals working for youth-serving organizations in your community, such as those in education, health, and even law enforcement, recognize that teenagers have unique needs, and it is time the library did so, too.

Details: Individuals who work with teens in urban environments as a part of their everyday jobs need a basic understanding of adolescent development. This helps ensure that teens receive quality and appropriate service. Survey youth-serving organizations in your area and have information on hand about how they train their staff to work with teens.

Why 6: Urban areas are diverse areas.

Details: Staff need training in successfully working with teens from different cultural and economic backgrounds.

If you are not sure about your library's own unique set of whys for training staff or are having difficulty articulating the reasons, a survey of both staff and teens can be a useful starting point. This survey will likely provide evidence supporting your push for initiating comprehensive staff training and offer useful ideas for developing training topics and priorities. The survey can also serve as a pre- and posttest evaluation tool. Staff members can take the survey before training is initiated and again after completion, and you will gain an understanding of the training's impact. Teen responses can also be evaluated before and after staff have completed the training. This will help you evaluate the real-world results and should validate the organization's continued administrative and financial support for ongoing training in this area.

Surveying Staff

Here are some suggested pretraining survey questions for staff. Keep it simple with yes/no and multiple choice questions. Busy staff members are more likely to respond to a short survey, and keeping it brief indicates respect for both staff feedback and their time constraints.

- Do large numbers of teens use your library location?
- Do you think teens are using the library differently than they did in the past?
- Do you feel you have the skills you need to effectively work with teens?
- How do your interactions with teen customers compare to your interactions with other customers?

  - More positive with teens.
  - More negative with teens.
  - About the same.

- Which best describes your feelings about working with teens?

  - I feel anxious with both individual teens and groups of teens.
  - I like working with individual teens but am anxious with groups of teens.
  - I love working with all teens.
  - I don't mind it, but could use ideas on how to do it better.

- Are you comfortable approaching teens at your library when they are in large groups?
- Do you think serving teens is an important part of what the library does?

- Do you feel like the library is supportive in helping you work with teens?
- Have you ever received any training in working with teenagers (through the library or any organization)?
- Would you voluntarily attend a training session focused on working with teens?

Surveying Teens

This list of suggested survey questions for teens may also be helpful when discussing the reason for offering staff training, developing training topics, and evaluating the impact on staff interactions with teenagers.

- How old are you?
- How often do you visit the library?
- What library location do you usually use?
- Do you like visiting the library?
- Do you attend programs and events at the library?
- How do think library staff members feel about teens?
  - Like teens in the library.
  - Are okay with teens in the library.
  - Dislike teens in the library.
- How do you feel about most library staff members?
  - Like them.
  - Dislike them.
  - No real feelings about them one way or the other.
- What is the best thing about the library?
  - Computers.
  - Staff.
  - Book, movies, and other stuff I can check out.
  - Activities and programs I can attend for free.
  - It's a great place to hang out with friends.
- Do you think most library staff members respect you?
- Do you respect library staff members?
- Do you think the library tries to be a good spot for teenagers to visit?

MAKING TEEN SERVICES TRAINING A REALITY

Coordinating with Managers and Administrators

To make training all staff in serving teens a regular part of your library's operations, you need significant management and administrative support. For organizations with no training currently being offered on the topic of teens, start by talking to managers, and share staff and teen survey results with decision makers. Explain how training staff to work with teens fits into your library's long-term goals and priorities. Suggest to management and administrative staff that the most effective way to realize long-term positive benefits for teen customers is to make training frontline staff in serving teens a priority by incorporating this training into standard new-employee orientation. If the initial response from managers and administrators is positive, be sure to build on this commitment by involving managers and administrators in determining what type of training program will be planned and who will be involved in presenting the training. Make sure the training reflects organizational values and that the training goals are reflected in administrative decisions. Work to find a reasonable way to make the plan fit within your library's resources and budget.

Involving Human Resources

The human resources department is often the foundation for the library's training program, particularly in large urban library systems. Human resources should be involved in planning training for all staff in serving teens from the start. Ask about the possibilities for incorporating teen topics into standard new-employee orientation information. Volunteer to be a part of or present this section of the training or to create resource packets. Make it clear that you are willing to supply whatever support might be needed to get the training started. In addition to planning for regular training in the area of teen services for all staff, take a look at your library's training calendar and find out if the topic of working with teens fits with any other scheduled training. If your library has an in-service training or staff development day, talk to the group charged with planning and organizing the session. Offer your services for helping create content for or present a session on working with teenagers. Be flexible and find a way to fit into their schedule.

Budget

Your plans for training must include specific budget projects, particularly if you are working with various divisions within your library. Questions to answer in your budget projections include:

- Will you have a keynote speaker? If so, how many sessions will he or she present and what is the cost per session? Will the speaker need lodging accommodations for more than one night?
- If you are having a speaker from your community, will you offer an honorarium or small gift of appreciation for his or her time?
- If your training includes a teen panel (discussed later in this chapter), strongly consider offering the teens gift cards in small amounts ($5 to $10) or other small tokens for their time and effort.
- Will your training include any sessions at which you will provide refreshments for staff?
- What is the cost of materials for attendees?
- Is there any material you would like to reproduce in color?
- What are your projections for the amount of staff time involved, including your time and the time of staff from other divisions like Human Resources?

Creating a Training Plan

Start by stating your library's mission and determine how your library's vision, values, and goals support training for teens. How does training teens fit into your library's mission? Do phrases such as *equal access* and *all users* appear in your library's mission, vision values, or goals? Look for key words that support your library being a dynamic, lively, and active part of the community and think about how you can tie these ideas to training staff to work positively with teens.

Find facts that support the need to train all staff in serving teens, such as demographic statistics. Include feedback from surveys of staff and teens. Emphasize community factors that support your training initiative. According to recent census data, the current generation of teens is one of the largest in U.S. history. This is probably true in your own community as well. Provide community assessments or report cards that evaluate the state of youth in your local area, including crime statistics, which will help paint a picture of the teens in your community.

Create your own vision of the training. How many sessions will be necessary? What topics will be covered at each session? Will all staff receive direct training on all topics, or is train-the-trainer a better approach for your situation? Investigate options for speakers and special presenters. A national presenter with a background in library service can be very helpful in motivating staff, but do not forget to look within your local community for an expert in serving teens. Find out if the speaker can provide multiple sessions for smaller groups of staff, perhaps at various branch library locations. Contact your state library organization for suggestions. Most urban areas have a local library consortium that offers services to libraries in the area. These local associations focus on training as one of their core services and can be very helpful in providing suggestions for presenters. Contact local hospitals for suggestions in the area of adolescent physiological and psychological development. Drug treatment centers, juvenile detention facilities, and alternative schools are excellent places to look for presenters who will speak about teens with special needs. Experts from parks and recreation departments can discuss various elements of working with teens in nonschool settings, and teachers, principals, and school guidance counselors can offer unique perspectives on teens, too. Outline your expected outcomes and the resources you will need to achieve these outcomes. The following are possible outcomes you might hope to achieve by the end of the training:

- All staff will gain a basic understanding of adolescent development.
- All staff will become more comfortable positively interacting with teens at the library.
- Staff will better understand the library's role in supporting healthy youth development.
- Staff will be better able to handle inappropriate teen behaviors in a positive, proactive way.
- Staff will more greatly appreciate the unique needs of the library's diverse teen population.

No training for staff in working with teens would be complete without offering staff a chance to talk to a teen panel. Teens are great teachers and are uniquely positioned to help staff to gain practical understanding of the concepts discussed in formal training on working with teenagers. Teens represent these concepts, live and in person. They can honestly and genuinely answer staff questions and help staff understand teens' perspective on a variety of situations. Teen panels offer all staff a chance for positive, productive interactions with engaged teens. These panel sessions also empower teens and help them understand how important their voice can be in shaping library practices.

Teens Speaking for Themselves: Putting Together a Teen Panel for Training

Step 1: Rely on teens you know to get things rolling. Teen advisory board members, regular attendees at anime clubs, and teens you see every day after school are prime candidates. Always be sure you have secured at least two or three teens. If you have only one teen, do not ask him or her to field questions from a room of adults.

Step 2: Consider offering teens an incentive for their service, especially because you should be doing your best to secure a wide variety of teens. Go beyond your circle of regulars and work on getting teens who do not often visit the library to agree to serve on your panel.

Step 3: Work with teens and their parents to figure out a viable time when teens can come to the library for the training session. Consider holding the panel later in day, after teens are finished with school and can find transportation to the library. Do not schedule your teen panel for 11:00 A.M. on a school day.

Step 4: Prepare a few questions in advance and let teens have a chance to think about their answers. Opening up the floor for questions from the audience is great, but letting teens have a chance to ease into the discussion can help make the situation less intimidating.

Step 5: When the teen panel is speaking and answering questions, set up the room in a less formal way. Arrange chairs in a circle to create an environment more conducive to discussion and open dialogue. Avoid chairs in rows or tables and chairs arranged classroom style. Establish clear guidelines and rules for expected and appropriate behavior by participants. These guidelines should allow for dialogue, but ensure that the discussion remain respectful and productive from all sides.

Specifically plan for how to evaluate the impact of the training. Consider attaching measurements to your stated outcomes, such as a 5 percent decrease in security incidents involving teens after the training program has been in place for one year or a 5 percent increase in the number of positive comments received by the library from teens.

ESSENTIAL TRAINING TOPICS FOR ALL STAFF

Bringing your organization together to help make teen services training a reality is a daunting task, but with careful planning and effective communication it is an achievable goal. What comes next, however, is the most important component: the content of the training itself. The following are a list of essential training topics that will help make the benefits of teen training a reality.

Training Topic 1: Understanding Teens Better = Serving Teens Better

A reluctance to change attitudes and behavior does not necessarily indicate that staff members are belligerent or antiteen. The larger issue may require taking a step back and realizing that difficulties in working with teens may involve staff expectations about the library environment. Many staff members, particularly those without professional training or a master's degree in library science, bring to their job whatever expectations of the library environment they have formed through their own life experiences. Staff members who have not been trained or educated about the changing library environment may rely on their long-held idea of what a library "should" be when forming expectations for teen customers' behavior. Educating staff about the physiology and psychology of teens will help them understand that teens often exhibit certain behaviors because of where they are developmentally.

When it comes to serving teens, think broadly. Answering a question and then expecting the customer to go away satisfied does not fit the model for how many teens use the library. Teens often do not ask library staff traditional reference questions. They frequently stay at the library for long periods of time, particularly during the after-school hours and in the summer months. The difference between traditional roles for the library and the needs of today's teen customers is a valuable discussion to include. Asking staff to reevaluate their role in serving teens by taking a broader approach to what their service might look like is a challenging task but is an important element in training staff to work effectively with teens.

Discussion Starters

- Ask staff to reflect on their own teen years. It can be helpful to ask staff to pick a particular age in order to help them really focus and remember.

  - What did they do after school?
  - Where did they go?
  - Who was with them?

- How did they complete their homework?
- Who were their friends?
- Did they have friends from outside their neighborhood? Their school?

- Ask staff to share some of their answers. Then ask them to take a moment and consider how teens would answer these same questions today.
- Give a little history of changing attitudes about teens, especially about teens exhibiting challenging behavior. Explain that ideas about what teens need have shifted, with researchers and policy makers changing their understanding and perspective of problem teen behaviors:

  - Teens need dynamic activities that engage them as individuals to succeed.
  - In recent years, instead of concentrating on programs designed to keep young adults out of trouble, funders and policy makers have shifted to programs designed to support positive youth development (U.S. Department of Justice 2003).
  - The library's role in serving teens is similarly changing. Funders and policy makers, as well as library administrators and the communities we serve, expect the library's role in the community to change as well. Adequate service to teens has to be more than merely checking out books.

- Libraries are just one part of the support network that has a role to play in supporting positive youth development.

  - What other agencies exist in the community to support teens?
  - Have these agencies changed over the last several years?
  - What does the library offer teens that these other agencies do not?

- Ask staff to make a list of the resources, services, and programs they think the library *should* be providing teens.
- Ask staff to make a list of what they think *teens* want the library to provide.
- In advance of the training, ask teens these same questions. Share the teens' answers with staff. Discuss the differences and similarities.

At your training, provide staff with easily accessible outlines of behaviors associated with each stage of teen development, such as the following one. Include suggestions on what to remember when working with teens at each stage. Suggest that staff consider creating tip sheets that can be kept on hand at each location or posted on the library's intranet. Following are sample tip sheets. Consider copying and cutting out the tip sections dealing with each stage of development. Include these sheets in staff orientation packets.

Developmental Tasks of the Teen Years:
It Is Not Easy

Teens are trying to figure out their:

- Identity.
- Autonomy.
- Intimacy.
- Sexuality.

Maturation is not just one big task, it is happening on many levels for teenagers, including:

- Physical/biological.
- Cognitive.
- Psychosocial.

Adapted, with permission, from the Children's Hospitals and Clinics of Minnesota, *Peaceful Parenting Tips* cards.

Adolescent Development: There Is a Lot Happening during the Teen Years

Younger Adolescence (Age 10 to 13) Is Characterized By

- Rapid changes, including growth spurts, causing younger teens to wonder if they are "normal."
- Desire for more independence from parents.
- Frequent mood changes.
- Spending hours interacting with friends.
- Not wanting to participate in family activities or being seen hanging out with parents.
- Often dressing exactly like friends.

Tips for working with teens at this stage of development:

- Allow chances to express their opinions.
- Offer mutual respect.
- Give privacy.
- Provide reassurance that they are normal.
- Because they can feel very awkward and unsure of themselves, younger teens may not be comfortable in large groups, especially if they are expected to talk or if unwanted or negative attention is being drawn to them.
- Give frequent breaks, including chances for physical activities, when working on projects or programs that require intense concentration.

Adapted, with permission, from the Children's Hospitals and Clinics of Minnesota, *Peaceful Parenting Tips* cards.

Middle Adolescence (Age 14 to 16) Is Characterized By

- Increased independence.
- Sexual development.
- Self-centeredness.
- Reaching full adult size.
- Interest in dating and romance.
- A desire to improve appearance and a willingness to spend time and money to do so.
- Challenging limits.
- Less childlike thinking.
- More ability to consider a variety of factors and reach good decisions.

Tips for working with teens at this stage of development:

- Set reasonable limits and explain these limits.
- Enforce rules in a consistent and fair manner.
- Make sure teens know the rules and understand consequences for breaking these rules.
- Encourage teens to discuss their opinions.
- Model appropriate adult behavior.

Adapted, with permission, from the Children's Hospitals and Clinics of Minnesota, *Peaceful Parenting Tips* cards.

Late Adolescence (Age 17 to 21) Is Characterized By

- Exploration of long-term relationships.
- High moral standards.
- Beginning to get involved in causes.
- Developing strong opinions.
- Lessening self-consciousness about their bodies and appearance.
- Lessening influence of peers.
- Developing self-confidence.
- Growing life experience.

Tips for working with teens at this stage of development:

- Respect each teen's uniqueness.
- Encourage independent decision making when appropriate.
- Listen when teens talk about goals and dreams for the future.
- Encourage teens to think and plan for post–high school education and careers.

Adapted, with permission, from the Children's Hospitals and Clinics of Minnesota, *Peaceful Parenting Tips* cards.

Where to Look for Help: Trainers in the Area of Adolescent Development

If you are looking for a speaker to talk about recent research in teen brain development or more in-depth discussion of the specific social, cognitive, and physical development of teens, there are a wealth of organizations in urban areas that can provide expert presenters. These organizations include but are not limited to local children's hospitals (particularly their adolescent development specialists), area high schools (high school principals and guidance counselors have a lot of relevant, direct experience), mental health counseling organizations, teen health centers, and organizations that offer parenting classes. If you are looking for a presenter familiar with teen development and with a background in library work, consider contacting a local state library consortium if there is one in your area, your state library, or your state's professional library association. On a national level, the Young Adult Library Services Association, a division of the American Library Association, offers experts in training staff for working with teens through the their Serving the Underserved program.

Serving the Underserved

In 1994, the Young Adult Library Services Association began offering members the chance to become Serving the Underserved (SUS) trainers. Initiated as part of the Serving the Underserved: Customer Services for Young Adults Project, the first class of SUS trainers was followed by several additional classes of SUS trainers, who have conducted more than 350 presentations to more than 20,000 library staff members (Young Adult Library Services Association, *Professional Development Center*). Among the many goals achieved by these trainers was empowering "paraprofessional staff by providing foundations of philosophy for YA services" (Le Conge 2004, 10). SUS trainers can be valuable, often affordable partners in training your staff to work more productively and positively with teens. A complete list of current trainers is available at http://www.ala.org/ala/yalsa/profdev/yalsatrainers.cfm.

Training Topic 2: Helping Teens Be Productive in the Library

As staff members increase their understanding of teens' unique developmental stages, they may realize that teens are not always completely "in control" of their behavior. A discussion of how to effectively work with teens in challenging situations can give staff a chance to discuss how their increased knowledge about teen development might change staff behavior.

Ten Tips for Leading Teens to Productive Behavior

1. Tell teens when you are pleased with their behavior.
2. Thank teens for cooperating with requests.
3. Always model respectful, calm behavior, the kind of behavior you want teens to emulate.
4. Avoid power struggles by offering teens choices.
5. Talk to teens, not at them.
6. Give difficult or challenging situations involving teens your undivided attention whenever possible, focusing on teens when they are talking to you about the problem.
7. You are the adult, they are the teens. Make sure you act like it.
8. Establish boundaries and expectations without being defensive or aggressive.
9. Do not panic if you need to address problem behaviors. Handle issues proactively as they arise.
10. Make sure to be consistent in your enforcement of rules and guidelines.

Essentials for Responding when Teen Behavior Problems Become More Serious

- Discuss with staff how to distinguish between mild behavioral problems that are a little disruptive (such as being noisy) and more serious problems (such as fighting, abusive or threatening language and behaviors).
- Make sure staff know the difference and respond appropriately, not overdoing the one but not underdoing the other.
- Include training exercises that remind staff not to stereotype, label, or make assumptions about teens based on their appearance. One often-used exercise is cutting photographs out of magazines, showing them to staff, and asking what assumptions staff made about each person based strictly on the appearance. Use this as a springboard for discussions about how appearance is not an accurate or useful tool when working with teens in the library.

- Talk to staff about options for enforcing limits on the number of people who can use a computer at a time. Use the training as an opportunity to develop strategies that result in consistent and reasonable enforcement of this rule for everyone, not just teens.
- Talk to staff about when it is appropriate to ask groups of teens who are going in and out of the library to either stay or to leave for the day.
- Bring a security expert in to discuss how to recognize and reduce nonverbal intimidation tactics. Talk to staff about how to address these behaviors.
- Make sure all staff are familiar with the library's policies for removing and suspending individuals and understand these policies should be enforced consistently across age categories.

Talking to Staff about Gang Activity

Including a section on the issue of gangs in staff training is worthwhile, as gang activity is an increasingly common occurrence in urban areas and staff need to be informed about smart and effective ways to ensure their own safety and the safety of their teen customers (many of whom may themselves be just as anxious about these issues as staff are). A frequent issue in working with teens in urban areas is the question of how staff should respond to suspected gang activity and interactions in and around the library. Staff may become aware of this activity through a variety of channels, some of which are reliable but others are not so reliable. Suspected gang problems may be occurring not in the library but in the parking lot or just outside the library building, but the tensions from those activities often spill over into the library building.

Training on this topic is not simple, and librarians are usually not experts in the area. Offering staff a chance to discuss the issue of possible and perceived gang problems and to receive realistic options from both library administration and safety and security personal is an important first step in proactively responding to this challenging issue.

Training Ideas and Resources

- Make sure all staff members know the library's security policies on when and how to write incident reports and what information should be included. Emphasize that staff need to communicate with one another about significant security problems, particularly when it comes to suspected gang activity in and around the library.

- Ask a community police officer to talk to staff about recent gang activity and related problems. Police officers, especially those specifically designated as community officers, are the experts on this issue, so you should work with them.

- Ask staff, and perhaps teens you know well and can speak to, in confidence, if they feel gang colors or symbols are being displayed in a confrontational way at the library.

- Recommend to staff that they watch for any tagging or gang-related graffiti, and recommend that they erase or report it as soon as it appears. This may require working with your facilities or cleaning staff to paint over it.

- Bring in ex-gang members to talk to staff and offer a firsthand perspective on the issue.

- Recommend that staff ask community officers or library security guards to check library landscaping and other hidden outside areas for weapons.

- Make sure staff are doing a good job of communicating with one another about the behaviors they are witnessing. This includes between shift changes as well as with other staff in the branch or department.

- Help staff understand that what happens outside the library and in the parking lot must be addressed as quickly as possible and that police officers and security guards should be the primary responders if at all possible.

- If teens are congregating outside, encourage them to come into the library or to leave.

- Explain how a schedule of staff roving the building can help stop problems before they begin. More people watching for suspicious activity helps set a tone that makes the library less attractive when it comes to gang and other illegal activity.

- Encourage staff to find out if their neighborhood has a gang task force and talk to police officers about the current state of gang activity in each branch's community.

Training Topic 3: Teens Deserve Excellent Customer Service

Once staff have become more knowledgeable in teen development and more comfortable with strategies to proactively and positively moderate and handle behavior issues, it is time to work on adapting the informa-tion about teen development, attitudes, and perceptions to deliver better customers service.

Six Simple Customer Service Tips for Serving Teens

- Look teens in the eye, smile, and greet them every day and every time they come into your library, no matter how you feel or how they behaved the day before. Follow up by asking teens how they are doing. If you know their names, use them.

- Congratulate young people whenever possible for their accom-plishments. Watch the local or community press and watch for teens' names on honor roll lists, sports highlights, or any other good thing happening. Congratulations do not have to be lim-ited to events occurring outside of the library. You can also con-gratulate teens for something as simple as honoring requests from library staff to moderate behavior for several days in a row.

- Engage teens about their interests and opinions. Books are a great thing to discuss, but you can also ask teens what they think about current events, celebrity news, video games, and sports.

- Have high but realistic expectations. Realize that teens are not adults and that their behavior may vary from day to day. Expect the best from teens every time you interact with them, however, and make it clear that you believe they are capable of moderating their behavior and responding to reasonable requests from library staff.

- Have a sense of humor and, when appropriate, do not be afraid to let your sense of humor show with teens. Teens love to see the silly and goofy side of adults!

- Lead by example. Every interaction you have with customers demonstrates to teens in your library what you think is appro-priate behavior. If you are nice to customers, even on the occa-sion when a customer might be yelling or complaining, teens will understand that, no matter the situation, everyone should be treated with respect.

Offering staff members a chance to role-play customer service scenar-ios is an easy way to help staff reflect on their customer service behavior with teens in a nonthreatening way. Create a handful of exaggerated situ-ations that allow staff to role-play. Base these scenarios on common expe-riences and have the trainer model two very distinct responses, one from a library likely to have success in serving teens and another in which teen problems seem much more likely to occur. Ask for volunteers from the audience to role-play the part of teen customers. Begin by modeling less-than-ideal customer service to the teen in each situation. Ask staff to list service behaviors they see that may have been more effective/successful/productive. Provide feedback and make suggestions for techniques and strategies that could be used, based on the information about teen development, attitudes, and perceptions discussed previously in this chapter. Trainers should be sure to provide plenty of examples. Role-play the same scenario a second time, asking staff to try out the techniques that were suggested. Last, initiate a discussion about how the suggestions they have received can positively affect the service they provide to teens and their own experiences working with teens as customers.

Scenario 1

You are a 13-year-old girl who needs help finding a biography that is at least 150 pages long. You have a crumpled piece of paper (with some gum stuck on it) that contains the actual assignment but are hesitant to talk to or interact with the librarian. When asked for help, you speak in general terms. For example, you might say you need a book or information that's "kind of longer and tells real stuff about a real person."

Suggestions for Trainer

Initially, you are unwilling to work with the teen. When you are given the crumpled paper, hold it between two fingers as if it is the most disgusting thing you have ever touched. Do not look the teen in the eye; instead, concentrate on your desk or computer. Do not bother to ask follow-up questions, instead just point in the general direction of the nonfiction shelves, being sure to use unexplained library jargon. Throw in a judgmental comment about how "you kids should take schoolwork more seriously" or "you should have started on this assignment a week ago!"

In the second run-through, look the teen in the eye, greet her, and smile. Patiently wait while the teen unfolds the wadded paper and do not let the gum faze you. Ask follow-up questions, even if the teen does not respond very enthusiastically. Walk with the teen to the shelves. Express empathy for the anxiety she is experiencing regarding their project assignment.

Ask staff to discuss different factors influencing the teen's behavior, making sure to reference points about physiological and psychological development. Discuss how the response of each staff member supports or detracts from helping teens and ensuring that teens and the library have a positive, productive relationship.

Scenario 2

You are a 15-year-old boy walking into the library at 8:50 P.M. The library closes at 9:00 P.M. You need a historical fiction book for school the next day. You have been unable to get to the library because your dad, who promised to take you to the library, had an emergency that caused him to work late. You do not usually ride the bus from home, but you managed to figure out the schedule and transfers that would get you to the library just before closing. You would prefer something quick and are a fan of paperbacks, but you do not know exactly what to tell the librarian. The one thing you do know is that you do not want a big, boring book.

Suggestions for Trainer

Remind the teen several times that the library is closing in ten minutes. While the teen talks, make sure to tap your foot or appear distracted. Check your watch. Interrupt the teen and point in the general direction of the fiction shelves, reminding the teen that they will have to hurry because the library will soon be closing.

In the second run-through, look the teen in the eye, greet him, and smile. Explain that the library is getting close to closing but assure the teen that you will work with him to find what he needs. Listen and nod as the teen explains the request. Continue the discussion as you walk with the teen toward the teen fiction section. Again, discuss how the response of each staff member supports or detracts from helping teens and ensuring that teens and the library have a positive, productive relationship.

Construct other scenarios to help staff in working in common situations involving teens. Ask staff to discuss what factors could be influencing the teen's behavior, especially factors that may not be readily apparent. Be sure to model appropriate responses and consider offering staff the chance to pair up, role-play scenarios with each other, and have some hands-on practice responding to situations involving teens.

Other Scenarios to Consider

- A teen and a very assertive parent who does not let the teen speak for him- or herself.
- A teen who mumbles or speaks very, very quietly with head down.
- A teen who will not take off a hat, cap or hoodie.
- A large group of teens huddled around a computer, laughing, hitting one another, sitting on each other's laps, and generally messing around.

- A customer who complains that teens are just outside the library door, not saying anything but physically crowding customers as they enter the building.

If your training session involves administrators or managers, talk with them beforehand and invite them to help direct responses.

You may also consider using scenarios as an online training tool for staff. Although seeing the behaviors modeled in person may be ideal, making the scenarios available via the Web or e-mail and then asking staff to comment, respond, and discuss virtually may work well, too. This is particularly helpful if there is a limit to the number of in-person training sessions your library or library system can realistically offer.

Training Topic 4: Reference Service to Teens

Homework and school-related questions constitute a significant portion of daily reference interactions with teens in many urban libraries. The quality and accessibility of school libraries varies greatly from location to location, with school libraries frequently being poorly funded, understaffed, and offering short or no after-school hours, so the public library becomes the de facto school library for students, especially students who do not have computers to do research at home. These reasons, along with the fact that in many urban areas middle and high schools are often located very close to public libraries, mean that at the end of the school day, students pour into the library, with many needing help with their homework assignments.

Good communication is the foundation of good reference service, and the customer service tips offered previously also apply to providing better reference service. In many cases, urban teens' reference needs are very similar to those of adults (especially young adults working on college projects). The major goal remains breaking down the communication barriers that occur between staff who do not possess the strategies described for providing quality customer service. The following list offers ideas for how to make teen reference service as successful as possible.

As an added note, if your library already offers basic reference training for all staff, propose that a segment of that training be dedicated to working specifically with teenagers. As with customer service training, additional tips for reference services staff on working with teens can be provided during a training session, through the library's intranet, or developed into an online Web-based training module.

Training/Discussion Points for Conducting Reference Interactions with Teens

- Teens spend a lot of time in classrooms where questions often have right and wrong answers. When conducting the reference interview, use open-ended questions in which teens will not feel as if you are expecting a right answer.

- Teens may be self-conscious and especially afraid to make a mistake. They may be asking for help on a homework question or trying to figure out an assignment they do not actually understand. Keep this in mind and be patient in working through the inquiry with them.

- Make sure you are approachable and responsive to teens. Listen first to the question being asked. Do not interrupt until it is clear that the teen has finished the thought or request.

- Repeat back to teens what you hear, using phrases such as "It sounds like you're asking..." If you are not sure what a teen said, do not be afraid to admit it; just ask nicely to repeat the request by saying, "I'm not sure I really heard your question. Can you say that again or tell me a little more?"

- If appropriate and you think it will help you more fully understand the question and get the teen the information needed, ask if the question is for a school assignment. Ask to see the homework assignment when appropriate. It will help both you and the teen more fully understand the context of the question.

- In fact, make sure all staff know about repetitive or mass homework questions and assignments so that they are prepared to answer teens' questions. This can be especially important in urban areas where multiple large classrooms of students often receive the same or very similar homework assignments.

- Do not judge what teens are asking for or hesitate to provide resources or answers; give them the information they want and need.

- Follow up with teens to be sure they have found the information they need.

- If a teen is at the library with a parent or adult, talk to the teen about his or her question.

- Do not use library jargon when answering questions or directing teens.

- Take the time to teach teens how to use resources, but do not force them to do more self-service than you would any other customer.

- Consider the role online and electronic resources can play in providing teens reference assistance, including blogs, instant messag-
  ing, and online homework and reference chat.
- Staff may not share the cultural background of teens requesting
  reference assistance. Do not judge teens by how they communicate their questions. Simply do your best to get them the information they are requesting.
- In many urban areas, English may be the second language of immigrant teens, and this can complicate reference interactions further. Remain patient and responsive while trying to help teens in
  these situations.

Scenarios and role-playing can also be helpful for training staff in
working with teens on reference questions. Consider inventing one or
two common reference situations involving teens that can create frustration for staff. Using the same techniques discussed earlier in the
chapter, encourage staff to role-play and practice their response to these
situations.

Training Topic 5: Reader's Advisory to Teens

Connecting the right teen with the right book is a challenge, no matter the setting. This challenge is complicated because reader's advisory
service is often delivered by staff with limited experience in providing
reader's advisory service to teenagers. Add to the mix the wide variety
of teen customers with diverse reading tastes served by libraries (is your
frontline staff ready with quick read-a-likes to the latest Zane or Nikki
Turner book?), and it quickly becomes clear why the basics of reader's
advisory for teens is a topic in which all staff need training.

Additional Reader's Advisory Resources for Staff

All staff should also be aware of where to look for the most up-to-date
information about current notable titles and award-winning books for
teens. Offer staff this list of resources to help them become familiar with
useful tools they can utilize when working with teens on reader's advisory questions such as *Teen Genreflecting* by Diana Tixier Herald (Libraries
Unlimited, 2003).

Michael L. Printz Award

> http://www.ala.org/ala/yalsa/booklistsawards/printzaward/Printz.cfm. Young Adult Library Services Association (division of the American Library Services Association). Award given for the best book for young adults in the preceding year.

Coretta Scott King Award

> http://www.ala.org/ala/emiert/corettascottkingbookaward/corettascott.cfm. American Library Association's Social Responsibilities Round Table. Best African American author and illustrator whose books promote an understanding and appreciation of the contribution of all people to the American dream.

Pura Belpre Award

> http://www.ala.org/ala/alsc/awardsscholarships/literaryawds/belpremedal/belprmedal.htm. Association for Library Service to Children of the American Library Association. "Presented to a Latino/Latina writer whose work best portrays, affirms, and celebrates the Latino cultural experience in an outstanding work of literature for children and youth."

Margaret A. Edwards Award

> http://www.ala.org/yalsa/edwards/. Young Adult Library Services Association (division of the American Library Services Association). Honors an author for lifetime contribution to the field of young adult literature and singles out one title from that author for special recognition.

National Book Award, juvenile category

> http://www.nationalbook.org/nbathisyear.html. National Book Foundation. Best book for children and young adults published in the United States in the previous year.

Golden Kite Award

> http://www.scbwi.org/awards/gk_main.htm. Society of Children's Book Writers. Best book for children and young adults written by a member of the society in the preceding year. Honors also awarded.

Edgar Allen Poe Award, young adult category (the Edgar)

> http://www.mysterywriters.org/index.htm. Mystery Writers of America. Best mystery/thriller for teens published in the United States in the previous year.

(continued)

(*Continued*)

Honor Lists

> http://www.ala.org/yalsa/booklists/bbya/. Best Books for Young Adults. Young Adult Library Services Association (division of the American Library Services Association).

Alex Awards

> http://www.ala.org/yalsa/booklists/alex/. Young Adult Library Services Association (division of the American Library Services Association). Best 10 adult books of interest to teenagers in the previous year.

Popular Paperbacks for Young Adults

> http://www.ala.org/yalsa/booklists/poppaper/. Young Adult Library Services Association of the American Library Association. One to five annotated list(s) of at least 10 and no more than 25 recommended paperback titles, selected from popular genres, topics, or themes.

Quick Picks for Reluctant Young Adult Readers

> http://www.ala.org/yalsa/booklists/quickpicks. Young Adult Library Services Association (Division of the American Library Services Association). Books for young adults who do not necessarily like to read.

Books for the Teenage. New York Public Library. Annual.

Booklist Editor's Choices. January issue.

School Library Journal Best Books of the Year. December issue.

Voice of Youth Advocates Top Shelf for Middle School Readers. February issue.

Frontline, nondegreed staff are sometimes (though certainly not always) the unacknowledged heroes of reader's advisory to urban teens. These staff members frequently read popular, mainstream novels and genre fiction—including urban/street lit—as compared to a lot of degreed librarians, whose tastes may be more literary or academic. These nondegreed staff may be the first people to read new graphic novels and urban authors. Think back to when Triple Crown books made a splash at your library. Who first noticed these titles, circulation and frontline staff or professional librarians? Frontline staff at small urban locations have a lot of informal reader's advisory interactions with urban readers during their day-to-day circulation work. Do not underestimate the knowledge of frontline, circulation staff when it comes to doing reader's advisory for urban teens.

Intellectual Freedom

Before tackling the topic of reader's advisory with teens, encourage staff to review your library's intellectual freedom policy (if it has one, and it should). Most libraries serving urban areas have policies addressing young people's rights when it comes to checking out material. Discussing reader's advisory for teens gives you an excellent opportunity to be sure staff members fully understand their role in helping teens find books and materials, especially when they come in asking for urban lit books with titles such as *Hustler's Wife.* Your staff members likely come from a variety of backgrounds and may not be familiar with the concept of intellectual freedom for teenagers. Reviewing your library's policies and discussing the concept that young people's reading requests should be respected and answered in a nonjudgmental manner are essential parts of preparing staff for doing reader's advisory with teens. Additional resources on intellectual freedom are listed at the end of this chapter.

Shelftalking

In chapter 5, you will find some helpful booklists for anyone working with teens in urban areas. For training purposes, select a few titles and ask staff to become familiar with one or two books in advance of their training session. Introduce the concept of shelftalking books to teens. This technique is an abbreviated form of booktalking. Shelftalks are usually shorter and more general that booktalks and can be very effective, especially in providing informal reader's advisory to urban teens. It can be especially useful for frontline staff who work with teens but are not specialists in this area because shelftalks require less in-depth knowledge of books and authors than more formal, lengthy booktalks. Additionally, many teens in urban areas may be in a hurry (rushing to catch a bus or hurried by a busy parent), so a quick, one- or two-minute shelftalk may be a good match for leading them to the right book. In shelftalking, staff use a few sentences to quickly sell a book by pointing out a unique or appealing aspect of the book or figuring out an angle or hook that might interest a teen. Encourage staff to practice shelftalking in pairs or groups, using the titles they have read in advance. If you do not feel comfortable asking staff to prepare by reading a title, bring several books with you, along with reviews and summaries for each. Ask staff to use this information to create a one- or two-sentence shelftalk.

Five Sample Shelftalks

Shattering Glass (Roaring Brook Press, 2002), by Gail Giles. Is there anyone at your school that everyone seems to pick on? Someone that no one likes, or sits next to at lunch? What if that person somehow became the coolest person in school?

First Part Last (Simon and Schuster, 2003), by Angela Johnson. Are there any girls at your high school, or do you know anyone, who got pregnant while still in high school? What if the girl couldn't take care of the baby after he or she was born? Would the baby's father step in? Meet Bobby—that's the choice he has to make, and he has to make it fast.

Black and White (Viking, 2005), by Paul Volponi. Two friends, best friends. They do everything together: play basketball, hang out, make plans for college, and steal. One is black, the other white. Soon they'll find out just how different the world can treat them.

The Perfect Shot (Carolrhoda Books, 2005), by Elaine Marie Alphin. When someone says "the perfect shot," a lot of people think of basketball. A shot with nothing but net. But there's another kind of perfect shot. The kind that involves a gun. One perfect shot, aimed at his girlfriend and her family, will change Brian's life forever.

Jason and Kyra (Jump at the Sun/Hyperion, 2004), by Dana Davidson. Jason is good-looking, a great athlete, and has a very, very hot girlfriend. Kyra, on the other hand, is not so cool. She's got bad hair and seems to spend all her time studying. But there's something about her that Jason just can't seem to resist.

Additional Booktalking Resources

Anderson, Shelia, and Kristine Mahood. 2001. "The Inner Game of Booktalking." *Voice of Youth Advocates* 24 (2) (June): 107–10.

Bromann, Jennifer. 2001. *Booktalking That Works*. New York: Neal-Schuman.

Bromann, Jennifer. 2005. *More Booktalking That Works*. New York: Neal-Schuman

Gillespie, J. T., and Corinne J. Naden. 2003. *Teenplots: A Booktalk Guide to Use with Readers Ages 12–18.* Westport, CT: Libraries Unlimited.

Guevara, Anne, and John Sexton. 2000. "Extreme Booktalking: YA Booktalkers Reach 6,000 Students Each Semester!" *Voice of Youth Advocates* 23 (2) (June): 98–99.

Mahood, Kristine. 2004. "Off the Page and Onto the Stage: Booktalking to Older Teens." In *Serving Older Teens,* ed. Sheila Anderson. Westport, CT: Libraries Unlimited.

Osborne, Marcia. 2001. "Booktalking: Just Do It!" *Book Report* 19 (March/April): 23–24.

Schall, Lucy. 2005. *Teen Genre Connections.* Westport, CT: Libraries Unlimited.

Schall, Lucy. 2007. *Booktalks and Beyond: Promoting Great Genre Reads to Teens.* Westport, CT: Libraries Unlimited.

Web Sites

Booktalking Ideas. http://www.albany.edu/~dj2930/yabooktalking.html.

Additional Resources about Young People's Intellectual Freedom

American Library Association. 2006. *Intellectual Freedom Manual.* 7th edition. Chicago: American Library Association.

American Library Association, Office for Intellectual Freedom. http://www.ala.org/Template.cfm?Section=oif.

Bodart, Joni Richards. 2002. *Radical Reads: 101 YA Novels on the Edge.* Lanham, MD: Scarecrow Press.

Harer, John B., and Jeanne Harrell. 2002. *People for and against Restricted or Unrestricted Expression.* Westport, CT: Greenwood Press.

Kids and Libraries: What You Should Know. http://www.ala.org/Template.cfm?Section=dealing&Template=/ContentManagement/ContentDisplay.cfm&ContentID=11099.

Kniffel, Leonard, ed. 1998. "Purveyors or Prescribers: What Should Librarians Be?" (Conference Call: Eleanor Jo Roger and Charles Robinson). *American Libraries* 29 (5) (May): 66.

Kravitz, Nancy E. 1998. "Young Adults and Intellectual Freedom: Choices and Challenges." In *Young Adult and Public Libraries: A Handbook of Materials and Services,* ed. Mary Ann Nichols and C. Allen Nichols. Westport, CT: Greenwood Press.

Minow, Mary, and Tomas A. Lipinski. 2003. *The Library's Legal Answer Book.* Chicago: American Library Association.

Pinnell-Stephens, June. 1999. "Libraries: A Misunderstood American Value." *American Libraries* 30 (6) (June/July): 76–81.

Symons, Ann K., and Carla J. Staffle. 1998. "When Values Conflict." *American Libraries* 29 (5) (May): 56–58.

(continued)

(*Continued*)

   Truly, Traci. 2002. *Teen Rights: A Legal Guide for Teens and the Adults in Their Lives.* Naperville, IL: Sphinx.
   Youthspeak. http://www.oblivion.net/youthspeak.

Training Topic 6: Diversity

Urban areas include teens from different ethnic, cultural, and economic backgrounds. Helping staff to be sensitive to the wide range of these urban teens' needs is an important task that must be a part of ongoing training in the area of teen services. Many of the techniques suggested in this chapter, such as role-playing and reenacting scenarios based on real-world experiences, can be useful in helping staff reflect on how they respond to and assist teen customers. Most people honestly believe they honor and respect diversity in their customers, and asking library staff members to reevaluate their reactions can create defensiveness and resistance. Invite an outside speaker to be a part of this training segment rather than having a library staff member lead the discussion. This can ease staff tension and provide a safe environment for staff to explore their responses to teens in various situations. The American Library Association's Office for Diversity (http://www.ala. org/ala/diversity/diversity.htm) is a great resource for speakers and staff training resources. REFORMA, the National Association to Promote Library and Information Services to Latinos and the Spanish Speaking (http:// www.reforma.org/), and American Library Association's Gay, Lesbian, Bisexual, and Transgendered Round Table (http://www.ala.org/ala/glbtrt/ welcomeglbtround.htm) are possible resources, depending on the focus of training. Your state library associations may include a diversity committee or section (or related committee) that can be an effective way to find local speakers on the topic of diversity. Examples include the Ohio Library Council Diversity Awareness and Resources Committee (http://www.olc.org/ diversity/best_prac.html) and the Minnesota Library Association Diversity Round Table (http://mladiversityroundtable.blogspot.com/).

An additional issue to consider when training staff is that of helping staff to appreciate cultural differences associated with teens' economic background. A simple, straightforward resource not to be missed on this topic is Ruby K. Payne's *A Framework of Understanding Poverty* (aha! Process, 2005). Although the author's background is in teaching, much of the information is relevant to librarians working in urban communities with high rates of poverty. Consider having staff read some or all of Payne's book as part of a diversity training session.

CONCLUSION

Training staff to work with teens in urban areas can be particularly complicated. All staff need to be trained in certain basic areas, and in large library systems that often serve urban communities, training everyone requires dedication, time, and planning. Training in the areas of teen services is also particularly important for staff working in urban areas. There are more teens, the facilities are often smaller, teens are often hanging out in the after-school hours for long periods of time, and staff specifically hired and dedicated as teen services librarians are not always on hand. These factors combine to make training essential in order for staff and teen customers to enjoy positive, productive experiences at the library.

WORKS CITED

Abram, Stephen, and Judy Luther. 2004. "Born with the Chip." *Library Journal,* May 1. Accessed March 31, 2007, available at http://www.libraryjournal. com/article/CA411572.html.

Children's Hospitals and Clinics of Minnesota. *Peaceful Parenting Tips Cards.* Accessed January 10, 2006, available at http://xpedio02.childrensmn.org/stellent/ groups/public/@xcp/@web/@forparents/documents/policyreferencepro cedure/web008431.asp.

Le Conge, Monique. 2004. "Ten Years and Counting: YALSA's Serving the Under served Project, 1994–2004." *Young Adult Library Services Journal* 3 (1) (Fall): 6–12.

Urban Libraries Council. 2006. *Learning in Libraries: A National Call to Action.* New York City: Urban Libraries Council.

U.S. Department of Justice, Office of Justice Programs, Office of Juvenile Justice and Delinquency Prevention. 2003. *2003 Report to Congress: Title V Community Prevention Grants Program.* Washington, DC: U.S. Department of Justice.

Young Adult Library Services Association. *Professional Development Center.* Accessed August 27, 2007, available at http://www.ala.org/ala/yalsa/profdev/under served/servingunderserved.cfm

FURTHER READING

Agosto, Denise E, and Sandra Hughes-Hassell. 2005. "People, Places and Questions: An Investigation of the Everyday Life Information-Seeking Behaviors of Urban Young Adults." *Library and Information Science Research* 27 (2): 141–63.

Anderson, Sheila B. 2000. "I Stink and My Feet Are Too Big! Training Librarians to Work with Teens." *Voice of Youth Advocates* 22 (6) (February): 388–90.

Gnehm, Kurstin Finch, ed. 2002. *Youth Development and Public Libraries: Tools for Success.* Evanston, IL: Urban Libraries Council.

Goldsmith, Francisca. 1999. "The Top 10 Things You Need to Know about Teens." *School Library Journal* 45 (January): 30–31.

Gorman, Michele. 2006. "The 'Terrible Teens': Understanding Adolescent Development Is Key to Successful Teen Services." *School Library Journal*, June 1. Accessed December 30, 2006, available at http://www.schoollibraryjournal.com/article/CA6338706.html.

Hersch, Patricia. 1998. *A Tribe Apart.* New York: Fawcett Columbine.

National Youth Anti-Drug Media Campaign, Office of National Drug Control Policy. 2003. *Pathways to Prevention: Guiding Youth to Wise Decisions.* Rockville, MD: White House Office of National Drug Control Policy.

Nichols, C. Allen. 1998. "Getting Started on the Right Foot: The Training Needs of Young Adult Staff." In *Young Adults and Public Libraries,* 239–50. Westport, CT: Greenwood Press.

Payne, Ruby K. 2005. *A Framework for Understanding Poverty.* Highlands, TX: aha! Process.

Rauner, Diana Mendley. 2000. *They Still Pick Me Up when I Fall.* New York: Columbia University Press.

Ried, Kimberlee, and Kaite Mediatore. 2003. "The 411 Is Now the Shiznit: Popular Culture and Teens." *Young Adult Library Services* 2 (Fall): 7–9.

Strauch, Barbara. 2003. *The Primal Teen: What the New Discoveries about the Teenage Brain Tell Us about Our Kids.* New York: Doubleday.

4

◈ ◈ ◈

MAKING SPACE FOR TEENS

Once while making plans at a teen department in a large central library located in a downtown area, I gave several teens a map of the proposed department and asked them to draw their ideal teen space. After working for nearly twenty minutes, one younger teen girl came back to me proudly carrying her finished plan. Just before handing it to me, she paused with a look of dawning realization on her face. "I think I have to start over," she said, "I have a plan for the whole thing, but I forgot to put the books in." Although the library's role in providing books and materials continues to be central to the services offered to teen customers, as this story illustrates, we must also appreciate how important having space to hang out and chill is to teens, especially in urban areas.

Teens need to have a space of their own where they feel welcome and where they have a sense of control. This is true in life, and it is certainly no less true in the library. As noted in *Connecting Young Adults and Libraries*, "Of all the things that teens treasure in their life, those that have their own room treasure that personal space" (Jones, Gorman, and Suellentrop 2004, 56).

Developmentally, teens need places that encourage "independence, learning, socialization and creativity" (Bolan 2006, 44). In reality, their options can be quite limited, particularly in urban communities. In fact, in many urban areas there are not many places where teens are welcome to hang out. Organizations and businesses may hesitate to embrace teens looking for a place to chill. Some businesses and institutions actively discourage groups of teens from staying in their facilities for very long and may even post signs stating that only one or two teens are allowed in a restaurant or store at time or requiring that everyone younger than 16 or 18 be accompanied by a parent or adult. Finding a place to hang out without participating in an organized activity or paying an entrance fee can be a real challenge for teens living in urban areas. And, unlike their peers living in nonurban communities, urban teens may have limited options for hanging out at their home or a friend's home. Many may live in smaller apartments that are not, simply because of a lack of space, a comfortable option for more than a few friends. More and more often, urban teens look to the library to fill this gap in their lives. In urban areas, the library's role as a place to go—and stay for long periods of time—may far outweigh the need for other materials, services, or programs we offer. The library is often the only option for teens looking for a place to just *be* in the community.

Throughout their history, libraries serving urban areas have faced the challenge of providing teen-friendly spaces to young people in the community. Chapter 1 discussed the history of serving teens in urban areas and included examples of libraries' experiments in creating spaces dedicated specifically to teens. Even though these experiments did not always produce long-lasting results, they clearly indicate that libraries in urban areas have had a long history of looking for ways to serve teens' need for space. In recent years, as teens have increasingly become recognized as an important customer group in their own right, this interest has become stronger than ever, with many libraries serving urban areas creating specific areas for teens and a number of them—Los Angeles Public Library and Phoenix Public Library, for example—achieving particularly notable results.

This chapter details why libraries serving urban areas need to create and maintain spaces dedicated specifically to teens; ideas for addressing staff concerns about creating and expanding these teen areas; the concept of the library as a so-called third place for teens in the community; technology, security, and marketing considerations; and concrete tips for making teen areas a reality (no matter the size of a facility).

WHY CREATE A TEEN SPACE?

During a recent discussion about reorganizing large, central libraries, a non-teen librarian who has worked in public libraries for many years asked me why teens would possibly need their own space. He was genuinely confused by this idea. I was surprised by his question, probably because the *whys* of creating teen areas have become so clear to me that I now spend most of my time thinking instead about *how* to make these spaces a reality. This conversation was a great reminder that teen librarians and advocates cannot bypass the necessary step of clearly and patiently explaining to co-workers and decision makers exactly why creating teen areas should be a top priority for libraries serving urban areas. Following are several easily communicated and compelling reasons why libraries serving urban areas need teen spaces. Although some may be relevant to libraries serving a variety of communities, all are particularly relevant to libraries serving teens in urban areas.

Teens need and deserve their own space. Teens have unique developmental needs, and the library should provide space that is appropriate for teen behavior and allows them freedom to be themselves. In urban areas, there are often limited teen-friendly places.

Teen spaces provide a place for teens to socialize and interact with peers. It can give them a place to chill, where they are not required to participate in organized behaviors and activities, as is often the case in after-school clubs or at community recreation centers where many urban teens spend their out-of-school time. In rural or truly suburban areas, teens may go directly home or even to a friend's house after school via a school bus or private transportation. In urban areas, many teens use a city bus or other public transportation to go to and from school. This offers teens time—between transfers or just because they have time on their hands before they are expected home—when they want to spend time with their friends and be in charge of choices about what they do. As Barbara Stripling, director of School Library Services for New York City's Department of Education (Library Media Services Division) recently said when discussing teens' library use in the after-school hours, "We [librarians] need to know what chilling looks like" (Urban Libraries Council presentation 2006). Once libraries appreciate chilling behavior for what it is, they need to step up and respond by actively recognizing the value of teens and reinventing the library so that it is a great fit for them.

Creating a teen area sends an important message from the library to teens about the library's commitment to serving teens. It is a way for the library to communicate to teens that "we know that you are here and we *want* you here." Developmentally, teens are very concerned with what is fair and what is right. In urban areas where they are not always welcome to hang out in stores or restaurants, teens as a group likely feel underappreciated and unfairly discriminated against because of who they are, not necessarily how they behave. Teens walking into a large central or main library usually find a children's room with staff working to assist kids and their families. They also will encounter one or more subject departments or reference areas packed with resources and materials for adults, with librarians answering questions and helping adults locate materials. These areas are, of course, open to teens but feel designed for adults. There may also be other large areas dedicated to popular fiction, movies, and technology. Is there a place in this library just for teens? The answer to this question will have a tremendous impact on the response that teens will have to the library, to its services, to its resources, and to the overall likelihood that teens will come back and keep coming back throughout their lifetimes. When teens look around the library, they almost certainly see many other young adults just like them, particularly in urban areas. If there is no teen area at all, or if the area dedicated to teens does not communicate a genuine appreciation of this age group through an adequate amount of floor space (for example, the notorious teen corner), designated staffing, and good-quality materials and furnishings, make no mistake about it, the inequity will not be lost on teens. If you do not see the difference in service, do not worry, the teen certainly will, and when library staff or a security guard asks a teen to cooperate and respect their surroundings but the library has not extended the same respect toward them, teens' reactions will reflect their feelings of frustration at being undervalued.

A separate teen space allows the library to clearly distinguish between materials for teens and materials for children. Libraries benefit by moving teen material to a separate area. This helps teens quickly identify the material that is specifically for them; it also helps children and parents understand that there is material specifically designed and written for teens that it is very different than material for kids. Most teen books are not intended for 10-year-olds, but the length and appearance of young adult books does not necessarily indicate the difference in the target audience. In smaller facilities, teen material is often shelved right next to juvenile fiction or nonfiction and is frequently located on the children's side of the library. The idea of young people graduating from juvenile books to teen books and having easy access to the young adult section when they are ready to move on to it is not a bad one. If the distinction between the two sections is not clear, however, problems and confusion can frequently result. A separate teen section, which is clearly for teenagers, makes this distinction much clearer. This is an especially good point to make when soliciting support for the creation of a teen area from children's services staff. All too often, juvenile fiction sections are underused because tweens in the 9- to 12-year-old age group jump to teen material without ever experiencing all the great reads located in the juvenile fiction section. Inviting and welcoming teen spaces that cater to the teen crowd help redirect the attention of tweens as well as the attention of their teachers and caregivers back to the juvenile section.

The process of building or redefining a teen space allows you to build partnership with teens and establish behavior boundaries. The planning process gives you and your staff a chance get to know teens' names and to find out more about the regular teen customers you see every day. Teens also have a chance to find out more about library staff members and appreciate them as individuals, too. Together, staff and teens can revisit the boundaries for activities like talking, socializing, and working collaboratively from the perspective of how things will work best in the new area. If a library has difficulties managing a large after-school crowd, as is often the case in urban areas, the creation of a new teen area is a chance to engage teens in a constructive dialogue about the library's role in their lives. Teens appreciate the chance to express their opinions, and the dialogue will produce a greater sense of ownership among teens about the new teen area. Furthermore, if teens feel they have a hand in creating a space, they are more likely to help with things like reminding their peers to act appropriately and respectfully. The collaborative process of creating a teen space provides staff an up close and personal look at how teens work as a group and reinforces the positive role that socializing and interacting can play in teens' lives.

Creating a teen space provides opportunities to expand services and increase staff understanding of teen needs. The new space will offer a place to have teen programs and activities. It will also serve as a starting point for opening a staff dialogue about teens' unique developmental needs.

ARGUMENTS YOU SHOULD BE PREPARED TO ANSWER

After patiently explaining to everyone why making room for a teen space is such an important task for libraries serving urban areas, it seems the path to doing so should be clear, and teen librarians should be on their way. Unfortunately, there may still be some bumps in the road. These bumps may come in the form of specific arguments (coming from other staff members) against creating a separate teen area. Following are suggestions for addressing some of the arguments you may face as you move forward on the road to creating or redesigning your teen space.

Argument 1: If teenagers cannot sit down and be quiet, they should just leave. Staff members may feel that active teens looking to connect with friends, work cooperatively, or play an online game while carrying on a discussion about it should either change their behavior or leave the library.

Response: In this case, staff may just generally disapprove of typical teen behavior. Explain that teens like to talk and socialize. It is part of who they are and where they are developmentally, and in urban areas places that welcome this kind of activity craved by teens are often very limited. The information provided in chapter 3 about the various stages of adolescent development is helpful in addressing this concern. Remind staff that the quiet, subdued, traditional environment of many libraries has gradually been changing for many years and that things like the Internet, word processing, and other new technologies have radically altered the landscape of libraries. There is no easy fix for what may basically be an objection to the idea of teens as customers in general, and teen librarians must be patient and persistent in their approach to staff.

Argument 2: Do teens really need a separate space?

Response: Another common staff objection is that teens, unlike children, whose physical size and development make it hard for them to negotiate adult-size furniture and shelves, are capable of using all areas of the library. In large urban central libraries, it is hard to argue that teens do not utilize the extensive collections of materials and resources in the adult collections for homework and school projects. But being able to reach the top shelf in the adult area or find a book on the shelves does not mean the library has provided teens access to what they need. Teens are not small adults, and it is important to recognize and provide for their unique developmental needs. Materials for teens will be packaged and formatted to address these unique needs, and the library has a responsibility to ensure that teens, like children and adults, can easily find and access the material targeted specifically to teens. In large central or main libraries with no teen area, it is not unlikely that this material will simply become lost in the shuffle and missed by the very teen audience for whom it was purchased.

Argument 3: If you make more space for teenagers, you will just attract more teens who act inappropriately.

Response: Sometimes staff group all teens together in their mind and assume behavior problems and teenagers go hand in hand. Remind staff that each teen customer is a unique individual. In the same way we would not make sweeping generalizations or broad assumptions about other groups of customers, we need to treat teens as individuals and address any behavior problems on an individual basis rather than basing service decisions on assumptions about teens as a group.

Argument 4: We do not have the money or resources to do it right, so why do it? What is the point of a few beanbag chairs in the corner next to the teen books?

Response: Creating or dressing up a teen area is just not about purchasing new furniture or building a new space. It is about making an effort to provide teens the space and services they need and deserve. There are simple ways staff can enhance a teen area, such as increasing display space by removing or rearranging shelves, moving a computer from one area of the library to the new teen space, and adding teen artwork to liven up a new teen area. As a matter of fact, something as simple as displaying art and creative work produced by teens themselves will help engender a greater respect for the area and may greatly decrease incidents of graffiti and other property destruction. Money is always helpful, but creative staff can send an important message to teens by making genuine efforts to enhance the teen area with the resources they have at hand.

Argument 5: Carving out a teen space will mean taking space away from other services.

Response: The focus of creating a teen space should be on the opportunity it provides to expand service to teens. Responding to this argument really starts by making sure staff appreciate the need to serve teens. If they do, they will be much more likely to have the ability to change gears and look at all the benefits to teens, instead of thinking of the new area in terms of its impact on other customers. The response to argument 2 in this section may be helpful in responding to this concern, too.

Argument 6: We are only talking about 50 books. Why create a whole space just for that many books?

Response: Talk to staff about the library's role in supporting teens' healthy development and how in urban communities, particularly those afflicted by poverty and with fewer available community services for teens, library staff are often the only positive adult role models available and accessible to teens. Discuss the Search Institute's 40 Developmental Assets and the library's role in helping teens achieve these skills. This is an opportunity to discuss with staff the broader place the library should have in teens' lives and in the community. Chapter 2 provides helpful talking points for this discussion.

Also be sure to confirm the reality of this statement. Recently, I had a discussion with a librarian from a large urban system, and he commented that although the budget for purchasing teen material had increased in the last few years, the space for displaying and shelving this material had not increased. Find out if your library's teen materials budget has increased recently, and, if so, be sure to point this out when answering this argument.

Argument 7: The low circulation of teen material must mean that teens do not really use the library or its collection, so why do we need to give them *more* space?

Response: Teen materials usually make up a relatively small percentage of the library's overall circulation, especially at large libraries with collections containing hundreds of thousands of volumes, a collection size that is typical of large urban library systems. Likewise, programming statistics for teen events are often dwarfed by the programming numbers produced through a large and active central library children's department or when compared on a large systemwide level. When viewed without the proper context, these traditional statistics do not immediately paint a picture that indicates a need to shift scarce resources to the creation or expansion of a teen area. This approach misses two essential elements to teen services in urban areas: the important role libraries can and need to play in supporting healthy youth development and a realistic understanding about how teens use the library's facility, which may be different than the use seen in nonurban areas. Teens may not be checking out dozens of books or attending weekly programs, but they are huge consumers of the library's space, computers, and technology. This type of use does not automatically generate statistics or hard data, particularly because much library data is based on measuring basic, traditional use of the library and library material. It is necessary for teen advocates to be creative when it comes to making the case about the need for an adequately sized and resourced teen area.

A useful technique to address this concern is to think of new ways to measure use so that the actual need for an area can be more easily demonstrated. Circulation statistics and collection size do not tell the entire story about who is using a library or how they are using it, and this is particularly true in the case of teenagers. It is not unusual for nonteenage customers in urban library settings to identify this kind of library use with comments such as, "This place is wall-to-wall teenagers today" or "I usually come in the mornings because in the afternoons the library is packed with teenagers." Library staff and administrators should take their cue from these customers by acknowledging and addressing this kind of use in urban areas. Circulation statistics may be low relative to the actual number of teens using the facility or browsing (but not necessarily checking out) library material on a daily basis. Set aside one month during which library staff take an hourly count of customers in the building. Ask staff to count customers in broad age categories: children, teens, adults, and senior adults, for example. In many libraries serving urban areas, these hourly counts will quickly provide a snapshot of the library use that is missed when looking at measurements like circulation. This snapshot will likely demonstrate that a surprisingly large numbers of teenagers use the building every day. Having quantifiable, consistent data demonstrating this teen use provides hard evidence that more space for teens makes sense.

And one final point, which is not exactly an argument against creating a teen area, but can present a challenge to making a teen area work is "As long as it will solve our teen problem I'm all for making a teen area."

Response: Some staff and library leaders may actually express support for creating a teen area but are doing so for the wrong reasons. Any staff support can be helpful, but staff sometime view the creation of a teen area as a way to "solve the teen problem" by creating a separate space in the corner of the library designed for teens that will prevent them from disturbing other customers. Successful teen areas do not start with the question of how a space can be used to make teens less of a problem for the library. Instead, the focus should be on what teens actually need and want from a teen area and how this area fits into the library's overall mission.

MAKING TEEN SPACES A REALITY

It takes planning, patience, and persistence to create a quality teen area, and anyone looking to do so should certainly consult the outstanding general resources that exist about this topic, including Kimberly Bolan's excellent and practical *Teen Spaces: The Step-by-Step Library Makeover* (American Library Association, 2003) and Virginia A. Walter and Elaine Meyers's *Teens and Libraries: Getting It Right* (American Library Association, 2003), which provide an outstanding overview of considerations for creating teen areas.

The following section offers additional concepts to consider through the lens of libraries serving urban teens. At the time of this guide's writing, several recent news stories have focused on libraries where teens' use of space has been discouraged, so much so that teens are required to have a parent or adult with them to be in the library after school. In one case, a library briefly considered closing completely during the after-school hours to avoid problems they were having with teens. These cases reveal a need for libraries to seriously consider their role in providing teens a relatively safe place to be in the community and to develop productive and manageable ways to fit this increasingly important role. This section is a good place to start that process.

Third Place

The first step in making your teen area a reality is to develop a vision of what you want the space to be and the purpose that you think it should serve in teens' lives. As discussed earlier, many teens in urban communities are looking for a welcoming place to go and just *be*. As you beginning planning and developing your teen space, keep in mind the idea of *third place*. Sociologist Ray Oldenburg describes third places as neutral ground in communities where people gather to discuss, interact, and enjoy the company of those they know (Project for Public Spaces, *Ray Oldenburg*). Most individuals consider their home to be their first place and consider work or, in the case of students or teenagers, school to be their second place. Is there actually a space somewhere in the community that is frequently used as a third place for teens? How might the library fill this role in teens' lives?

Having access to a quality third place can be an invaluable part of young adults' lives, allowing them to connect with their friends and to feel like a part of a larger community, essential elements for healthy youth development. Libraries in urban settings in particular can embrace their role as third place for teens by becoming familiar with a few basic elements commonly found in successful public spaces and incorporating them into their design and services. Take a minute to imagine what your library's space could become. Think beyond standard library activities such as studying, using technology, providing reader's advisory services, or providing reference assistance. Think about ways to support these activities by encouraging and capitalizing on teens' natural tendencies to gather and interact, and make your teen area a great third place. Do not miss the opportunity to consider the library as a third space, as doing so is one of the unique opportunities for working in an urban area. Unlike libraries serving rural and truly suburban areas, libraries in urban communities that successfully create a third space can provide a comfortable, neutral meeting place for a wide variety of teens from many different backgrounds and neighborhoods.

Simple steps like having furniture that is easily moved around is a great example of proactively working to create a public space that is a perfect fit for teens. Whether the furniture supports it or not, teens will make the space work for them by sitting three to a chair designed for one, sitting on the edges of tables, or sprawling across the floor. Is it possible to make your area so adaptable that teens can be comfortable doing these things, not in spite of the furniture and design but because of it? Are there furniture designs that embrace this kind of use instead of fighting it? Although this type of furniture may be conducive to some unacceptable teen behaviors such as inappropriate displays of affection and teens sitting on each other, these problems should be addressed through behavior management, not by limiting the potential of the space by avoiding some types of furniture. Along with mobile furniture, consider how you might make some sections of your collection more mobile. For example, in one larger urban library at which I worked, the graphic novel collection began to grow so quickly that I was forced to use a book truck to temporarily house new graphic novels. I made it a priority to weed the collection, and in a few weeks I was able to comfortably fit all of the graphic novels back onto the shelves. Much to my surprise, several teens complained. They explained that they actually loved having the new graphic novels on a cart! They had gotten into the habit of settling in at a large comfortable table and wheeling the cart to them while they sat and browsed, rather than having to stand at the shelves while they looked at the new material. I apologized for not asking before eliminating the movable graphic novel collection, worked with my branch manager to find a cart that I could permanently dedicate to the teen section, and then asked the teens to load the cart with the graphic novels they liked and to decorate the cart to make it teen friendly.

Other options to consider include program rooms and space. This may be an option more likely available to larger branches and central libraries. How close is your teen area to a designated programming space or room? Is it possible to have more than one room available for teens to use, perhaps a larger programming space and one or two smaller spaces for tutoring or studying? Remember, if these types of space are available, in the interest of safety and security all of the room or space must be clearly visible to staff.

Teens in urban areas often carry around large book bags and other personal belongings that cannot be left at a table or on the floor because of theft concerns. Staff in urban areas are frequently asked by teens if it is possible to leave these personal items behind the service desk. When creating or redesigning your teen area, consider options for lockers or other places to put book bags, backpacks, coats, and jackets.

Additional considerations that may be particularly important to incorporate into the planning for your teen area is homework supplies. Basic homework supplies such as a stapler, tape, paper, pens, and paper are always in demand. Find a way to stock a homework supply center with these kinds of supplies for teens. The supplies may disappear quickly, so be prepared to find resources to replenish these on a regular basis.

Teens' technology needs are discussed in detail later in this chapter, but it is worth mentioning here that when considering how to make your teen area a dynamic, functioning third place, include viable options for teens bringing in their own technology. Outlets to plug in computers and free Wi-Fi access should be incorporated in designing and reengineering space for teens. In the same way it is worth considering how to provide teens storage options for their backpacks and book bags, think about what you can offer teens for storing their own technology, like laptops and, perhaps more commonly, handheld gaming devices.

Finally, there is the issue of telephone use. Public telephones were once a staple at many libraries in urban areas. With the rise of cell phones, public pay phones are not as common as they once were. And in many urban areas, teens do not have money to pay for a phone call. A recent survey indicates that 51 percent of urban teens own cell phones, a higher percentage than both their suburban or rural peers (Lenhart, Madden, and Hitlin 2005). Urban teens may not, however, always have minutes available and so may not be able to consistently use their cell phones to call for a ride or talk to their parents. Allowing teens to use staff phones is often a contentious issue with staff. If your library is serious about making the teen space a truly functioning public space for teens in your community, however, teens' ability to count on using the phone to contact parents cannot be ignored. One option for addressing this issue is setting clear, time-based guidelines for phone use. Another option that I have seen successfully used in public parks in urban areas is providing a free courtesy phone for teens. These phones do not require any payment but have a very short time limit, perhaps two or three minutes. When the time is up, the phone automatically disconnects.

Take steps to encourage use of the space by a diverse group of individuals. Setting a tone of zero tolerance for any intimidating or threatening behavior from the start is essential for ensuring that all teens feel welcome and comfortable using the space. Library staff members do not need to be intrusive or insert themselves, uninvited, into the conversations or lives of teens hanging out in the library to do this; however, they should work proactively to maintain a comfortable, inviting atmosphere that preserves the purpose of the teen space. Successful public spaces are free from a sense of fear or anxiety, and in the teen area everyone should feel a relative sense of comfort and ease.

Think of ways to give the feeling that the area has a real beginning and end. The teen space should have a clear entrance and feeling of having definite boundaries. This does not necessary involve putting up barriers between the teen room and the rest of the library, although some libraries may choose a movable partition of sorts that can be used during particularly busy or noisy time periods. If you choose to include a partition as part of your teen area, think about making the partition clear. This will achieve the desired noise control and also maintain the ability of teens in the area to check out what's happening in the rest of the library. If possible, locate your teen area in a place where teens have a view of passing activity and people. Teens like to see who is in the library and what is going on in and around the building. Can you arrange the space so that teens have access to windows overlooking either the outside or the inside of the library?

The teen area must be clean, neat, and attractive, just like any other successful urban third place. Do not underestimate this when developing your teen space. Practically every conversation I have ever had with teens about developing teen areas includes the teen saying something along the lines of, "It just has to be clean." Many people are surprised when they hear this. Teens so often are associated with being messy, so adults may not place cleanliness on the top of the priority list when making a space for teens. But in talking with teens, especially teens who live in crowded or economically disadvantage neighborhoods, you will likely find that they are very concerned about their library space being clean. This does not mean it must be pristine and appear never used. The area can still have the necessary lived-in feeling of heavily used public spaces while appearing to be cared for and respected by those who use it and those charged with maintaining the area. Consider having teen volunteers do periodic cleanup detail around the area, particularly during and after periods of heavy use. It is also vital that librarians and security guards model the "pick up after yourself and others" behavior while in the teen area. It is never acceptable for staff to walk by obvious trash without gathering it up and tossing it in a garbage can. The goal should be both to keep the area clean and to publicly set the example that shows it is everyone's responsibility to care for the area, even if it sometimes means taking care of somebody else's trash.

The need to keep the teen area clean and attractive is complicated by the issue of food. Inviting third places often allow visitors to have snacks and drinks. Libraries have a variety of policies regarding food, however, with some central libraries offering coffee bars or a vending machine area, whereas others do not allow food or drink at all. Regardless of the policy, however, it is a reality that food is likely to make an appearance in a teen area, especially if it is a successful area that draws in teens after school. At the very least, make waste cans and trash receptacles readily available. If sandwich wrappers, French fry containers, and other fast-food carnage begins to be a serious issue, ask a teen advisory board or teen volunteers to help spruce up the trash cans as a group project. They could also work on an antilittering slogan campaign to help remind other teens, even if they are breaking rules by eating, to at least throw away their trash when finished. Another option, and one that I have often heard recommended by teens, is to accept that teens are going to eat and to designate a part of the teen area as a food-allowed section. This makes managing trash and leftover food more manageable for staff, volunteers, and the cleaning crew. It also offers a compromise option for teens who are going to eat in the library regardless of policies and the staff trying to enforce these policies.

Remember that many teens come to the library by themselves. Readily available parking and transportation information for teens can help make the journey to the library less confusing, and it should be readily available in the teen space. The New York Public Library, for example, includes specific information about bus routes and public transportation options on small postcard-size advertisements for the Nathan Straus Young Adult Center at the Donnell Library Branch. Include this kind of transportation information, including parking options if possible, on all print and Web pages advertising the teen areas.

Walk around your teen area and ask yourself the question, "How does this space feel?" Truly successful third places often have a feeling of fun and whimsy. When it comes to teens, it is okay to venture a little into outright weirdness, especially if you have been careful to take your clues from the teens. If your teen area seems to have a sense of humor or does not appear to be taking itself too seriously, you are probably on the right track!

Although everything is easier with a large budget, it is certainly possible to create a great third place without extensive funding. As Kathleen Madden, senior vice president for the Project for Public Spaces, said, "All too often, lack of money is used as an excuse for doing nothing. In fact . . . too much money might actually discourage the inventiveness and creativity required to create a great place" (Madden 2001, 3).

Technology

Technology is part of teens' lives today as never before. Providing all teens access to technology is a critical role for libraries, and this may be particularly true for libraries in urban areas serving lower-income communities. According to Pew Internet Research, 78 percent of teens who have Internet access say they believe it helps them with schoolwork, with 71 percent reporting that they used the Internet as the major source for their most recent school project or report (Lenhart, Rainie, and Lewis 2001). A 2005 study reported that 86 percent of young people age 8 to 18 have a computer in their home (Rideout, Roberts, and Foehr 2005). Low-income families are more likely to depend on library computers, and for many teens the library may be the primary source for a viable computer (Gordon et al. 2003). Even for those who have a computer in their home, that computer may not be able to support commonplace needs, such as downloading a study guide, something 34 percent of online teens reported doing in Pew's 2001 survey (Lenhart, Rainie, and Lewis 2001). A number of factors, including home computers with outdated hardware and PCs shared by too many family members, are reasons teens, like other customers, might turn to the library for their technology needs (Gordon et al. 2003).

Ensuring teens have access to computers can be a difficult task. Small libraries in urban areas often have only a handful of computers, and, unlike in many truly suburban communities where library users also have computer access at home, in many urban areas the library is the only computer access available to neighborhood residents. Long waiting lists quickly develop, with many teens waiting to use the limited number of available computers. This situation becomes even more difficult to manage during the busy after-school hours. Add a few frustrated adults complaining that teens are just using the computers to play games into the mix, and the situation can become stressful and unpleasant for everyone.

But teens do need the technology. Teachers may require students to word process an assignment. Perhaps a teenager is required to prove he or she has run their assignment through an online plagiarism check site such as Turnitin.com before submitting it. Access to research databases and online tutoring services can be essential to a teen trying to finish pressing homework. These are timely problems, and teens want and need to use the library's technology to complete their assignments.

Unfortunately, there is no perfect solution to these problems. Small libraries are often stuck with the limited number of computers they have. Space, funding, wiring, and electrical problems can make it virtually impossible for some libraries to install more or newer computers. In larger facilities with more workstations, arranging computers so that the teen area includes at least a few computers designated for teens is one possible way to improve the situation. Teens can also be given priority use of computers in their area. Having a few teen computers supports giving teens the opportunity to comfortably use at least some of the library's computers in large groups. Regardless of the arrangement, staff should make sure to monitor sign-ups and waiting lists to be sure teens are receiving equal access to whatever technology is available. One example for an innovative way to address this issue is the Austin Public Library's Wired for Youth Centers (http://www.wiredforyouth.com). These grant-funded centers designed for people age 8 to 18 provide a model for the equipment, staffing, and institutional capacity necessary to address teens' need for a variety of technology.

Large central libraries have a slightly different set of challenges when it comes to teens' use of technology. Usually, these larger facilities offer customers access to more computers than smaller branch libraries, so trying to make sure teens have access to the technology they need is not a daily struggle. Rather, teens may have ready access to computers but want to use them for very different purposes or may use them in ways that differ from the expectations of the staff who work in the areas where the computers are located. Some may be focused on schoolwork. Others may choose to spend their time in groups browsing MySpace and other social networking sites.

Arrange computers that support multiple kinds of computer use by teenagers. This may mean having separate banks of computers clearly designed for each kind of activity, in which one group of computers is arranged in a circle or other arrangement that is conducive to group work and other computers are set up in a classroom or computer lab style or spread farther apart for teens wanting to have lots of private space to spread out. These teens may be doing schoolwork or may just want to have some time by themselves after a busy day at school. Ask yourself what kind of arrangement *you* would like best if you were an after-school user of the library's computers. But most important, ask your teens what *they* think is the best way to arrange the computers.

Any discussion of technology would not be complete without talking about social networking. Many libraries that serve urban teens are using MySpace pages to reach their teen customers in a new way. Although libraries in a variety of settings consider social networking sites to connect with teen customers, libraries serving urban teens may wish to reflect on many of the points discussed in the introduction to this chapter about shrinking options for teens to just hang out in their communities when considering the new virtual landscape of social networking. For many teens, social networking sites may be filling the need discussed earlier for a third place in their lives. Social networking and other interactive online activities, such as online gaming, are extremely popular in many libraries. Eighty-one percent of online teens report playing games (Lenhart, Madden, and Hitlin 2005). These kinds of online activities can involve a lot of interaction, both online and in person. Teens engage in an activity online while talking about it with other teens in the library. Often, this social interaction spills over into the real-world library. When this happens, the response should be the same to all socializing in the library: embraced and encouraged when acceptable and managed when behavior issues make it necessary to do so.

Although the library is not in a position to manage online behavior beyond compliance with individual library Internet and technology usage policies, it is essential to offer opportunities for teens and parents to broaden their knowledge about how teens can be effective and productive users of all technologies, including social networking. This is particularly important in urban areas where parents may not have access to a computer at home and may have little or no real experience with the many emerging social networking technologies popular among teenagers. Providing instructional programs is one option, although it is often difficult to generate attendance for formal programs focused on online safety.

Another avenue for raising awareness about this important issue is to provide educational materials such as bookmarks with online safety suggestions along with consistent informal instruction whenever possible. Initiate a discussion of safe and unsafe online behaviors as a part of all technology-related programs or even as part of a discussion during a teen advisory board meeting. After the discussion, a teen-generated list of safety tips may be gathered and posted or reproduced in a bookmark format. When students visit the library as part of a school group or tour, include online safety materials in any take-home resource packets that are offered. Finally, libraries in urban areas can make it a point to celebrate Teen Tech Week, a national initiative sponsored by the Young Adult Library Services Association, as a way to raise awareness annually about online safety and social networking. Teen Tech Week is also an excellent opportunity to educate teens about a variety of related technology issues, such as privacy and identity theft. You may consider hosting a local law enforcement officer specializing in online crimes for a teen program focused on these important safety issues.

Libraries Serving Urban Teens with MySpace Pages

Carnegie Library of Pittsburgh. http://www.myspace.com/clpteens.
Denver Public Library. http://www.myspace.com/denver_evolver.
Glendale Public Library. http://www.myspace.com/teenlibrariansgpl.
Hennepin County Library. http://www.myspace.com/hennepincounty library.
Lansing Public Library. http://www.myspace.com/lansingpubliclibrary.
ImaginOn (Public Library of Charlotte and Mecklenburg County). http://www.myspace.com/libraryloft.

Displays and Marketing

A great teen space has a lot of room for displays. These displays can focus on books or other materials that are teen-driven or created, such as teen artwork, poetry, or teen collections. Room for displays may not be readily available. This does not mean you cannot use face-out shelving or create other small display spaces, but it will require real creativity and painful choices on where to make the room. In facilities where the rule is one item in, one item out because of serious space constraints, it is still worthwhile to open up an area by removing a shelf or two and creating an area to display books. This area can be decorated with fabric and props. It will mean a little less shelving, but the results will be worth it.

If you have space to dedicate to displays, work with teen volunteers, advisory board members, or the after-school crowd to come up with ideas. If your programming attendance is consistently lower than you would like, consider using interactive displays to relate to and get to know the teens who are using your area. Instead of a traditional book club, do a Grab It, Read It, Post It passive program display, featuring multiple copies of one book and a bulletin board where teens can post their thoughts about the title. Utilize the library's Web site for an online version of this interactive display, with teens posting thoughts to a library-moderated Web page. Use quizzes, matching games, and trivia contests to draw attention to the teen area and collection. Change the interactive displays often and offer small prizes weekly. Teen customers will quickly develop a habit of checking daily for new displays and chances to enter contests. In large systems, develop a process by which interactive displays can be shared between branches in order to maximize creativity and resources. The potential for connecting with teens through regular displays of books, which may make up the majority of displays in teen areas, should not be overlooked or underappreciated. Carefully consider the books and topics for displays. Chapter 5 provides lists of material of particular interest to urban teens and will be helpful to staff looking for ideas on creating displays. Change these book displays frequently, making sure to note what is and is not being taken (for future displays). If a display is not drawing teens in and the books or material are not moving, get rid of it and try something else.

Marketing online is another way to increase teen awareness of your teen space. Consider a teen-created podcast or blog advertising and discussing the new teen area to help generate excitement and communicate the teen-driven nature of the new area. Ask teens involved in the planning process to discuss the things that they are particularly excited about and make this into a podcast featured on the library's Web site. You might also create a Flickr photo-sharing account featuring before photos of the proposed teen area, photos of teens working during the planning process, and weekly updates of the area as furniture arrives and other improvements are made. This will heighten anticipation among teens and will also help sell the story of the new teen area to the media. Once the newly created or expanded teen area is complete, ask teens involved in the process to help produce a MySpace page or blog that reflects their feelings about the results.

Consider using different lighting in different areas of your teen space to highlight displays or unique features. Perhaps one of the specially designed display areas will be the focus of the room or the first thing that jumps out at visitors when they enter the area. Or an exhibit board or case featuring teen art or creative work might be the focus. No matter what you choose to do, finding a unique or dynamic feature to highlight helps create a sense of anticipation for the entire space.

Signage in the teen area is important, as it is in all areas of the library. But signage in the teen area needs to be for more than just directions and labels for various parts of the collection. Signs can subtly communicate behavioral expectations and guidelines without coming across as mean, disrespectful, or heavy-handed. Teens can and should be a part of creating both the design and content of signs. The "World Cafe" exercise in Walter and Meyers's *Teens and Libraries: Getting It Right* provides excellent suggestions for signs that might be scattered throughout the area. Any sign that communicates behavior expectations and guidelines should be short. The longer the list of rules, the less likely it will be that teens, particularly teens that may not have a history of positive interactions with authority figures, will comply with these rules. The length of the rules list and the rate of compliance with that list is inversely proportional. Limit your list to three to five points.

Part of marketing your teen area involves deciding how to arrange and lay out the collection. Some collections, particularly at large central libraries, focus on material that is associated with supporting school curriculums and homework. In your newly created or redesigned teen space, think of ways to highlight the popular, high-demand material by moving it to the front and increasing the shelf space dedicated to these collections. Take into consideration the demographics of your community and be sure that prominently displayed material reflects the diversity of the urban area and allows a variety of teens to immediately see themselves reflected in the material you are promoting. What is the first thing teens see when they walk into your teen area? What message does this send?

In larger facilities like central or main libraries, there may be an option to create genre and pullout collections. Whether this is the best way to serve teen customers is a challenging and oft-debated question. One of the first steps in answering it is to, once again, ask the teens! Weigh their responses with your own ideas and with staff feedback. If you do decide to create pullout collections, make the arrangement as intuitive for your teen customers as possible. For example, *historical* for a librarian may mean books focused on events that happened during or before World War II. But for teens, the 1970s may seem historical. The teen area should make the library experience a positive one for teens whenever possible, and so it is important to avoid pullout collections that will create confusion or frustration.

Safety Concerns

Security is often an issue when designing a teen space in any library, whether it is located in a rural, truly suburban, or urban area. When considering creating or expanding a teen area in an urban setting, especially a large central library, however, security issues should be realistically assessed and play a part in design decisions when appropriate, which likely will make it a part of many planning discussions. Take a look at recent security and incident reports in order to have a firm grasp on whether security is a major issue and what the nature of possible security problems might be. Making design decisions that discourage possible security problems and inappropriate behaviors is a good thing to do. Nooks and crannies are cool features for a teen area, but the security and behavior problems these kinds of design elements create should not be ignored. Isolated areas or areas without clear lines of sight from a public floor or service desk can be tempting places for anyone, teens or adults, who might be looking for a private space to engage in inappropriate behavior. A teen area does not have to be located right next to a security station or reference desk in order to avoid possible safety and security issues. But if you are building an area designed to attract teen customers, who may be hanging out for several hours every day, it is worth considering design options that aid in creating a comfortable and relatively safe environment. Simple decisions, such as replacing surfaces in the library that are easily marked with material that is more graffiti- and scratchproof, may help the library remain neutral territory that is open and inviting for everyone.

Interestingly, though Carnegie buildings have limitations when it comes to rearranging collections and floor plans to accommodate a teen section, these older buildings do have the benefit that they were often built with "good visibility down sightlines emanating from the central desk in the rotunda" (Shuman 1996, 37). Do not be to too hasty to ignore this conventional wisdom. If natural sightlines have been lost, consider rearranging furniture and stacks to regain a clear view of the entire building or area.

As noted earlier, some libraries use meeting rooms as de facto teen lounges. If you choose to do this, staff should monitor the area, particularly if it is removed from the rest of the library. Keep doors to meeting rooms and study rooms open when they are being used by teens. If a teen area is designed with separate study rooms, all areas of these rooms should be clearly visible to staff at all times. Consider glass or clear walls without shades or blinds.

INVOLVING TEENS IN THE PLANNING

Informal and formal focus groups with teens are an excellent way to find out what teens want and need in a library space designed just for them. Walter and Meyers's *Teens and Libraries: Getting It Right* provides a detailed model for "moderated teen panels" that can be adapted when working with teens to gather input in a number of situations. Be creative in your marketing of this event to teens, particularly in an urban library that does not have a history of reaching out to, engaging, or welcoming teens. Go beyond the usual offer of snacks or pizza for participants and offer a $5 gift certificate to a local coffee shop or fast-food restaurant as an incentive for teens to attend. Piggyback on existing programs by working with teens before or after some other activity, like an anime night or gaming program.

The more input you can gather, the better! Give yourself four to six weeks to plan and promote a focus group. During that time, visit programs at various locations and ask teens the focus session questions. Involve teen librarians, staff at locations hosting programs at which you will be talking to teens, and teen advisory groups in recruiting teens for the focus sessions.

Sample Focus Session Checklist

Explain the background of the project to teens. Many teens are not familiar with what their role in a focus or input session might be. Explain the purpose and what you are hoping to do during the session very clearly.

Set expectations for focus group participants, including how long the session will last, that there are no right or wrong answers, and there is no need to respond to every question.

Ask group members to introduce themselves.

Include a short icebreaker before the session begins.

Possible Focus Group Questions

1. Think about a public place—the park, school (or area of school)—you enjoy visiting. What is it that you like about that place? How is the library like and not like that space? How could the library be more like that space?

2. When you think of the ideal library place for teens, what comes to mind?

3. What is your highest priority while visiting the library, the thing that is the most important to you?

4. What kinds of material do you use when you are at the library? How do you choose that material?

5. What kinds of things are you looking to do immediately after school? How might the library help support these things?

6. What kinds of things happen at the library that you do not like? Why do you think these kinds of things happen? Is there any way you would arrange a teen area to keep them from happening?

Working with teens in the planning helps build ownership and support for the area. Ensuring that teens feel they have been listened to requires keeping teens involved throughout the process. If possible, formally recruit and select a group of teens that is charged with working with library staff and architects during the planning and design process. Be sure this group represents the diverse nature of your urban community. Consider hosting a reception for the teen planning group to meet staff members. Build in opportunities for teens to discuss their ideas with the architect or interior designer on specific ideas about furnishings and color schemes. Ask teens about their ideas for hosting a grand opening of the teen area and invite them to be involved in planning any activities or ceremonies for the day.

Finally, be sure to evaluate the success of your teen area once it has been established. Conduct yearly focus groups to generate ideas for continually improving your new teen area. If possible, work with members of the original teen planning team when evaluating the area, asking them how successfully the library achieved the original goals described by the planning group.

CARVING OUT A TEEN SPACE
Smaller Facilities

In order to come up with a plan for accommodating and encouraging teens' energy and social needs in a small urban facility where large numbers of teens congregate, particularly during after-school and out-of-school hours, take a step back and rethink your library's overall arrangement. Think about how you might rearrange the entire library, instead of simply how to rearrange your existing teen section. This may be easier said than done. Older branch libraries in urban areas that have not been recently updated or renovated often have shelving units and ranges built along or into the walls, as is the case with many Carnegie libraries still operating today. This kind of construction makes significant rearrangements of the collection difficult.

Even if rearrangement is a viable option, arguing that the prime real estate currently used to house high-circulating, high-demand adult or children's collections should instead be dedicated to teens is not always an easy sell. The problem is not necessarily that people just do not like teens. The bottom line is that space is essential to all services. In a library that already feels overcrowded and is not expected to be renovated any time soon, *something* will have to shrink if room is to be found to create or expand a teen section. Adult customers may like the concept of giving teens a place of their own, but if it means the magazine section will not be right next to the sunniest window in the building or that a favorite reading table will be replaced by a circular computer table designed for teenagers, these same customers may not be quite as supportive of the new and improved teen area idea.

Step 1: When considering the options for a teen area, start by reenvisioning the library. Just because the teen materials have been located in one corner or along one wall as long as you can remember, do not fall into the trap of thinking that is the only space with which you can work.

Walk around the entire library and weigh every option, regardless of what material is currently located where. Remember the point made previously, that sometimes it may even be better if the teen area is not directly adjacent to the children's area. Do not forget to elevate your ideas up the ladder to managers and administrators, especially if the changes are likely to involve technology and furniture.

Step 2: Ask a trusted teen to also reconsider all of the options for the location of a teen area. Put this reenvisioning activity on the agenda for a teen advisory board meeting or enlist the aid of teen volunteers. If you do not have formal volunteers or teen advisory board members, ask the after-school teen crowd what they think.

Step 3: Compare your thoughts and the feedback received from teens with reality. What areas have real potential for working as a teen area and why?

Step 4: Think about where teens currently congregate. This can be a great clue to what teens find appealing, such as privacy from other customers (and maybe from staff), a window or aisle that offers a clear view of who else is hanging out in or near the library, and tables, chairs, and computers that allow for socializing and communal work.

Step 5: Make a list of all the things you would like to see in your dream teen space. How could you position the teen area to make some of the items on your wish list a possibility? For example, if you would love to have a bulletin board where teens could post information and express their creativity, look for a large blank wall that might work well for this purpose. Do not worry if it is located right in the middle of the adult nonfiction. Think about *what could be* instead of *what is*.

Step 6: Narrow down the choices for teen areas and ask staff their opinion. If you are hoping to move the teen material from its current location, ask staff what they think are the possible limitations of the current area. Use their answers to support your ideas for relocating the teen material.

Step 7: Discuss with staff the difference between separating teen material from the rest of the collection and creating a distinct teen area. Make sure staff members understand that simply putting teen books and materials on separate shelves is not the same as making a teen space.

Step 8: Consider options for linking the teen area with technology access. Is it possible to dedicate a few computers to the teen area and give teens first priority for using these terminals, at least during the after-school hours or other times when the building is brimming with teens?

Step 9: Bring together all of your thoughts and run your final plan by teens and staff. Listen to feedback and carefully consider any concerns that are raised. Do not let these concerns derail the process, but do your best to discuss issues productively and build support for the change. Do not be defensive; just ask staff or teens to clearly and specifically explain what it is that has them worried.

Step 10: Snap several before and after photos of the teen area. Be sure to submit photos and any positive teen comments to internal staff communications tools, like newsletters, blogs, and Web updates. Also, share this information with local community or neighborhood newsletters and newspapers.

Large Central or Main Libraries

Large urban central libraries pose a slightly different kind of dilemma than their small-library counterparts. Many have plenty of floor space, but the floor plan and arrangement of service points and materials are not always flexible. Large service desks and in-depth reference collections often dominate central library landscapes. Most have a children's room that may stray from the design of the rest of the building, but outside of that children's area, shelving, furniture, and the arrangement of computers and other technology is designed for reference and research use, not necessarily for teens' comfort. And, unlike smaller urban facilities where the resistance to a dedicated teen area may be related to an overall lack of space, the issues at central or main facilities are sometimes related to a feeling that teens simply do not belong in the building.

Responses to an informal survey reveal that the kinds of spaces created at large urban libraries vary widely, with respondents reporting sizes ranging from 100 to 4,000 square feet. Survey respondents frequently reported that they did have a teen area at the central library, but that it was extremely small or that, relatively speaking, the teen space was smaller than other collections serving specific populations or needs. Lay the groundwork for creating your teen area by carefully reviewing the arguments section of this chapter. If the root cause of the problem is staff (and possibly library leaders) not fully understanding how many teens use your central library on a daily basis or the nature of this use, start educating staff about these topics. Work to help staff have a better understanding of teens' need for space (or at the very least help staff develop a more open-minded view). Once you do, these practical steps can help you through the process of creating or expanding your existing teen area.

Step 1: What are teens already doing to make the library space fit their needs? How can you piggyback on these adaptations that are being developed organically by teens to make a teen space successful? Where in the building are teens congregating? What are the common elements to the spaces in which they are already choosing to hang out?

Consider the atmosphere of the library and attitude of staff. Laying the foundation with staff for embracing the development or expansion of a teen area is as important for long-term success as picking the right colors for furniture or making good decisions about collection layout.

Step 2: Push the point on money. For library systems with multiple branches serving large urban areas, the central library is likely the largest location and the best equipped for supporting an adequately sized area for teens. Unlike other, smaller locations that must do the best they can with limited space, a larger facility has the capacity to be a system- or citywide resource for all teens. Find out what the options are for grants, partnerships with other community agencies, and working with the library's friends group or foundation for securing a real budget for creating the teen area. Do not accept that there simply is not any funding available. Instead, think strategically about how to build support for creating an appropriately sized teen area. If you move forward without doing so, you may never get a second chance to improve it.

Step 3: Start focus groups with teens sooner rather than later. As soon as there is discussion of creating or expanding a teen area, begin your dialogue with teens. If you can set up meetings with teens specifically for the purpose of discussing the teen center options, do so. If you have a teen advisory board that meets at the main or central library, put the creation or expansion of the teen center at the top of the agenda. Or start informal, casual conversations with teens at the library whenever possible. Circulate a survey and discuss the results with teens in person.

Step 4: Do not settle for too little room. It is easy to become overjoyed at the prospect of having a real, live teen space, but make sure that there really is enough space for your teens! It is not just about having enough linear feet of shelving to house the collection or enough paperback racks to store the books. Teens need room to move, socialize, and interact. They need access to technology. And they need quiet areas where they can work independently, especially teens living in crowded urban areas where they do not always have access to private space for themselves.

Step 5: Find out if an architect or interior designer is going to be involved in the creation or expansion of the teen area. If so, be sure it is clear that you and your teens will need to be involved in discussions about the design and layout of the area.

Step 6: House all material of interest to teens in the proposed space. Proposals for fiction-only or fiction-with-high-interest-nonfiction collections for teens may be considered in smaller facilities where there are serious space limitations. In a large central library, however, all of the teen material should be located in the teen space. This makes it easy for teens to take advantage of one-stop shopping rather than being forced to hunt around a large facility for multiple items.

Step 7: Think about music. Even if there is not music in the rest of the library, having the ability to play music in the teen area should be strongly considered. It will help separate the space from the rest of the building and also set the tone that, in the teen area, a certain level of noise is not only okay, it is encouraged!

Step 8: Investigate the options for making the teen area open to teens only. In a large facility, children and adults have plenty of space and resources available to them. A teen-only policy will make the teen space inviting and provide a sanctuary where teens can be themselves without worrying what the rest of the world thinks.

Step 9: Flexibility is the key. Consider ways to make the furniture and shelving movable if possible. Although safety and security issues should also be kept in mind, tables and chairs with wheels can be helpful when it comes to using the teen area for programming activities. Staff members may be initially concerned that wheeled furniture will produce possible behavior problems. If so, an alternative is to consider furniture that is lightweight or small. This will still make it easy for furniture to be moved around for programming. It will also give teens the option to rearrange the space to suit their needs on a daily basis.

Step 10: Make the opening a big deal. Work with your library's public relations staff to build excitement and interest months before the newly created or expanded space is scheduled to open.

Midsize or Large Libraries

Urban teens are often served by midsize and large libraries. These libraries may be part of a multibranch library system and located in inner-ring suburbs that are not too far from a major metropolitan area. Or these mid-size and large libraries may not be part of a large system, rather they may be an independently operated library located in a smaller city or urban area. Libraries fitting either of these descriptions may wish to borrow specific steps from the previous suggestions for small and large libraries, depending on each library's unique situation. The following are three important additional considerations for libraries in this category.

Consideration 1: With a larger collection, there may be more materials of interest to teens spread throughout the library in different sections. This is especially true for audiovisual material of interest to teens, like popular music CDs and anime DVDs. Bring these materials together in the new teen area. Is it possible to receive multiple copies of the latest anime, for example, with one copy always being placed in the teen area?

Consideration 2: Think about dedicating a reasonable amount of your library's available technology to teens. Designate one or more computers as teen and move these to the teen area. Give teens priority for using these computers.

Consideration 3: Can your library serve as a resource for other libraries in the area that are not able to develop a separate teen area? While researching this book, I sent an informal survey to libraries serving urban areas (included in the appendix), and some multibranch systems indicated that teen areas were being developed on a more of a regional basis. Rather than creating teen areas in every location, in this system several midsize or large branch libraries focus on creating spaces for teens. Selecting a few libraries at which to create teen areas allows larger systems to concentrate efforts and limited resources in locations that may be more suited, in terms of available space, to support these new areas. Creating teen areas in a limited number of branches is a great way to start the process of making space for teens a part of a library systems culture. Long term, libraries should continue to move toward the goal of developing teen areas at all locations, however, especially as some small urban locations are those most in need of inviting, welcoming space for large numbers of teens.

If a Separate Area Is Just Not an Option

One respondent to the informal survey questions summed up her library's situation about the amount of space dedicated to teens in their urban branch facility, by noting "most of our branches have little space for anyone." If your situation is similar, do not give up hope just yet.

Consider serving teens in smaller urban facilities by moving after-school teen activity and chilling to a meeting room. Many libraries are already dedicating meeting rooms or other separate space for teens to use, especially after school. The Multnomah Public Library, for example, has reconfigured community meeting rooms into teen-only computer labs and hangout spaces called Teen Lounges. A few branches of the Saint Louis County Library now offer teens access to meeting rooms on weekdays during the after-school hours. This may not be your idea of the perfect solution, but for small urban facilities with limited space and furniture a meeting room may realistically be the only place teens can hang out, work together, play board games and card games, or socialize.

If the meeting-room-as-teen-space concept works for your library, allow teens to decorate the room in the same way they might help decorate a teen area. Encourage teens to put up posters or find a bulletin board you can hang in the room. Put high-demand and appealing items like graphic novels, manga, anime, and paperback books on shelving trucks and wheel these movable collections into the meeting room while teens are using the space. Bring in board games and comfortable chairs, if possible. Allow teens to select and play music in the room. Investigate the options of incorporating technology like computers, laptops, and gaming consuls for teens' use in the meeting rooms. Be sure to consider the security measures and staffing necessary to manage this situation, too.

CONCLUSION

Urban libraries are in a unique position to serve teens. Recognizing the importance of a space specifically designed for and with teenagers will have a positive ripple effect on a variety of services. Although programming and outreach play an invaluable role in building teen services in urban communities, it is the space that is often at a premium and is just as often the first and perhaps only impression of the library many teens receive. Do not miss your chance to have the teen area make a distinct, long-lasting, and positive impression on your teens.

WORKS CITED

Bolan, Kimberly. 2006. "Looks Like Teen Spirit." *School Library Journal* 52 (November): 44–48.

Gordon, Andrew C., Margaret T. Gordon, Elizabeth Moore, and Linda Heuetz. 2003. "The Gates Legacy." *Library Journal* 128 (March 1). Accessed March 31, 2007, available at http://www.libraryjournal.com/index.asp?layout=article&articleId=CA276674.

Jones, Patrick, Michele Gorman, and Tricia Suellentrop. 2004. *Connecting Young Adults and Libraries.* New York: Neal-Schuman.

Lenhart, Amanda, Mary Madden, and Paul Hitlin. 2005. *Teens and Technology: Youth Are Leading the Transition to a Fully Wired and Mobile Nation.* Washington, DC: Pew Internet and American Life Project.

Lenhart, Amanda, Lee Rainie, and Oliver Lewis. 2001. *Teenage Life Online: The Rise of Instant-Message Generation and the Internet's Impact on Friendships and Family Relationships.* Washington, DC: Pew Internet and American Life Project.

Madden, Kathleen. 2001. "Creating 'Places' that Work." *Planning Commissioners Journal* 43 (Summer): 1–3. Accessed November 26, 2006, available at http://www.pps.org/pdf/placesthatwork.pdf.

Project for Public Spaces. *Ray Oldenburg.* Accessed March 31, 2007, available at http://www.pps.org/info/placemakingtools/placemakers/roldenburg.

Rideout, Victoria, Donald F. Roberts, and Ulla G. Foehr. 2005. *Generation M: Media in the Lives of 8–18 Year-Olds."* Menlo Park, CA: Kaiser Family Foundation.

Shuman, Bruce. 1996. "Designing Personal Safety into Library Buildings." *American Libraries* 27 (August): 37–39.

Urban Libraries Council presentation. 2006. "Learning in Libraries: Brooklyn, Queens and New York" panel discussion. *Learning in Libraries: A National Call to Action.* New York City: Urban Libraries Council.

Walter, Virginia A., and Elaine Meyers. 2003. *Teens and Libraries: Getting it Right.* Chicago: American Library Association.

FURTHER READING

Bernier, Anthony. 2000. "A Library TeenS'cape Against the New Callousness." *Voice of Youth Advocates* 23 (3) (August): 180–81.

Bishop, Kay, and Pat Bauer. 2002. "Attracting Young Adults to Public Libraries." *Journal of Youth Services in Libraries* 15 (Winter): 36–44.

Bolan, Kimberly. 2003. *Teen Spaces: The Step-by-Step Library Makeover.* Chicago: American Library Association.

Brehm-Heeger, Paula. 2006. "A Tie for Third Place." *School Library Journal* 52 (July). Accessed November 22, 2006, available at http://www.schoollibraryjournal.com/article/CA6348397.html.

Edwards, Margaret A. 1994. *The Fair Garden and the Swarm of Beasts: The Library and the Young Adult.* Chicago: American Library Association.

Galehouse, Maggie. 2004. "Teen Sections Are Changing." *Arizona Republic,* October 18, 2004.

Jenson-Benjamin, Merideth. 2003. "Club Fishbowl." *Voice of Youth Advocates* 26 (2) (June): 120–21.

Kendall, Karl. 2003. "Safe, Structured, and Teen-Friendly." *Voice of Youth Advocates* 26 (5) (December): 380–81.

Kenney, Brian. 2006. "A Challenge to Library Directors." *School Library Journal* 52 (November). Accessed November 26, 2006, available at http://www.schoollibraryjournal.com/article/CA6386666.html.

Lushington, Nolan. 2002. *Libraries Designed for Users: A 21st Century Guide.* New York: Neal-Schuman.

New York Public Library. *Teen Central.* Accessed November 26, 2006, available at http://www.nypl.org/branch/central/dlc/dna/.

Pedersen, Martin C., and Paul Makovsky. 2002. "The Power of Place: A School Play." *Metropolis Magazine*, October. Accessed November 22, 2006, available at http://metropolismag.com/html/content_1002/lib/index.html.

Project for Public Spaces. *Hanging Out: Teens Search for the Perfect Public Space.* Accessed November 22, 2006, available at http://www.pps.org/articles/hanging_out.html.

Project for Public Spaces. *Safety and Security in Public Space.* Accessed November 22, 2006, available at http://stage.pps.org/info/placemakingtools/issue papers/safety_security.

Project for Public Spaces. *Teen Central at Burton Barr Library.* Accessed November 22, 2006, available at http://www.pps.org/tcb/teen_central.htm.

5

COLLECTION DEVELOPMENT

While in the process of setting up a new partnership with a juvenile detention center serving young men age 12 to 18, I received a call from the coordinator of the center. "A new boy just checked in today and he's a reader!" she exclaimed. "I told him about the visits the library was going to be making and explained to him that the librarians would be bringing books. He was really happy and even has a few requests." Of course, I was thrilled to hear this and said that we would do our best to bring the young man the books he wanted. "Well," the coordinator said after a pause, "the thing is that I'm concerned about what type of books these might be. As you know, we cannot have books that are too violent or edgy. Can you tell me if these books would be okay? The first title is *A Hustler's Wife* by Nikki Turner." The books on the rest of the list were, like Turner's book, street lit titles, too. I volunteered to bring copies for the coordinator to read or browse but told her I thought the titles might not fit her criteria for books that she wanted the young men to have access to while in the detention facility. "But," I said, "I really think I can find several other books that might interest your new reader, even if they are not the exact titles he requested."

As this story illustrates, librarians working in urban areas face a challenging task when connecting teens with the books they want. Working in an urban area often means serving an extremely diverse group of teens and representing a wide variety of racial, ethnic, and economic backgrounds with a wide variety of interests and needs. New immigrants often make up a significant portion of your customer base. Some of the teens you serve will be enthusiastic readers, eager to pick up almost any book you might offer to them, whereas other teens you serve will want to read only one kind of book or genre or be reluctant to read anything at all. Some, as in my juvenile detention center example, will have truly unique needs that require real reader's advisory skill on the part of the librarian to come up with just the right book for their situation. Diversity is a staple of life in urban areas, and no place is it more essential to recognize and celebrate this diversity than when building your library's collections for teens.

Building a collection with appeal to a wide variety of teens is no easy task. Make no mistake about it, the library's collection is a key factor in determining teens' perception of the library's relevance and value to their everyday lives. When a teen walks into the public library (or visits the Web site), she should be confident that material she wants will be available on the library's shelves. If a teen is not sure what it is he is looking for, he should be able to rely on a display or booklist promoting titles that interest him. Teens should have confidence that, if needed, a knowledgeable and friendly librarian will be there to assist him or to spark her interest. This may seem like a tall order. Remaining relevant to today's sophisticated urban teen customers means that libraries must provide teens what they want when they want it. Having current, high-demand teen material available and in good condition helps your library send a positive message to teens. It is a way of saying, "We care about you and take serving you seriously."

This chapter gives you an overview of some of the most popular genres and titles frequently recommended for and requested by teens in urban areas. Most recommendations are titles and series that have been published in the last five to seven years. You will also find ideas on how to ensure your organization's collection development process supports the creation of high-interest and high-demand teen collections, tips for involving teens in the collection development process, and suggestions on how to evaluate your collection. The further reading section at the end of this chapter offers ideas on where to look for more information and materials.

HOW MATERIAL IS ACQUIRED

Many public libraries, particularly large public libraries in urban areas, use centralized methods of collection development. This may happen in a variety of ways, but for many organizations the days of multiple librarians from different locations and departments reading reviews and placing orders is gone. Instead, libraries often employ teams of specialized collection development librarians whose sole or primary job duty is collection development. These collection development librarians order materials for an entire library or library system. The way centralized collection development duties are assigned varies from library to library. Some libraries have professional positions dedicated to selecting material based on the target audience of the material. At other libraries, the collection development librarians are generalists, and duties are not based on the age of the material's target audience but, instead, are assigned based on Dewey decimal numbers or subject areas. Librarians select for all age levels in these assigned subject areas.

Whatever the structure, teen material should receive the same careful treatment and consideration that adult and juvenile materials receive. Resources should be dedicated to teen material in terms of collection development specialist's time and attention as well as funding. In libraries with centralized collection development, in which positions are designated to selecting material exclusively to certain audiences based on age groups, a position should be specifically designated to collecting material for teens.

If collection development positions are generalists, teen librarians and frontline staff serving teens must communicate openly and frequently with collection development librarians about the needs of their teen customers. Make sure there is a mechanism for quickly communicating teen customer requests directly to staff in a position to respond to these requests quickly. If a teen asks about a book or anime DVD, frontline staff must have a way not only to pass that request along but also to receive an answer about whether the library will be purchasing the material. Creating clear communication channels for discussing collection needs positions libraries to receive extremely useful information about teens' ever-changing pop culture interests. Making sure teens receive a definite answer in response to their request also helps build teens' trust that the library values their opinions and takes their requests seriously. Your library's collection development structure must be flexible and responsive in order to address teens' needs.

Teen material usually makes up a smaller portion of your library's overall collection when compared to material for adults or children. Because this is often the case, you will probably be asked why one person should be designated to collection specifically for teens. Here are five simple reasons staff should be specifically designated to perform collection development exclusively for teens:

- Teens have distinct developmental and educational needs. Building collections for this unique audience requires knowledge of teen material, adolescent development, and teens' educational and curriculum needs.

- In urban areas, there is great diversity when it comes to teens' collection needs. Responding to these needs requires specific attention, dedicated resources, and specialized knowledge.

- There has been an explosion of publishing in all format types for teens in recent years. Young adult literature is one of the fastest growing segments of publishing (Beatty 2005). Staying on top of this growing segment of publishing requires time and attention.

- As discussed in chapter 4, teen areas have traditionally not been part of the original design and construction of public libraries. This may be particularly true in libraries serving urban areas that have not been redesigned or remodeled in decades. Building collections that strike the necessary balance between space constraints and extending collections to meet the needs of teens requires time, attention, and knowledge of teen materials.

- Dedicating staff specifically to building and developing collections for teens is a necessary component to making an overall organizational commitment to teens. If a library is serious about serving teens, a dedicated and consistent focus is needed to ensure effective development of its teen collections.

TEEN PARTICIPATION IN COLLECTION DEVELOPMENT

Make teen input a part of your collection development process whenever possible. If your library or library system has one or more active teen advisory boards, regularly ask these teens for feedback about your library's collection. Talk to teens about new formats, series, and authors of interest. Ask teen advisors to bring at least one recommendation for a teen book or series to each meeting. If you are able to attend professional library conferences, pick up galley or advance reader copies of books, often available free of charge on the exhibit floor. Some publishers offer librarians the opportunity to sign up directly to receive advance reader's editions of books, such as Random House's Library Marketing Reading Group Advisory List at http://www.randomhouse.biz/libraries/. Share these advance copies with your teen advisory board. Consider other ways to get galley or advance copies of items in the hands of your teens, including applying to be a part of the Young Adult Library Services Association's Young Adult Galley project. Teen discussion groups selected to participate in this project receive copies of recent titles and evaluate these titles for publishers. This valuable teen feedback can also be shared with collection development librarians.

Although smaller libraries may have the opportunity to ask teens for direct input about what items to purchase, this kind of direct feedback may not be quite as easy to get at large urban libraries. Institute a formal method for sharing teen feedback about your library's collection with collection development staff. Create an internal blog on which teen librarians can share information. If a blog is not an option, an e-mail form can be an effective way to communicate with collection development librarians, too. Set aside time at teen librarian meetings to discuss collection issues directly with collection development staff.

BUDGET

Teen material, both print and audiovisual, should be funded through distinct teen budgets. Separate funding makes it more likely that a proportionally appropriate amount of money will be dedicated to purchasing teen material. Determining what proportion of funds should be set aside for teen material can be a challenging task. Start by examining circulation figures along with any data you have gathered through other output measures that capture teen library use, such as the observations discussed in chapter 4. If teen circulation is counted separately, use these statistics to figure out what overall percentage of circulation comes directly from teen materials. If your library is expanding teen service, one output goal you may have identified is to increase circulation. Include this projected increase in your budget figures. And use this to make the case for why your teen budget should be increased (especially because teen circulation represents a valuable growth opportunity for libraries). If your library utilizes any automatic ordering options, determine the ideal quantities of certain series, graphic novels, manga, and anime that your library should receive to meet customer demand and develop a budget that can support this kind of automatic ordering. It is easier to convince decision makers about the need for a separate teen budget if you have a concrete figure and tangible examples of the material that will be purchased from this separate budget.

TARGET AUDIENCE

The Young Adult Library Services Association defines teens as people age 12 to 18. This age range is frequently viewed as the target age group for teen collections in public libraries, including those serving urban areas.

Is this the target audience for your library? If so, how are you currently doing in attracting teens from the entire 12-to-18 age range?

To answer this question, gather information about the age of teens actually using your teen collection. Ask staff for input, and create a survey aimed at teens to gather data about the average age or age range of teens currently browsing and using your teen collection. This input can be useful when making collection development decisions. It will help you determine what kind of material needs to be purchased to expand the collection.

You may find that on average it is younger teens, age 11 to 14, who most frequently browse and use your teen collection. There are a variety of reasons for this. For example, in many libraries with large juvenile collections, some titles are cataloged and placed in both the teen and juvenile collections. This is a great service to the 11-year-old reading in the teen collection and also to the 12-year-old who still enjoys series found in the children's area. If a book is located in both places, more young people are likely to find it. Including books in a teen collection that push the upper age limit of juvenile fiction provides a bridge from the kids' to the teen collection for young people transitioning from one collection to the next. But including these titles in your teen collection can also make it more difficult to convince older teens that the teen collection is also for them. Make it a priority to purchase and include titles and materials that appeal to an older teen audience in your teen collection. Consider expanding the teen collection to include adult material of interest to older teens as well. Including this material in the teen collection can help lure older teens into your teen area. Once they are there, they are far more likely to discover the wide variety of teen books published for high school students. They will begin to consider the teen collection a viable browsing option, full of material that satisfies their more sophisticated reading tastes.

Keep in mind that placing material of interest to the entire spectrum of people age 12 to 18—a large and developmentally diverse population—in one area will require a significant amount of staff and customer education about the wide variety of material and information that your library considers "teen." Some libraries have a long-standing, though not formalized, tradition of not emphasizing material for older teens, perhaps because of concerns about younger teens finding these books in the teen collection. Information regarding the age range for your library's teen collection should be clearly stated and communicated to staff, particularly those who actively build and maintain teen collections. Communicate why it is important for the teen collection to appeal to a wide variety of teens, including older teens. Make sure staff are aware of resources that offer book suggestions for younger teens, such as *Serving Young Teens and 'Tweens* by

Sheila B. Anderson (Libraries Unlimited, 2007). This can help ease concerns and ensure that staff are able to effectively serve all teen customers.

MOVE IT OR LOSE IT

Collection development does not end once new books are on the shelves. Keeping a collection fresh and current is an essential part of the collection development process. Teens, particularly reluctant readers and savvy urban teens, will have little use for overcrowded shelves that are full of worn-out or outdated items. No matter how many great new books arrive every day, if teen area shelves are overloaded or stocked with items badly in need of weeding, teens have a difficult time browsing and locating the good stuff they really want.

In smaller facilities found in many urban areas, weeding material that does not circulate is a must for creating and maintaining a successful teen area. This means that at smaller locations items have a shorter shelf life than those at locations with more space, especially when it comes to genres that are not popular in your library. Focus on maintaining a high-circulation collection to keep teens coming back to the area again and again, confident that they will quickly be able to find what they want, including genres popular with urban teens, such as manga, narrative nonfiction, horror, romance, realistic fiction, and books featuring diverse characters, particularly African American and Latino characters.

Finally, no matter how small your shelf area, arrange or remove shelves to create a display area. Teens need help when they are browsing. You may be reluctant to remove shelving when you are already short on available space, but removing that one shelf will open up an area in which you can highlight new items or create a small rotating face-out display. In the long run, you will gain use despite losing space. Staff may not always be in the area or on hand to provide that assistance, but a dynamic display space will provide a surprising amount of reader's advisory. It will also serve as a place for regular teen customers, volunteers, or advisory board members to highlight their favorite material.

THE COLLECTION

The following lists represent a sampling of materials likely to appeal to many teens served by libraries in urban areas. These lists are suggestions designed to help staff at all levels when working to assist teens with reader's advisory. New librarians or those working for the first time in libraries serving urban areas will find these lists useful when looking for booktalk and shelftalk ideas. Titles requested by sophisticated urban teens are often considered edgy. Librarians using the following suggestions should be aware that this preference is likely reflected in many of the titles listed in this chapter.

Manga

There is little doubt that manga is among the most popular material on the shelves at libraries in urban areas. In fact, at a recent library conference, Rollie Welch, teen librarian for the Cleveland Public Library, listed "the library has manga" as one of the top 10 reasons urban teens visit the public library (Welch and Brehm-Heeger 2006).

Staying ahead of the curve when it comes to manga series requires a lot of knowledge and determination. The popularity of manga varies over the life of a series. One day *Death Note* is the hottest thing in your library, only to be replaced the next day by an entirely new series—sometimes a series you did not even know about until 10 teens ask about it in one day! Collection development librarians who do not work on a public desk need to hear about new series from frontline staff. Similarly, collection development staff can offer updates to staff about the forthcoming series soon to hit the library shelves and that will be popular with various segments of the teen population.

The following lists represent series popular at the time this book was written. By publication, at least one or two newer, more popular titles are likely to have been published!

Popular Manga Series

Anzai, Noboyuki. 2003. *Mar.* San Francisco: Viz.

Ginta spends much of his time daydreaming about a fantasy world where he is a hero. One day he is magically transported to the world of his dreams.

Gerard, Anthony. 2004. *Tsubasa Reservoir Chronicle.* New York: Del Rey.

Princess Sakura is about to tell Syaoran that she loves him, until a strange symbol robs her of her memories.

Kohta Hirano and Duane Johnson. 2003. *Hellsing.* Milwaukie, OR: Dark Horse Comics.

The adventures of the top secret Hellsing Organization, whose job it is to protect England against vampires, monsters, and other ghoulish creatures.

Minekura, Kazuya. 2005. *Saiyuki Reload.* Los Angeles: Tokyopop.

Continues the adventures chronicled in the original Saiyuki series as a band of four *youkai* hunters travels the countryside battling *youkai*.

Moxhizuki, Minetaro. 2006. *Dragon Head*. Los Angeles: Tokyopop.

After a terrible train wreck, Aoki Teru is stranded in a sealed tunnel with only two companions left alive, neither of whom is in much condition to help him.

Ohba, Tsugumi, and Obata Takeshi. 2005. *Death Note*. San Francisco: Viz.

When Light Yagami finds the Death Note, he intends to use the book's deadly power to make the world free of evil. Things do not go as planned.

Takahashi, Rumiko. 2004. *Inu Yasha*. San Francisco: Viz.

Traveling back to feudal times, high school student Kagome Higurashi accidentally releases part-demon Inu Yasha, binding the Kagome and Inu Yasha together in a grand quest.

Takei, Hiroyuki. 2003. *Shaman King*. San Francisco: Viz.

Teenage shaman Yoh Asakura's talent of at seeing ghosts and communicating with spirits comes in handy as he continues his training to someday be the shaman king.

Toriyama, Akira. 2005. *Dr. Slump*. Los Angeles: Viz.

Mad scientist Dr. Senbei Norimaki's newest invention is a "perfect" robot girl with some unusual skills, including super strength and a knack for getting into trouble.

Yoshizaki, Mine, and Fukami Yuko. 2004. *Sgt. Frog*. Los Angeles: Tokyopop.

Cut off from contact with his home planet, Sgt. Korero does his best to continue plans to help aliens invade earth from his new home, the Hinata family's apartment.

Five Manga Series for Guys

Anzai, Nobuyuki. 2003. *Flame of Recca*. San Francisco: Viz.

Hanabishi Recca's greatest dream is to be a ninja, but discovering he is descended from a long-extinct clan of ninja's does not make his life any easier.

Kishimoto, Massashi. 2003. *Naruto*. Los Angeles: Viz.

Shunned in his home village, teenage ninja Naruto's life changes when he successfully graduates from Ninja Academy and learns the truth about the demon locked inside of him.

Sadamoto, Yoshiyuki. 1998. *Neon Genesis Evangelion*. Los Angeles: Viz.

Teenage Shinji Ikari is unwittingly recruited to pilot one of the giant Evangelions as humanity wages a fight for survival against the terrifying and monstrous Angels.

Togashi, Yoshihiro. 2003. *Yu Yu Hakusho*. San Francisco: Viz.

Yusuke Urameshi is not the kind of person anyone, including inhabitants of the Spirit World, would ever have expected to die sacrificing his life to save someone else.

Yuy, Beub-Ryong. 2003. *Chronicles of the Cursed Sword*. Los Angeles: Tokyopop.

(continued)

(*Continued*)

If Rey Yan has any hope of using the PaSa sword to save the world, he must first figure out how to keep its unusual cravings satisfied.

Five Manga Series for Girls

Akino, Matsuri. 2003. *Pet Shop of Horrors*. Los Angeles: Tokyopop.
Buying a pet from Count D's pet store results in terrible consequences for anyone who breaks their contract.
Kamio, Yoko. 2003. *Boys over Flowers*. San Francisco: Viz.
The F4 or Flower Four, a snobbish clique of wealthy boys, rule the Eitoku Academy and do not make life easy for new, working-class student Tsukushi Makino.
Miyasak, Kaho. 2002. *Kare First Love*. San Francisco: Viz Communications.
Shy Karin Karino is accustomed to people ignoring her; and she is surprised when two boys she meets become rivals for her affections.
Pak, Sang-son. 2005. *Tarot Café*. Los Angeles: Tokyopop.
A variety of supernatural beings seek Pamela's help because of her tarot card reading skills and ability to see the future.
Takaya, Natsuki. 2004. *Fruits Basket*. Los Angeles: Tokyopop.
Taken in by Shigure and his family when she is discovered living on the family's estate, Tohru Honda is invited to become a member of the household if she can keep the family's unusual secret.

Five Manga Series for Younger Teens

Anno, Moyoko. 2006. *Sugar Sugar Rune*. New York: Ballantine Books.
Witches Vanilla and Chocolat, both hoping to be the queen of the Magic World, decide that the witch who attracts the most human guys will become the queen.
Elder, Joshua (Erich Owen). 2006. *Mail Order Ninja*. Los Angeles, Tokyopop.
Bullied and bothered at school, Timmy McAllister's life changes forever when he wins a contest and his ninja hero shows up in the mail.
Higuchi, Daisuke. 2004.*Whistle!* San Francisco, Viz.
Sho is determined to win a spot on the starting soccer team and, with the help of the rest of the second-stringers, challenges the team's star captain to a match.
Konomi, Takeshi. 2004. *Prince of Tennis*. San Francisco: Viz.
Ryoma Echizen may be the best tennis player at Seishun Gakuen, but his insistence that students be allowed to represent the school in tournaments during their freshmen year does not sit well with his older classmates.
Obata, Takeshi. 2004. *Hikaru No Go*. San Francisco: Viz.
When sixth grader Hikaru Shindo finds an abandoned Go Board, he unlocks the spirit of legendary Go player Fujiwara-no-Sai.

Looking for Anime? Try These Helpful Sites

Anime Addicts. http://www.animeaddict.org.
Anime club information along with information on new releases.
Anime Café: A Parent's Guide to Anime. http://www.abcb.com/parents.
Includes discussion about age-appropriate anime for kids and teens.
Anime Encyclopedia. http://www.abcb.com/ency/index.htm.
Includes A to Z reviews of hundreds of anime series.
Anime Insider. http://www.wizarduniverse.com/magazines/anime.cfm.
Articles and reviews about all things anime.
Anime News Network. http://www.animenewsnetwork.com.
Reviews, recent releases, and articles about the happenings in the world of anime.
Anime on DVD. http://www.animeondvd.com.
Recent DVD releases, news, and more.

News, reviews, and resources on anime

Librarians Guide to Anime and Manga. http://www.koyagi.com/Libguide.html.
Offers a very thorough explanation of the various elements of anime, discusses content and age appropriateness, and offers ideas on how to run an anime club and suggestions on what to purchase.
TheOtaku.com. http://www.theotaku.com.
Includes a cosplay (costume play) division with photo and unusual anime and manga-related quizzes.

Collection/Programming Tie-In: Tips for Running an Anime Club

Many teens who read and browse manga also love anime. Style and content similarities, not to mention series overlaps, result in the two formats sharing fans. Capitalize on this overlap by providing manga fans the chance to enjoy anime at the library. Before launching an anime film series or undertaking regular anime showings, however, it is important to become familiar with anime as a format and think about the most effective way to program for anime fans.

Review the Films

- Anime films are not necessarily full-length movies. Most of them originated as TV shows and are in episodes. Inu Yasha has well over a hundred episodes.

- Do not forget to get permission! Request permission well in advance if possible of showing the title.

- Get permission for a number of dates so you can show numerous episodes.

(continued)

(*Continued*)

- Check the company Web site for contact person or fan support tab.
- Find out if your library has a license to show movies from certain companies and distributors.
- Join a fan support club online.
- Be ready to explain to anime club participants why you cannot show the films they bring in without receiving permission from the movie producers and distributors first.
- Snacks are a must, but they do not need to be to elaborate. Be sure to pick up Pocky, a long, thin, biscuit-type confectionery treat dipped in various flavors, including chocolate and strawberry, originally introduced in the 1960s by Japanese company Glico (http://www.glico.co.jp/en/).
- If you receive free stuff from the film companies, have drawings or a contest to distribute these items.
- Encourage teens to come dressed as their favorite characters or hold a cosplay, a program idea discussed in chapter 6.

Nonfiction

Highly readable nonfiction should be a top collection priority for libraries of all sizes serving urban areas, and every effort should be made to include this kind of nonfiction in the teen area. Including these nonfiction titles in the teen collection may be particularly difficult in smaller facilities, where the majority of nonfiction that appeals to teens is frequently shelved in either the juvenile or adult collections due to space constraints. But do not let that stop you! Start by moving a sampling of nonfiction titles likely to be popular with teens to your teen collection or by creating a display of high-interest nonfiction. When selecting nonfiction for teens, include individual or collected biographies about musicians, titles about hip-hop, humorous books, and titles focused on sports, particularly basketball and streetball.

The following is a list of nonfiction titles with teen appeal:

Bastfield, Darrin Keith. 2002. *Back in the Day: My Life and Times with Tupac Shakur.* New York: Ballantine Books.

An intimate portrait of the legendary hip-hop star written by someone who knew Shakur before he was famous.

Benton, Jim. 2004. *It's Happy Bunny: Love Bites.* New York: Scholastic.

The first book in the popular Happy Bunny series offers tips on love and dating from the famous cartoon bunny.

Discovery Channel. 2003. *Monster Garage: How to Customize Damn Near Everything.* Saint Paul, MN: Discovery Channel, Motorbooks International.

Based on the popular television series, this title gives ideas on how to customize a variety of vehicles and includes photographs, illustrations, and instructions to help make these ideas come to life.

Gantos, Jack. 2002. *Hole in My Life.* New York: Farrar, Straus and Giroux.

An autobiography describing the circumstance surrounding the award-winning author's two-year prison sentence for drug smuggling.

Gottlieb, Andrew. 2003. *In the Paint: Tattoos of the NBA and the Stories behind Them.* New York: Hyperion.

The strange stories behind many NBA stars' unusual tattoos are revealed in this title.

Hart, Christopher. 2002. *Anime Mania: How to Draw Characters for Japanese Animation.* New York: Watson-Guptill.

This title provides background on careers in animation along with detailed demonstrations of drawing and art techniques used in creating anime.

Hoye, Jacob. 2003. *Boards: The Art and Design of the Skateboard.* New York: Saint Martin's Press.

Color photographs demonstrating the impressive graphic art displayed on today's coolest skateboards are featured in this visually inviting book.

Kenner, Robert. 2003. *VX: 10 Years of Vibe Photography.* New York: VIBE Books in association with Harry N. Abrams.

Hip-hop's greatest stars appear in striking and unusual full-color photographs.

Myers, Walter Dean. 2001. *145th Street.* New York: Laurel-Leaf.

Ten short stories describe life on a dynamic block in a Harlem neighborhood.

Perel, David. 2006. *Batboy Lives!: The WEEKLY WORLD NEWS Guide to Politics, Culture, Celebrities, Alien Abductions, and the Mutant Freaks that Shape Our World.* New York: Sterling.

This unusual compilation highlights strange and entertaining news stories from the popular tabloid.

Platt, Larry. 2002. *Only the Strong Survive: The Odyssey of Allen Iverson.* New York: ReganBooks.

An intimate look at one of the NBA's best-known and sometimes most controversial stars, from his poverty and crime-ridden childhood to his success as a professional athlete.

Sampson, Davis, George Jenkins, Rameck Hunt, and Sharon Draper. 2005. *We Beat the Street: How a Friendship Pact Led to Success.* New York: Dutton.

Recounts how a promise made to one another as teenagers helped three African American men from a poverty-stricken Newark, New Jersey, neighborhood graduate from medical school and go on to careers in medicine.

Seckel, Al. 2006. *The Ultimate Book of Optical Illusions.* New York: Sterling.

Hundreds of fun, fascinating, and eye-catching optical illusions draw in even the most reluctant readers.

Singer, Marilyn, ed. 2004. *Face Relations: Eleven Stories about Seeing beyond Color.* New York: Simon and Schuster Books for Young Readers.

Short stories from well-known young adult authors explore the complicated issue of racial identity.

Slichter, Jacob. 2004. *So You Wanna Be a Rock and Roll Star: How I Machine-Gunned a Roomful of Record Executives and Other True Tales from a Drummer's Life.* New York: Broadway Books.

A look at the truth behind the life of a rising rock star from a member of the band Semisonic.

Weiss, Jerry M., ed. 2002. *Big City Cool: Short Stories about Urban Youth.* New York: Persea Books.

Fourteen stories, featuring diverse teen characters from a variety of ethnic backgrounds, explore urban life.

Westbrook, Alonzo. 2002. *Hip Hoptionary.* New York: Harlem Moon.

Provides definitions of hip-hop terms along with biographical information about famous people in the hip-hop world.

Always in Demand

Some titles never go out of style. These titles are perpetually popular with a wide variety of teens, including reluctant readers served by libraries in large urban areas. Buy multiple copies of these titles in paperback and watch them fly off the shelves.

Canfield, Jack, ed. 1997. *Chicken Soup for the Teenage Soul: 101 Stories of Life, Love and Learning.* Deerfield Beach, FL: Health Communications.

The first book of the popular series offers advice on love, friendship, families, and more.

Draper, Sharon. 1994. *Tears of a Tiger.* New York: Atheneum Books for Young Readers.

When his close friend and fellow basketball team member dies in a drunken driving accident, Andy, who was driving the car, is overcome by guilt and unable to move on with his life.

Draper, Sharon. 1997. *Forged By Fire*. New York: Atheneum Books for Young Readers.

When Gerald's mom shows up on his ninth birthday after a six-year absence from his life, Gerald's world is turned upside down.

Flake, Sharon. 1998. *The Skin I'm In*. New York: Jump at the Sun/ Hyperion Books for Children.

Teased because of her dark skin, Maleeka reexamines her life when a new teacher shows up.

Guinness Book of World Records. 2007. London: Guinness World Records.

The classic series now comes with an eye-catching cover, numerous photographs, and more unusual world records than ever before.

Myers, Walter Dean. 1996. *Slam*. New York: Scholastic Press.

High school basketball star Greg Harris can handle anything on the court, but life off the court is beginning to slip out of control.

Myers, Walter Dean. 1999. *Monster*. New York: HarperCollins.

Sixteen-year-old Steve recounts his experience as the defendant in a trial told through a screenplay-style diary.

Pelzer, David. 1995. *A Child Called It: An Abused Child's Journey from Victim to Victor*. Deerfield Beach, FL: Health Communications.

A dramatic account of the author's abusive childhood and his journey to overcome his mistreatment.

Pelzer, David J. 1997. *The Lost Boy: A Foster Child's Search for the Love of a Family*. Deerfield Beach, FL: Health Communications.

The sequel to *A Child Called It* follows the author after he leaves his own difficult family situation, navigates foster care, and enters his adult life.

Shakur, Tupac. 1999. *The Rose that Grew from Concrete*. New York: Pocket Books.

Collection of poems written by the legendary rapper before he became famous.

Soto, Gary. 1997. *Buried Onions*. San Diego, CA: Harcourt Brace.

His cousin's recent murder and his family's desire for revenge may ruin Eddie's plans for a peaceful life.

Fiction Featuring African American Characters

Libraries in urban areas serve a diverse teen customer base. Titles featuring African American characters are often in high demand. Some libraries may use spine labels to help customers locate books featuring

African American characters, but many do not. This list offers staff at all levels a place to begin their search for these often-requested titles.

Adoff, Jamie. 2005. *Jimi and Me.* New York: Jump at the Sun/Hyperion.

After his father's death, Keith and his mother give up the family's apartment in Brooklyn and move to Ohio.

Barnes, Derrick. 2007. *The Making of Dr. Truelove.* New York: Simon and Schuster.

Diego would do anything to win back his girlfriend, Roxy, even pose as "Dr. Truelove," a guru offering advice on how to make relationships work.

Crutcher, Chris. 2001. *Whale Talk.* New York: Greenwillow Books.

Japanese African American high school senior T. J. Jones forms a swim team of outsiders at a high school with no swimming pool.

Davidson, Dana. 2004. *Jason and Kyra.* New York: Jump at the Sun/Hyperion.

Star athlete Jason is surprised by his feelings of attraction for brainy Kyra.

Davidson, Dana. 2005. *Played.* New York: Hyperion Books.

Ian's acceptance into an elite fraternity depends on his ability to make unpopular Kylie fall in love and sleep with him.

Draper, Sharon. 1999. *Romiette and Julio.* New York: Atheneum Books.

African American Romiette is head-over-heels in love with Hispanic Julio, but a local gang threatens violence if the two do not stop their romance.

Draper, Sharon. 2001. *Darkness before Dawn.* New York: Atheneum Books for Young Readers.

Excited by a mutual attraction to her high school track coach, Keisha is stunned when the relationship takes an unexpected and unwanted turn.

Flake, Sharon. 2003. *Begging for Change.* New York: Jump at the Sun/Hyperion Books for Children.

After her mother is attacked, Raspberry's drug-addicted father re-emerges and complicates Raspberry's life.

Flake, Sharon. 2004. *Who Am I without Him? Short Stories about Girls and the Boys in Their Lives.* New York: Jump at the Sun/Hyperion Books for Children.

Teen girls' feelings about love and romance are captured in 10 short stories.

Flake, Sharon. 2005. *Bang.* New York: Jump at the Sun/Hyperion Books for Children.

After his son is killed in a neighborhood shooting, Mann's father decides to toughen up his remaining son by taking him camping and leaving him stranded.

Frost, Helen. 2003. *Keesha's House.* New York: Farrar, Straus and Giroux.

Seven troubled teens with nowhere else to go describe their experiences at Keesha's House, the one place where they can take shelter, be safe, and figure out what to do with their lives.

Grimes, Nikki. 2002. *Bronx Masquerade.* New York: Dial Books.

Weekly English class open-mic poetry sessions lead to surprising revelations about 18 high school students.

Johnson, Angela. 2003. *First Part Last.* New York: Simon and Schuster Books.

On his 16th birthday, Bobby learns that his girlfriend, Nia, is pregnant. The story traces the couples' struggle about how to handle the pregnancy, beginning with the end of the story and flashing back to fill in the blanks.

McDonald, Janet. 2001. *Spellbound.* New York: Frances Foster Books.

Trying to keep her dreams for a positive future alive, 16-year-old Raven, a new mom, enters a spelling bee that offers the winner a chance to go to college.

McDonald, Janet. 2006. *Harlem Hustle.* New York: Frances Foster Books/ Farrar, Straus and Giroux.

Eric Sampson decides to end his days as a petty criminal and rely on his rapping and rhyming skills to build a future.

Myers, Walter Dean. 2006. *Street Love.* New York: Amistand.

The unlikely romance between Damien and Junice, two teens from very different worlds, is told through short poems.

Sitomer, Alan Lawrence. 2005. *Hoopster.* New York: Hyperion Books for Children.

A writing assignment for a national magazine causes talented writer and athlete Adre to reevaluate his belief that racism does not affect his daily life.

Sitomer, Alan Lawrence. 2006. *Hip Hop High School.* New York: Hyperion Books for Children.

With the help of the inspirational words of her favorite hip-hop artists, Theresa works to achieve her goal of attending the University of Southern California.

Thomas, Jacquelin. 2006. *Simply Divine.* New York: Pocket Books.

When Divine's famous family falls apart, the whole world is watching. Sent to live in a small Georgia town with her pastor uncle and his family, Divine expects to hate life in "the sticks" but is surprised to find her new home offers many things that were missing from her life.

Volponi, Paul. 2006. *Rooftop*. New York: Viking.

Cousins Clay and Addison are both enrolled in a day drug treatment facility. Clay is clean. Addison is not and continues to deal drugs. When tragedy strikes and Addison is killed in a police shooting, Clay decides to face his own demons head-on.

Williams, Lori Aurelia. 2005. *Broken China*. New York: Simon and Schuster.

Determined to repay the debt for her young daughter's funeral, China gets a job as the coat check girl at a local strip club.

Wolff, Virginia Euwer. 2001. *True Believer*. New York: Atheneum Books for Young Readers.

LaVaughn pursues her dreams of college and a better life while coping with confusing feelings about love and faith.

Woods, Brenda. 2004. *Emako Blue*. New York: G. P. Putnam's Sons.

Everyone believes 15-year-old Emako is destined for a bright future, until a drive-by shooting aimed at someone else ends Emako's life.

Woodson, Jacqueline. 2002. *Hush*. New York: Putnam's.

When Toswiah's police officer father, an African American, testifies against a fellow white officer in a murder case, Toswiah and her family must enter the Witness Protection Program.

Historical Fiction Featuring African American Characters

Historical fiction is fairly low on the popularity scale among urban teens (Chelton 2006), though students often receive school assignments that require them to read in this genre. This list offers suggestions for teens who want or need to read historical fiction but who also have an interest in titles featuring African American characters.

Draper, Sharon. 2006. *Cooper Sun*. New York: Atheneum Books for Young Readers.

Sold into slavery in the 1730s and given as a birthday gift to the son of a South Carolina plantation owner, 15-year-old Amari dreams of escape.

Houston, Julian. 2005. *New Boy*. Boston: Houghton Mifflin.

Hoping for a better future, Rob Garrett becomes the first African American student at an elite Connecticut boarding school in the 1950s.

Lester, Julius. 2005. *Day of Tears: A Novel in Dialogue*. New York: Hyperion Books for Children.

The tragic story of an 1859 slave auction, the largest slave auction in U.S. history, is recounted in dialogue format.

Mosley, Walter. 2005. *47*. New York: Little, Brown.

A young slave boy in the 1830s with only a number for a name is changed forever when he meets an unusual runaway slave, who turns out to be an alien from "beyond Africa."

Moss, Sheila. 2006. *Return of Buddy Bush*. New York: Margaret K. McElderry Books.

In this sequel to *The Legend of Buddy Bush* (Margaret K. McElderry Books, 2004), Pattie Mae travels to Harlem in 1947 hoping to find her Uncle Buddy and bring him home.

Taylor, Mildred. 2001. *The Land*. New York: Phyllis Fogelman Books.

In this prequel to *Roll of Thunder, Hear My Cry* (Puffin Books, 1976, 1991), Paul-Edward, the son of a white plantation owner and his black slave, lives his life caught between two worlds in the Reconstruction-era South.

Wilson, Diane. 2005. *Black Storm Comin'*. New York: Margaret K. McElderry Books.

When Colton's father abandons his biracial family on the wagon trail heading west in 1860, Colton takes a job with the Pony Express.

Fiction Featuring Latino or Hispanic Characters

Many urban areas have seen a large increase in their Latino and Hispanic populations in recent years. The following titles provide a starting point for providing reader's advisory for this growing group of teen customers.

Alvarez, Julia. 2002. *Before We Were Free*. New York: Knopf.

Living in the Dominican Republic during the turbulent early 1960s, 12-year-old Anita must deal with her father's involvement in a plot to assassinate the country's dictator.

Alvarez, Julia. 2004. *Finding Miracles*. New York: Knopf.

Until Pablo arrived at her school, Milly never gave much thought to her birth family or her native country, but when Pablo speculates that Milly may be from his hometown, she begins to wonder what other secrets her past may hold.

Canales, Viola. 2005. *Tequila Worm*. New York: Wendy Lamb Books.

When Mexican American Sofia is offered the chance to attend an elite boarding school, she must convince her mother and family that leaving home does not mean she will forget her heritage.

Cofer, Judith Ortiz. 2004. *Call me Maria*. New York: Orchard Books.

Hoping for a chance at a better education in the United States, Maria leaves her home in Puerto Rico to live with her father in New York, where she adjusts to urban life and learns to speak "Spanglish."

Herrera, Juan Felipe. 2005. *Cinnamon Girl*. New York: Joanna Cotler Books.

When her uncle is gravely injured in the attacks on September 11, 2001, Yolanda copes with her fear and grief by facing her own difficult past and by gathering ashes and dust from those who died in the attack.

Jaramillo, Ann. 2006. *La Linea*. New Milford, CT: Roaring Book Press.

Fifteen-year-old Miguel has been waiting years to get the word from his parents that it is time for him to leave Mexico and join them in the United States. Unbeknownst to Miguel, his little sister follows him on his journey, creating problems and putting their lives in danger.

Osa, Nancy. 2003. *Cuba 15*. New York: Delacorte Press.

Fifteen-year-old Violet did not intend to have an extravagant *quinceanera*, complete with a fluffy dress, but when her grandmother proposes the idea, Violet is swept up in the planning, discovering a lot about her Cuban heritage along the way.

Pagliarulo, Antonio. 2006. *A Different Kind of Heat*. New York: Delacorte Press.

Sent to a Boys and Girls Home after inciting violence at a protest following her brother's death in a police shooting, former gang member Luz Cordero chronicles her life and attempts to cope with her feelings of anger in a diary given to her by Sister Ellen.

Saenz, Alire. 2004. *Sammy and Juliana in Hollywood*. El Paso, TX: Cinco Puntos Press.

Growing up in Hollywood, New Mexico, in 1969, Sammy works to finish high school and go onto college while dealing with the tragic murder of his girlfriend, Juliana.

Saldana, Rene. 2003. *Finding Our Way: Stories*. New York: Wendy Lamb Books.

These 11 short stories feature Hispanic teenagers growing up and figuring out who they are and who they want to be in life.

Sanchez, Alex. 2004. *So Hard to Say*. New York: Simon and Schuster.

When Xio develops a crush on her close friend Frederick, things become awkward as he struggles to tell her about his attraction to another boy.

Soto, Gary. 2003. *The Afterlife*. Orlando, FL: Harcourt.

After dying from a stab wound suffered in a bathroom, Chuy observes life in his neighborhood, visits unknowing family and friends, and meets other ghosts, including one young suicide victim with whom Chuy falls in love.

Soto, Gary. 2006. *Accidental Love.* Orlando, FL: Harcourt.

During a tense exchange in an elevator, Marissa accidentally picks up the cell phone of an uninvolved observer, thinking it is her own. She soon learns the phone belongs to Rene, a less-than-cool guy who does not live in her rough neighborhood and for whom she begins to feel an unexpected attraction.

Urban/Street Lit

Anyone who has worked in a public library serving an urban area in the last few years is already well aware of the emergence of the popular street lit (or hip-hop) genre. Gritty and often violent, most (although not all) street lit titles feature African American characters. Common elements in street lit include strong language along with explicit sex. The fact that these books are published for adults has not prevented many teens, especially older teens, from reading and requesting street lit titles. David Wright, reader services librarian at the Seattle Public Library, recently speculated that the age range of street lit readers is approximately 14 to 34 years old (Fialkoff 2006). Despite their popularity, including titles from this genre in your teen collection (or sometimes even in the library at all) can be controversial. This may be particularly true for smaller libraries where the children, teen, and adult collections are frequently located very close to one another.

Not having street lit titles located in your teen section is no excuse, however, for ignorance about them, and if you are to maintain credibility with teens, it is vital to have knowledge about the latest and hottest street lit titles and authors. The following series and titles are of interest to fans of street lit. Although the language and subject matter can still be quite mature, the target audience is teens rather than adults.

Bluford High Series

Set in an urban high school named after the first black astronaut, this series explores the lives of students and their families.

Booth, Coe. 2006. *Tyrell.* New York: Push.

When his father goes to jail for the third time, 15-year-old Tyrell and his family are forced to move into a dirty, run-down homeless shelter. Despite dropping out of high school, Tyrell resists pressure to sell drugs and does his best to help his family out financially without doing anything illegal.

Langan, Paul. 2007. *The Fallen.* West Berlin, NJ: Townsend Press.

Langan, John. 2007. *Search for Safety*. West Berlin, NJ: Townsend Press.
Langan, Paul. 2007. *Shattered*. West Berlin, NJ: Townsend Press.

Drama High

One of only a handful of African American students bussed to a wealthy school where most of the student body is white, Jayd deals with romance, heartache, and the drama of everyday high school life.
Devine, L. 2006. *The Fight*. New York: Dafina.
Devine, L. 2006. *Second Chance*. New York: Dafina.
Devine, L. 2007. *Jayd's Legacy*. New York: Dafina.

Platinum Teen

Friends Dymond, Kera, and Porsha learn life lessons about guys, love, and betrayal.
Hardrick, Jackie. 2004. *Imani in Never Can Say Goodbye*. Vauxhall, NJ: Enlighten, 2004.
Imani's senior year is full of concern for her future, while many of her friends face difficult challenges.
Juwell, Precious. 2005. *Ab-Solute Truth*. Bear, DE: Precioustymes Entertainment.
Juwell, Precious. 2006. *Runaway*. Bear, DE: Precioustymes Entertainment.
King, Katina. 2006. *Ride wit' Me*. Fort Lee, NJ: Young Diamond Books.
A modern day Romeo and Juliet love story blossoms when wealthy, 16-year-old Mercedes comes to stay with her father in Chicago for the summer and falls in love with Dalvin, the son of one of her father's business rivals.
Knight, Khadijah, Ashley Jones, et al. 2005. *Teenage Bluez: A Collection of Urban Stories*. Brandywine, MD: Life Changing Books.
Six stories featuring teens dealing with love, crime, and high school life in an urban setting. Fans might also try Marketa, Salley, Darnell C. Jackson, et al. 2006. *Teenage Bluez II*. Brandywine, MD: Life Changing Books.
McDonald, Janet. 2004. *Brother Hood*. New York: Farrar, Straus and Giroux.
After winning a scholarship to an elite boarding school in upstate New York, 16-year-old Nate does his best to remain true to his Harlem roots while attending his new school.
McKayhan, Monica. 2007. *Indigo Summer*. New York: Kimani Tru.
Just when things are looking up for Indigo, her new football star boyfriend drops her. Fortunately, her always reliable friend and neighbor Marcus is there to lend a hand and offer a shoulder to cry on.

Van Diepen, Allison. 2006. *Street Pharm*. New York: Simon Pulse.

With his dad in prison, Ty tries to maintain his father's drug-dealing business and begins to wonder what he really wants for his future.

Williams, KeShamba. 2004. *Dymond in the Rough*. Bear, DE: Precioustymes Entertainment.

Twenty-Five Urban Fiction Authors You Should Know

Nicole Bailey-Williams
Tracy Brown
Chunichi
Donald Goines
Shannon Holmes
La Jill Hunt
Angel Hunter
Brenda Jackson
Jihad
Solomon Jones
K'wa
Thomas Long
Karen Miller
Y. Blak Moore
Daaimah S. Poole
Iceberg Slim
Sister Souljah
Vicki Stringer
Kiki Swinson
Nikki Turner
Omar Tyree
Carl Weber
Anthony J. Whyte
KaShamba Williams
Teri Woods

Street Lit Resources on the Web

Borders African American Urban Fiction. http://www.bordersstores.com/features/list.jsp?list=afamurbanfiction.

Includes publication information and, with just one click, brief synopses of current popular urban fiction titles.

Carl Weber. http://www.carlweber.net/.

Offers a biography of the popular author and links to other urban fiction resources, including urban authors' Web pages and a publisher of urban African American Christian books.

Essence Magazine Best Selling Books. http://www.essence.com/essence/books/.

(continued)

(*Continued*)

Excellent site to find out what titles are new and hot on the urban lit scene.

Kimani Tru. http://www.kimanitru.com/.

Publisher of books of interest to teen fans of street lit.

Precioustymes Entertainment. http://www.kashambawilliams.com/home New.htm.

Includes author information.

Q-Boro Books. http://www.qborobooks.com/.

Includes author information and a photo gallery

Teri Woods Publishing. http://www.teriwoodspublishing.com/main.html.

Offers information about the author, her books, and upcoming appearances.

Triple Crown Publications. http://www.triplecrownpublications.com/about.php.

Includes information on several popular authors and articles about the rise of Triple Crown Publications.

Urban Fiction/Street Lit/Hip Hop Fiction Resources for Librarians. http://www.libsuccess.org/index.php?title=Urban_Fiction/Street_Lit/Hip_Hop_Fiction_Resources_for_Librarians.

Section from Meredith Frakas's Library Success: A Best Practices Wiki offering booklists and places to look for additional resources.

Urban/Street Lit Fiction Reading List Suitable for School Library Collections. http://dolphin.upenn.edu/~vmorris/SchoolUrbanFictionReadingList.htm.

Suggestions from Clarion Professor Vanessa J. Morris for teens looking for urban fiction titles.

Multicultural and Mixed Heritage

Libraries located in urban areas serve a very diverse population. The following titles may be of interest to teens looking to see themselves and their lives reflected in characters and stories and also to those teens ready to explore the diverse, multicultural world in which they live.

Desai Hidier, Tanuja. 2002. *Born Confused.* New York: Scholastic Press.

Dimple Lala, a 17-year-old Indian American teenager, tries to fit in with her American friends despite her immigrant parents' disapproval of her new American habits.

Gallo, Donald R. 2004. *First Crossing: Stories about Teen Immigrants.* Cambridge, MA: Candlewick Press.

Teens from a variety of backgrounds and countries explore the immigration experience and life in the United States in this collection of short stories.

Marston, Elsa. 2005. *Figs and Fate: Stories about Growing Up in the Arab World Today.* New York: George Braziller.

Five short stories explore life as a teenager living in various Middle Eastern countries, including Egypt, Lebanon, Syria, Iraq, and Palestine.

Ortiz Cofer, Judith. 2003. *Riding Low through the Streets of Gold.* Houston, TX: Pinata Books.

Poems and stories by both established and newer authors explore the familiar experiences of many Latino teenagers growing up balancing life in two cultures.

Placide, Jaira. 2002. *Fresh Girl.* New York: Wendy Lamb Books.

Returning to the United States after living in Haiti for nearly a decade, Mardi does her best to maintain her Haitian heritage.

Whelan, Gloria. 2003. *Homeless Bird.* New York, HarperCollins.

When 13-year-old Koly is widowed by her new groom, she no longer has a place in her Indian society.

Sports

Books focusing on sports are popular with a variety of teens. These books frequently have strong appeal to guys, particularly guys living in urban areas where sports—whether it be shooting hoops at the neighbor-hood court or playing football for a large high school—are an everyday part of life. Reluctant readers uninterested in most titles are often willing to give a sports-themed book a try.

Alphin, Elaine Marie. 2006. *Perfect Shot.* Minneapolis, MN: Carolrhoda Books.

When his girlfriend is killed, high school basketball star Brian does not believe the police are after the right suspect.

Coy, John. 2005. *Crackback.* New York: Scholastic.

Football season does not turn out as expected for high school junior Miles when he gets a new, verbally abusive coach and his best friend begins pushing him to take steroids.

De La Pena, Matt. 2005. *Ball Don't Lie.* New York: Delacorte.

Stick takes his game to the courts of a tough Los Angeles neighborhood, dreaming of making it as a pro basketball player.

Deuker, Carl. 2005. *Runner.* Boston: Houghton Mifflin.

Everything is going great with Chance's job picking up and delivering packages for a stranger, until the stranger disappears and Chance is stuck with a mysterious package.

Nelson, Blake. 2006. *Paranoid Park.* New York: Viking.

A 16-year-old skateboarder recounts the guilt and remorse he feels after being involved in the events that led to the accidental killing of a security guard.

Volponi, Paul. 2005. *Black and White.* New York: Viking.

High school basketball stars Marcus and Eddie do everything together, even commit the occasional crime. But when a robbery goes bad, the two boys, one black and the other white, have very different experiences in the criminal justice system.

Reluctant Readers

Reaching a reluctant reader is one of the toughest challenges librarians face. Some reluctant readers do not like to read because they are not very good at it. Others do not read because books do not interest them or because they do not have the time to read. Still others do not want to engage in an activity like reading that may be judged as uncool by their peers. Whatever the case, most libraries serving urban areas face the challenge of finding the right book for a reluctant teen reader nearly every day.

The following suggestions have many of the elements that appeal to reluctant readers. The plot lines are engaging. The books feature eye-catching covers or illustrations. Although shorter books often have high reluctant reader appeal, not all of the titles here are short. Rather, this is an eclectic sampling of fast-paced, often edgy titles for librarians to consider when working with reluctant readers, particularly older teen reluctant readers.

There are other superb resources focusing on titles for reluctant teen readers. One not to be missed is the Young Adult Library Services Association's annual "Quick Picks for Reluctant Readers" list.

Baskin, Julia. 2006. *Notebook Girls: Four Friends, One Diary, Real Life.* New York: Warner Books.

This real-life shared diary started by four friends during their freshman year at a New York City high school includes photos, scribbles, and the truth about their high school experience.

Buckhanon, Kalisha. 2005. *Upstate.* New York: Saint Martin's Press.

Harlem teenagers Natasha and Antonio are separated when Antonio is sent to prison during his senior year for killing his father. The story of love and very different lives is told through the letters they exchange over the next several years.

Cohn, Rachel, and David Lefithan. 2006. *Nick and Norah's Infinite Playlist.* New York: Knopf.

One night changes everything when Nick meets recently heartbroken Norah and the two travel across Manhattan together.

Giles, Gail. 2004. *Playing in Traffic.* Brookfield, CT: Roaring Brook Press.

Why would a girl like Skye Colby even notice someone like Matt, much less want to be his girlfriend? The truth behind Skye's sudden attraction is even more stunning than Matt could have imagined.

Goobie, Beth. 2002. *Sticks and Stones.* Custer, WA: Orca.

High school freshman Jujube is not "that kind of girl," but that does not seem to matter when a nasty rumor about her starts and Jujube develops and an unwarranted and unwanted bad reputation. Be sure to also check out other books from the Orca line.

Olin, Searn. 2005. *Killing Britney.* New York: Simon Pulse.

Life should be good for Britney now that she has changed from a geeky outsider into a slim, beautiful member of the popular crowd. The only problem is that everyone around Britney is dying. Who is the killer, and is Britney next?

Polhemus, Ted. 2004. *Hot Bodies, Cool Styles: New Techniques in Self-Adornment.* London: Thames and Hudson.

A unique look at tattoos and body art, including eye-catching photographs and safety tips for anyone considering a tattoo.

Stone, Tanya Lee. 2006. *A Bad Boy Can Be Good for a Girl.* New York: Wendy Lamb Books.

The local library's copy of Judy Blume's *Forever* becomes the place several high school girls scribble their warnings about a popular jock whose romantic intentions are not as pure as they seem.

Audiobooks

One important and often-overlooked resource for teens, and especially reluctant readers, is audiobooks. The Young Adult Library Services Association publishes an annual "Selected Audio Books for Young Adults" list that is an excellent starting point for determining what to buy. Purchase a range of audiobooks for teens. If possible, consider buying multiple copies of the most popular titles. A key for success in serving reluctant readers is having the material on the shelf. Although other teen customers may be willing to wait a day or a week for an item, reluctant readers who do not walk out of the library with the audiobook they want when they want it may be disinclined to return.

Many libraries now offer downloadable audiobooks. Reluctant teen readers who own an MP3 player or have technology at home that allows them to easily access and use the library's downloadable book collection are a good target audience for these new resources. Teens can access them anytime, even when the library is closed. They do not accumulate fines, another issue that often affects teens' library use. Although downloadable audiobooks clearly have a number of benefits for teens, reluctant readers' use of this collection may depend on how easy it is for these teens to locate and use your library's collection of downloadable books. If this collection is not easy to navigate, an unenthusiastic teen reader will not spend much time trying to figure out your system and procedures. And many teens served by libraries in large urban areas do not have ready access to the technology necessary to use downloadable audiobooks at home. For this reason, books on compact disc remain, at least for the time being, an important option for all reluctant teen readers.

Magazines

Ask a roomful of teens if they read, and many will immediately answer no or shake their heads. Follow up by asking, "Do you read magazines?" and nearly every hand in the room will immediately shoot up. Magazines are a staple of existence for many teens. In libraries serving urban areas, having a wide variety of magazines readily available and on display in your teen area is a must. Although not every title on this list is specifically published with teens in mind, these titles are likely to be among your teen customers' favorites and should be easily located by teens who are browsing and hanging out in your library.

Black Beat Magazine

Monthly magazine that is "the ultimate source for teens and college age fans of the urban music scene." Bimonthly. $29.94 per year.

Offers interviews with well-known and successful black women; entertainment, music, and culture news; along with short stories and poems. Bimonthly. $24.00 per year.

Brio and Beyond. http://www.briomag.com/briomagazine/briobeyond/.

Christian magazine aimed at an older teen than the original, its companion magazine, *Brio.* Monthly. $22.00 per year.

Draw! http://www.drawmagazine.com/.

This "step-by-step magazine on drawing for comics and animation" will appeal to fans of anime and manga. Quarterly. $20.00 per year.

Giant Robot

Covers cool aspects of Asian and Asian American pop culture. Quarterly. $30.00 per year.

J-14. http://j-14.hollywood.com/.

Celebrity news aimed at teen girls. Ten issues per year. $16.95 per year.

Mad Magazine. http://www.dccomics.com/mad/.

This subversive, perennial favorite never goes out of style. Monthly. $16.00 per year.

Newtype USA. http://www.newtype-usa.com/.

Provides in-depth articles and discussions related to anime as well as reviews of the latest anime releases. Monthly. $89.95 per year.

Shojo Beat. http://www.shojobeat.com/.

A manga magazine featuring stories driven by character and mood often of interest to girls. Monthly. $29.95 per year.

Sister 2 Sister. http://www.s2smagazine.com/.

News and interviews with prominent African American women, with a focus on the entertainment industry. Monthly. $14.99 per year.

Skateboarder Magazine. http://www.skateboardermag.com/.

A must for skateboarding fans, includes news from the world of skateboarding along with photos and interviews with the sport's top stars. Monthly. $11.97 per year.

Teen Ink. http://teenink.com/.

Written for and by teens, includes many forms of creative expression from poetry to short stories. Monthly. $25.00 per year.

XXL. http://xxlmag.com/.

"Hip Hop on a higher level." Interviews, news, and more from the world of hip-hop. Monthly. $12.00 per year.

Word Up

Covering all the latest news from the world of rap music. Monthly. $29.00 per year.

CONCLUSION

Developing a collection that addresses the wide range of urban teens' interest and needs is no easy task. Lists and resources created by professionals are essential tools for librarians searching for materials with high appeal to a diverse and sophisticated teen audience, but the value of keeping the lines of communication open between teens and library staff members purchasing material and maintaining current teen collections cannot be overstated. Asking teens for their input about the existing collection and new titles is a surefire way to engage teens and keep your collection dynamic and relevant.

WORKS CITED

Beatty, Sally. 2005. "You're Reading What?" *Wall Street Journal,* June 24, W1.

Chelton, Mary K. 2006. "Perspectives on Practice: Young Adult Collections Are More than Just Young Adult Literature." *Young Adult Library Services* 4 (2) (Winter): 10–11.

Fialkoff, Francine. 2006. "Street Lit Takes a Hit." *Library Journal* 131 (February 1). Accessed March 7, 2007, available at http://www.libraryjournal.com/article/CA6299839.html.

Welch, Rollie, and Paula Brehm-Heeger. 2006. Serving Teens in Urban Libraries at the Ohio Library Children's/Young Adult Conference, Columbus, Ohio, August.

FURTHER READING

Ammon, Bette, and Gale Sherman. 1999. *More Rip-Roaring Reads for Reluctant Teen Readers.* Englewood, CO: Libraries Unlimited.

Anderson, Sheila. 2005. *Extreme Teens: Library Services to Nontraditional Young Adults.* Westport, CT: Libraries Unlimited.

Angier, Naomi, Rebecca Cohen, and Jill Morrison. 2001. "Juvenile Justice Outreach: Library Services at Detention." *PNLA Quarterly* 66 (1) (Fall): 16.

Arnold, Andrew. 2004. "Drawing in the Gals: Move Over Guys. Graphics for Girls Are the Hot New Genre in Japanese Comics." *Time,* February 16, 97.

Bartel, Julie. 2005. "The Good, the Bad and the Edgy." *School Library Journal* 51 (July). Accessed March 7, 2007, available at http://www.schoollibrary journal.com/article/CA621754.html.

Bodart, Joni Richards. 2000. *The World's Best Thin Books: What to Read When Your Book Report Is Due Tomorrow.* Lanham, MD: Scarecrow Press.

Brenner, Robin E. 2007. *Understanding Manga and Anime.* Westport, CT: Libraries Unlimited.

Cai, Mingshui. 2002. *Multicultural Literature for Children and Young Adults: Reflections on Critical Issues.* Westport, CT: Greenwood Press.

Campbell, Kim. 2004. "Gritty 'Street Lit' Makes Noise in the 'Hood." *Christian Science Monitor,* September 9. Accessed March 7, 2007, available at http://www.csmonitor.com/2004/0909/p11s02-bogn.html.

Court, Ayesha. 2003. "Edgy Stories Echo the Streets, 'Ghetto Fiction' Lures Big Publishers." *USA Today,* July 2, 1d.

Delatte, Monique, and Deborah Anderson. *Ten Ways to Build a Reluctant Reader Library.* Accessed March 1, 2007, available at http://www.randomhouse.com/highschool/RHI_magazine/pdf/delatteanderson.pdf.

Doyle, Miranda. 2002. "Tough Girls: Fiction for African American Urban Teens." *Voice of Youth Advocates* 25 (3) (August): 174–75. Accessed March 31, 2007, available at http://pdfs.voya.com/Af/ric/AfricanAmerFiction.pdf.

Doyle, Miranda. 2005. "Sex, Drug Deals, and Drama: More Books Like *The Coldest Winter Ever.*" *Voice of Youth Advocates* 28 (3) (August): 190–93. Accessed March 31, 2007, available at http://pdfs.voya.com/VO/YA2/VOYA 200508SexDrugs.pdf.

Fallis, Chris. 2005. "Graphic Generation." *Young Adult Library Services* 4 (3) (Summer): 16.

Fletcher-Spear, Kristin, and Kat Kan. 2005. "The Anime-ted Library." *Voice of Youth Advocates* 28 (1) (April). Accessed March 7, 2007, available at pdfs.voya.com/VO/YA2/VOYA200504AnimetedLibrary.pdf.

Flectcher-Spear, Kristin, and Merideth Jenson-Benjamin. 2005. "Get Animated @ Your Library." *Young Adult Library Services* 3 (4) (Summer): 32-38.

Goldsmith, Francisca. 2003. "Graphic Novels as Literature." *Booklist* 99 (11) (February 1): 986.

Gorman, Michelle. 2002. "What Teens Want: Thirty Graphic Novels You Can't Live Without." *School Library Journal* 48 (8) (August): 18.

Guild, Sandy, and Sandra Hughes-Hassell. 2001. "The Urban Minority Young Adult as Audience: Does Young Adult Literature Pass the Reality Test?" *New Advocate* 14 (4) (Fall): 316–77.

Hughes-Hassell, Sandra and Christina Lutz. 2005. "What Do You Want to Tell Us about Reading? A Survey of the Habits and Attitudes of Urban Middle School Students toward Leisure Reading." *Young Adult Library Services* 4 (2) (Fall): 39–45.

Jones, Patrick. 2004. "Reaching Out to Young Adults in Jail." *Young Adult Library Services* 3 (1) (Fall): 16–19.

Jones, Patrick, Maureen L. Hartman, and Patricia P. Taylor. 2005. *Connecting with Reluctant Teen Readers: Tips, Titles and Tools.* New York: Neal-Schuman.

Kan, Kat, and Kristin Fletcher-Spear. 2002. "Showing Anime in the Library." *Voice of Youth Advocates* 25 (1) (April): 20–23.

Kilgannon, Corey. 2006. "Street Lit with Publishing Cred: From Prison to a Four-Book Deal." *New York Times,* February 14. Accessed March 7, 2007, available at http://www.nytimes.com/2006/02/14/books/14rele.html?ex=1297573200&en=eae95f3764cc841f&ei=5088&partner=rssnyt&emc=rss.

Libretto, Ellen V., and Catherine Barr. 2002. *High/Low Handbook: Best Books and Websites for Reluctant Teen Readers.* Westport, CT: Libraries Unlimited.

Madenski, Melissa. 2001. "Books behind Bars." *School Library Journal* 47 (July): 40.

Marech, Rona. 2003. "Hip-Hop Lit Is Full of Grit: New Literary Genre Is Emerging from Underground Authors." *San Francisco Chronicle,* October 19. Accessed March 7, 2007, available at http://www.renayjackson.com/articles/sf chronicle101903.pdf.

Matherson, Whitney. 2004. "What Animates Teens About Manga?" *USA Today,* May 12.

Memmott, Carol. 2005. "Japanese Manga Takes Humongous Step: Comics Go Mainstream." *USA Today,* July 6.

Reid, Calvin. 2006. "Selling Urban Fiction." *Publishers Weekly* 253 (January 23). Accessed March 7, 2007, available at http://www.publishersweekly.com/article/CA6301171.html.

Rosen, Judith. 2004. "Street Lit: Readers Gotta Have It." *Publishers Weekly* 251 (December 13). Accessed March 7, 2007, available at http://www.publishersweekly.com/article/CA486531.html.

Ryan, Laura T. 2005. "Hip-Hop Fiction Drawing More Readers to Black Lit." *Seattle Times*, "Entertainment and the Arts," February 22. Accessed March 7, 2007, available at http://seattletimes.nwsource.com/html/artsentertainment/2002186046_blacklit22.html.

Snowball, Clare. 2005. "Teenage Reluctant Readers and Graphic Novels." *Young Adult Library Services* 4 (3) (Summer): 43–45.

Suellentrop, Patricia. 2006. "Book It: A Detention Center Booklist." *YAttitudes* 5 (3) (Spring). Available at http://www.ala.org/yalsa/yalsamemonly/membersonly.cfm.

Sullivan, Edward T. 2002. "Race Matters." *School Library Journal* 46 (4) (June): 40–41.

Walker, Rob. 2004. "Comics Trip: What Are American Kids Looking for in the Cultural Mix and Match of Japanese Manga? *New York Times Magazine*, May 30: 24.

Weeks, Linton. 2004. "New Books in the Hood." *Washington Post*, July 31, C01.

Welch, Rollie. 2006. "Cleveland Teens' Top Ten Manga Series." *Young Adult Library Services* 3 (4) (Spring): 11.

Wolk, Douglas. 2001. "Manga, Anime Invade the U.S." *Publishers Weekly* 248 (11) (March 12): 35–36.

YoungadultARCs. Accessed March 7, 2007, available at http://yaarc.blogspot.com/.

6

◇ ◇ ◇

PROGRAMMING

Several years ago while working at a large central library located in an urban area, I hosted a cosplay (costume play). This program involved inviting teens to come to the library dressed as their favorite anime or manga character. I knew that at least a few of the branches of the multibranch system hosted active anime clubs (actually a member of one of these clubs had suggested the cosplay idea). Still, I did not know what to expect. Would teens actually come to their nonneighborhood library dressed somewhat outrageously to hang out with people they did not know? It turned out to be one of the most successful programs I have ever had, both in terms of numbers and in the individual responses from teenagers. Several young people rode the bus, bringing their costumes in plastic bags and changing in the library's bathrooms. Immediately following the first cosplay, I was bombarded with e-mails asking when we would be hosting the next one. Why did teens respond so positively to this program? The ingredients for success included teen input, a topic of interest to teens, giving a group of teens in a large urban area with a specific interest the chance to meet and socialize with peers having a similar unique interest, and providing teens a chance for creative expression and independence. Clearly, these are essential considerations when program planning for urban areas.

Teens are bombarded with messages from businesses and organizations competing for their attention and time. Even in areas where it seems there are inadequate community spaces for teens to spend time, the mall and, increasingly, the Internet are serious competitors for the library's teen area. Unlike adults looking to check out books by their favorite mystery writer or parents and children who choose to make the library an established weekly outing by regularly attending story time, the library's appeal to teens is something that cannot be taken for granted. Furthermore, when teens do visit the library, making that initial contact and then establishing the types of relationships that lead to teens becoming regulars who value the library and make it a part of their everyday lives can be serious challenges. Programming for teens can really pay off in terms of breaking the ice and building these relationships.

Urban areas provide many such opportunities for creating unique and innovative programming and are home to an array of resources and organizations that can be utilized when planning events and activities. The large staff size of many of these libraries also presents a wealth of easily accessible expertise and knowledge. Effective documentation and evaluation of replicable programs help staff share ideas and resources, making it much easier for multiple locations to reproduce successful programs with minimal staff planning time. This is not to say that planning and implementing programs in urban areas are without their own sets of obstacles. But if you are determined, you can find creative ways to overcome any potential roadblocks.

Libraries in urban areas commonly offer programming for teens. Some libraries offer programs at all locations, others at a handful of branches with interested and enthusiastic staff, and still other libraries concentrate their programming efforts at a central or main facility in a designated area designed for teens. No matter what your library's current situation or whether you are a beginning teen programmer looking for ideas on generating support, finding funding, and planning regular teen programs or an experienced programmer looking for new ideas, fresh perspectives, suggestions for adapting programs for greater success, and methods for effectively sharing program resources, this chapter has something for you. Ideas for implementing regular programming at individual locations are discussed, and methods for starting or enhancing large, systemwide programs are offered.

WHY OFFER TEEN PROGRAMMING?

Teen advocates believe in and understand the value and importance of quality teen programming. But decision makers or other staff not directly engaged in serving teens or staff with long-standing negative feelings about teens often need convincing. In many libraries serving urban areas, resources are stretched thin. Arm yourself with compelling reasons that are easy to explain and understand when discussing proposals for beginning, enhancing, or expanding teen programming. Objectives and goals for teen programming should clearly and concretely match library goals and objectives and should be easily connected to helping build teen developmental assets.

Here are six quick, understandable, and compelling reasons staff serving teens in urban areas can offer when discussing the need for teen programming.

- Dynamic, meaningful teen programming is a cornerstone of creating the bridge that leads the dedicated story-time toddler to becoming a lifelong library customer and supporter. The teen attending a program today is only a few years away from voting on the tax levies of tomorrow.
- Programming provides a productive and welcoming environment for teens looking for much-needed positive peer social interactions and adult role models.
- Programs offer library staff and teens the opportunity to naturally and comfortably collaborate on building successful services.
- Programs help teens see the library in a new light. Many libraries located in urban areas do not have the resources or funds to renovate library facilities. Creative programs offered on a regular basis can give the library a face-lift even when the physical building cannot be updated or changed.
- Programs bring teens into the library and help them become familiar with using the library and its resources.
- Teens need constructive ways to spend their out-of-school hours. For teens age 12 to 17, the risk of being the victim of a violent crime peaks in the hours immediately following the close of school. This is also a time when many teens are unsupervised or have few opportunities to engage in structured activities. Teens whose after-school hours lack supervision and structure are more likely to engage in unproductive behaviors and may result in poor school performance or dropping out of school altogether (Snyder and Sickmund 1999).

Successful programs are essential for building confidence in those directly serving teens and in helping skeptical staff members see firsthand that when the library offers high-quality, fun, and developmentally appropriate activities for teens, teens will respond positively. Supporting and witnessing teens engaged in and enjoying library events create an environment in which all staff can become comfortable and enthusiastic about serving young adults. This in turn leads to staff treating teens with respect on a daily basis.

GETTING STARTED

As mentioned earlier, urban areas provide unique opportunities for creating dynamic and innovative programming because of the wide range of resources and potential partners available in these communities. Chapter 7 offers ideas for partnering and collaboration that will enhance services and includes specific examples of award-winning programs from libraries in urban areas that draw upon these resources. In addition to these partnership opportunities, there are several other unique factors to keep in mind when planning programs in urban areas.

One important point is to consider your diverse audience. Teens come from a variety of backgrounds and represent an array of ethnic, cultural, and racial groups. Your programming and the presenters and partners with whom you work should reflect this diversity. What kinds of cultural centers are represented in your neighborhood? Contact these groups and discuss options for shared programming or ideas for how the library can create programs that will attract young people associated with these various cultures. Take a look at the demographics of your community on a regular basis. Make sure that your current programming is in line with this information and not based on outdated assumptions about the makeup of the community.

Take into consideration that teens coming together for a program in an urban area will probably not only be strangers but will also come from very different backgrounds and have widely divergent life experiences. Build extra time into programs for icebreakers like those found later in this chapter and other opportunities for teens to build trust and familiarity with one another. Conversely, if a group of several teens who know each other begins to dominate the program activities or discussions, leaving out those teens who may not know anyone else, be prepared to intervene with solutions that will draw in the entire group. For example, you may ask teens to partner or work with someone they do not know, if only for a very short segment of the program. On occasion, I have requested teens sit next to someone they have never met, but I caution in using this device very often because one of the most treasured elements of teen programs is often teens' ability to make their own choices about their participation.

Finally, programs in urban areas need to be fluid, flexible events. Unlike activities in nonurban areas where teens are frequently dropped off at the library specifically to attend a program and picked up when a program is scheduled to conclude, in urban areas many members of your audience will be teens who are already in the library and have decided to (or been persuaded to) stop in and check out an activity. Teens in this situation are more likely to leave at various times because they are using public transportation or catching an already scheduled ride home. Other elements of the programming in urban environments that need to be flexible include how refreshments are handled and whether there is a limit on the number of times a teen may leave and return to a program (both issues are discussed later in this chapter).

Discuss programming ideas with a small group of teens or create a general survey to generate feedback from a large numbers of teens. This is a great place to start the process of planning teen programs. Feedback is an essential step in planning any program or initiative for teens and can be easily gained through paper surveys and online survey tools such as Zommerang.com and SurveyMonkey.com.

If you are working in a library system with multiple branches, take a look at what programs are currently being offered and ask staff involved at those locations how the programming is being received. Ask about past attempts at programs to find out if staff can share any thoughts on what went wrong or right. It is likely that things like book clubs, anime clubs, scavenger hunts, and game nights have already been tried, and feedback from other staff members about these experiences can be invaluable in planning future programs.

Getting started with teen programming involves taking a realistic look at the current level of organizational, staffing, and financial support for teen services. Ideas for expanding teen programming should not be abandoned if the organizational response lacks enthusiasm or if staffing and financial resources are not readily available. Do not let taking a good, hard look at where your library is in its support of teen programming keep you from pursuing plans to do more. The ideal time to pursue doing additional teen programming may never come, especially in libraries where extra funds or increased budgets are not commonplace. An examination of your organization's current capacity for supporting teen programming simply gives you a realistic starting point for planning.

This initial big-picture planning for more teen programming helps you develop a long-term vision and strategy for how existing resources might be shifted to achieve this new vision. For example, part of the long-term vision may be to have caring, competent staff members offer teen programming

Sample Teen Programming Survey Questions

Have you ever come to a library program? If you have, what was the program? Did you like it? Why or why not?

If you have not, why not?

What kind of activities would you like to do at the library?

Learn to draw.

Volunteer.

Meet and author.

Talent show.

Read to little kids.

Read or write poetry.

Meet with other teens to plan library events.

Watch anime with other teens.

Make a craft.

Other ideas:

What is the easiest time for you to get to the library for a program?

Weekdays, after school.

Weekdays, in the evening.

Weekends, in the morning.

Weekends, in the afternoon.

on a *regular, consistent* basis. The plan may also call for money to support purchasing snacks and other supplies. Interested and enthusiastic staff with a plan and a vision can help build your organizational capacity for programming by clearly and specifically presenting resource needs and goals to decisions makers who control staffing and financial resources. Working to generate the institutional support that often comes through planning and communication can ensure that a simple change in staffing, such as a teen librarian leaving, will not result in regular teen programming being significantly cut back at a location or discontinued altogether.

Budget

Determine a systematic and consistent method for how costs for supplies, presenters' fees, and refreshments will be handled. It may be possible for you to scrape together resources for programming through donations from organizations in the community, other library divisions, or a friends group, but to truly implement successful and sustainable teen programming, a yearly teen programming line must be part of the library's overall programming budget.

When developing a yearly teen programming proposal for your library's decision makers, present them with a budget worksheet that projects estimates of how much programming will cost, taking into account how programs are currently paid for by your library, what additional outside opportunities exist for funding teen programming, and what types of savings can be realized by utilizing low-cost or possibly free program presenters (such as the library's own teen librarians or other talented staff).

Individual programs are not generally planned at the beginning of a yearly budget cycle, but having a general idea of costs associated with presenters is essential when it comes to long-term planning. This is especially true when planning involves asking decision makers to shift resources to support something new. If results of a teen programming interest survey are available, use these ideas to help determine when outside presenters or experts might be necessary. Look around your community to find a suitable presenter. Make a quick inquiry phone call or e-mail to develop estimates on costs associated with outside presenters and include these costs in budget planning and requests for funding. Be sure to consider other costs associated with the program beyond the cost of the presenter. These costs might include:

- Supplies.
- Food and refreshments.

- Graphics such as paper for flyers and posters.
- Public relations promotional work such as billboards or ad space on buses or mass transit.
- Giveaways.
- Any costs for adding books or other material to the collection to support the program.

Remember, when thinking about the types of teen programs that will be offered, your teen program schedule will include both programs given by staff and programs offered by outside presenters. Some programs, like teen advisory groups and anime clubs, can and should be planned and presented by library staff. Others, like a video gaming program or poetry slams, can be planned and coordinated by staff, with the actual presentation being given by a paid performer or expert from the community.

Consider partnerships, discussed in detail in chapter 7, when developing your teen programming budget plan, too. Oftentimes, community partners can be called upon to provide presenters and experts for library programs and are willing to do so free of charge or at a very low cost. Be sure to consider all partnership options when thinking about programming and budget. You can also hire teens to do programs for peers or slightly younger tweens. Often teens are looking for a place to try out their many talents, and presenting programs at the library gives them an opportunity to do that. The cost is probably reasonable if not free, the presentations are usually good, and hiring teens "shines the spotlight on their talents...and gives younger kids someone to whom they can look up to" (Suellentrop 2006, 39).

As you build your program plan, keep in mind how programs are funded at your library. Are they funded from a specific budget category that is developed on a yearly basis? If so, make sure your request for teen programming funds coincides with the yearly programming budget cycle. Is a friends group primarily responsible for funding? Are donations or trust funds used to fund specific types of programs? If so, do any of the specifications include funding for the teenage range? Sometimes generous patrons will donate funds to the library intended to support activities for specific age groups. The specified age ranges may or may not mirror library designations of children and teen. Often these funds are utilized to fund children's activities, but the donation may specify only that the money be used in serving youth. Find out if a portion of such funds can be dedicated to funding activities and programs for teens, particularly younger teens. If your library has a development office, approach the development director with specific ideas for funding. Although donations often provide funding for only a finite time period and are not ideal for supporting teen programming in the long term, sizable gifts can be used to initiate programs that, once they are proved to be successful, the library will want to continue.

It is not essential, at least initially, that the library dedicate exactly the same monetary amounts to teen programming that is budgeted for children's services or other long-standing programs; however, creating a separate budget line for teen programming is a significant first step and a real gesture of organizational support and commitment. It also creates an expectation that the money set aside for teen programming is utilized on a yearly basis. Once this budget line has been established, larger organizational factors, such as budget variations or staffing changes, are less likely to result in a library completely abandoning or severely reducing teen programs. Once the money has been dedicated to teen programming, someone will be expected to spend it.

The following budget worksheets offer examples for yearly program planning. Each worksheet includes supplies and staff as well as projected outcomes, a way of evaluating programs that is discussed in the "Expected Results" section of this chapter. A budget worksheet provides decision makers a snapshot of teen programming and helps them make decisions about funding. It also offers staff planning the programs an overall plan of action, including what should be achieved through each program.

Estimated Yearly Budget for Teen Programming Worksheet
(Total Amount of Request: $705)

Program:	Monthly Anime Club
Staff:	Teen librarian or interested staff member(s)
Supplies:	Refreshments, including Pokey sticks, chips, pretzels, soda, water, and grapes for six meetings per year and pizza for the other six meetings per year
Estimated cost:	$40 for pizza months, $25 for nonpizza months
Estimated attendance:	15 to 20 teens
Outcomes:	Developmental assets: Supports the external asset that young people receive support from three or more nonparent adults, in this case the anime club advisor who is the teen librarian; increased awareness among teens of the library and its resources; expanding teens' concept of the library to include a place offering dynamic and engaging activities

(continued)

(*Continued*)

Total cost per year:	$390 per year
Program:	Poetry Contest for National Poetry Month in April
Staff:	Teen librarian
Supplies:	Gift certificates for grand prize winners, ribbons and certificates for multiple honorable mention winners
Estimated costs:	Gift certificates for 2 grand prize winners = $50 total; ribbons and certificates for 15 honorable mention winners = $25; refreshments for award ceremony = $40
Estimated attendance:	50 entries; award celebration for winners = 50 attending
Outcomes:	Developmental assets: Supports the external assets of creative activities with young people spending three or more hours per week in lessons or practice in music, theater, or other arts and empowerment with the celebration of teen achievement and the perception that adults in the community value youth
Total cost per year:	$115
Possible variation to include outside presenter or expert:	Poetry workshop or slam
Staff:	Poet from the community
Supplies:	Refreshments
Estimated costs:	$25 for refreshments, $75 per location for presenter
Estimated attendance:	6 to 10 people for workshop, 20 people for slam
Total cost per year:	$100
Program:	Teen Advisory Board
Staff:	Teen librarian
Supplies:	Refreshments, including chips, pretzels, soda, water, grapes, T-shirts with TAB slogan or TAB design, end-of-year celebration/recognition of TAB work
Estimated attendance:	12
Estimated costs:	$25 per 11 meetings, $50 for year-end celebration, $50 for T-shirts
Total cost:	$375

Staff Support

Although enthusiasm and willingness to try something new are invaluable, careful consideration of staff attitude and management support are also required. It is tempting for enthusiastic teen services staff to launch an ambitious programming schedule. If staff feel stressed by an overambitious programming schedule requiring additional desk or public service hours, however, negative attitudes may develop and ultimately make it difficult to attract teens to the library for new programs being offered. Realistically assess staff capacity and support before instituting regular programs. It may seem to slow down the implementation or expansion of regular, consistent programming for teens, but it is a vital step in building long-term teen success. Talk with staff and management to develop a programming structure that builds in time for communicating with staff about upcoming events, involvement of all staff in the in-house promotion of programs, and a chance for staff to offer their feedback about teen programs.

Who is qualified or permitted to offer teen programs? Should only degreed staff be involved in planning and presenting programs? Should staff position or enthusiasm be the primary factor in assigning programming duties? Staffing structures (chapter 2) vary greatly from library to library, but regardless of the formal staffing structure, utilizing the skills and expertise of everyone on staff is a great way to involve the entire team in teen programming. Remember, energy and enthusiasm are the most important ingredients for success.

Promotion

Once your program plan is in place, the next important step is setting up plans for program promotion. Work with graphic designers, which many libraries have on staff, to design teen-friendly flyers and posters. This may be as simple as making a standard request for flyers or posters in the same way all printed promotional material is requested. If your library does not offer teen programming on a regular basis, however, work closely with graphic designers and artists to be sure that the material produced is teen friendly and inviting. Ask for sample promotional material to be sent out for testing with teens. If a particular flyer or poster design is well received by teens, request that it be used as a template for future flyers. If you do not have a graphics department, consider inviting teens to help design flyers. If your library has public access to software that can be used for designing promotional items, utilize these resources when working with teens on creating flyers and posters. If you are in a large library system with multiple branches, make sure that any systemwide programming calendar has an easy-to-find and easy-to-identify section highlighting teen programs. In these large library systems, staff at individual branches should strongly consider making monthlong calendars that are specific to teen events. Because many teens in urban areas may walk or use mass transit to get around, promotional material should be compact and easy to stick in a pocket or backpack.

Librarians working in urban areas are sometimes dismayed by the lack of attention their programs receive from major media outlets, but in urban areas, many newspapers and television stations receive hundreds of press releases each week from a wide variety of organizations. No matter how exciting an event or program may be, it is sometimes difficult to get noticed in such active and competitive public relations environments. Sending a simple letter or notice to a major newspaper or TV station is unlikely to produce results or coverage. Many libraries employ very skilled and savvy public relations experts who, if given enough time and presented with organized, quality information about teen programs, can work with newspaper, radio, and television reporters to get advance coverage of upcoming events. Be sure to stay in contact with the library's public relations staff or department and keep teen events on their radar. Work with public relations staff to produce standard information pieces focused on teen programs that can be included in any press kit promoting the library. Such kits often contain a CD with photos, flyers, and information.

It is a great idea to have press kits about teen programs on hand because major media outlets in urban areas sometimes contact the library at the last minute on a slow news day or when they have unexpected room in their newspaper or evening newscast. If the library's public relations department has received clear communication about upcoming teen events, quality photographs of teens enjoying themselves at past activities, or follow-up summaries of teen programming successes, teen events are more likely to be the place public relations staff look when they need quick information for high-profile publications. This kind of press is invaluable in generating interest in teen programs and in raising the profile of teen services within the library and in the community.

Small neighborhood or community papers are often willing to run stories or features about new and exciting teen programs. Although major newspapers receive many press releases and a large number of requests for coverage of events across the city, neighborhood presses are frequently looking for new information to highlight and include in their publications. Some smaller newspapers even have a policy of accepting all submissions for publication. Talk to your library's public relations department and ask if you can work with small neighborhood newspapers directly to promote teen programs.

Send fliers to or post information at places and venues where teens frequently visit and hang out in the community. Look for natural partners in promotion like the parks department, recreation or community centers, free health clinics, venues for concerts, coffee shops, and fast-food restaurants that might be willing to post flyers or posters. If possible, post flyers on bulletin boards around the community. Many bookstores and coffee shops frequented by urban teens post flyers and information in bathrooms; do not be afraid to use these venues to promote your library events, too! If possible, give flyers to teens you know well, such as teen advisory board members, volunteers, or just members of the regular after-school crowd. Ask these teens to post a flyer at school, at their church or other place of worship, or at another community agency they visit. Along with teen advisory board members, teen employees can be great partners in promoting programs, particularly because teen employees have a real working knowledge of how library programs work. Teen employees can easily find out the details about any particular event by informally talking to library staff and can talk up the parts of the program most likely to appeal to their friends and other teen library customers.

Highlight program information on the library's main Web page, in any events section, and on the library's teen page. If the library has a blog, be sure to include information about upcoming programs. If possible, post photos of teens enjoying themselves at recent programs. If your library does not post individual teens' pictures, post photos of any cool program props or sets that might generate interest. For example, if the library recently offered a teen mystery night, take photos of the crime scenes. If a program included a lot of pizza or snacks, take photos of the boxes of pizza before the program and the carnage of empty boxes left after the program.

Get out to the schools. Dropping off promotional material at a school office is a good first step, but it is far more effective to actually go to a school and talk to students directly. Combine program promotion with booktalks. If schools do not permit outside organizations to pass out flyers or promotional material, focus on making visits to individual classrooms. Be sure to talk about upcoming programs during booktalks or presentations about library resources. Keep in regular contact with school media specialists to promote programs. Sending an e-mail with program information or a flyer is one way to make it easy for a school librarian to promote public library programs. Invite a school librarian to bring a class or group to the library or to offer extra credit for students attending an event. Ask school contacts and media specialists for their thoughts on the best dates and times to hold programs, too.

Space Limitations

Some smaller libraries, especially those in urban locations, do not always have an area in their facility specifically dedicated for teens. Some do not have space dedicated to programming or even a separate meeting room. If this is the situation you are in, do not let this be a reason to limit or abandon ideas for regular teen programs. Instead, think of options for offering teens the chance to experience the library in a new way. Consider holding programs after hours, when the library is closed to the public. If the library closes at 6:00 P.M. on Fridays, investigate options for holding teen programs from 6:30 P.M. to 8:30 P.M. on Friday nights. Work with management to develop a schedule that supports two or three staff members working these monthly after-hours programs. Emphasize the limitations for programming during open hours and focus on the benefits of having the after-hours aspect as a programming hook to use when convincing urban teens to attend a library program.

If space is not available at the library and after-hours programs are not an option, look for a community partner willing to offer space for library events. Recreation centers are often eager to host quality events, and frequently teenagers are already hanging out at these locations. Taking a program off-site is a great way to reach teens who may not otherwise have contact with the library.

Coordinating Efforts

When planning teen programs in a large metropolitan library system that includes a number of branch locations, determine how potentially limited programming resources will be divided among branches. Will staff at every location offer regular teen programming? Will programs be offered at only some locations, and if so, which locations and why? Responses from an informal survey indicate this decision varies greatly among urban library systems, with some urban libraries focusing all programming efforts for teens at a main or central location. Staffing structures and space limitations affect this decision.

If your staffing and resources are limited for teen programming, effectively organizing, planning, and coordinating efforts across libraries and branches is vital. Teens in urban areas have a variety of choices when it comes to deciding how and where to spend their time. Even libraries that have a large after-school crowd sometimes find it challenging to attract teens to organized programs and events. Focusing efforts can help in several ways. Determine what locations are staffed to support regularly scheduled programs. If staffing is an issue, is there a way to coordinate efforts to maximize opportunities for teens living in neighborhoods in close proximity to attend programs? Can locations be paired or grouped so that resources and staffing are shared? Working as a pair or a group, libraries unable to support teen programming independently due to resource and staff limitations may be in a better position to offer regular teen programming to neighborhood teens.

Offer staff members who are responsible for providing teen programming a chance to brainstorm and share ideas and resources. One way to do this may be through quarterly or monthly meetings focused exclusively on planning programs. Utilize available staff communication tools such as the library intranet or e-mail distribution lists for programming discussion among teen services staff. Share ideas about what trends are particularly hot with teens and investigate options for working cooperatively to plan and present a large-scale program focused on one current popular topic. Make sure that staff document programs and share ideas, results, and resources with one another. Many library systems have instituted structured methods for sharing among children's services staff, including central storage locations for flannel boards, puppets, and various craft supplies. Using this same organized approach to teen programming can help improve efficiency and alleviate staff stress about teen programming. For example, if one staff member plans and presents a program on beading, he or she should be encouraged to develop simple instructions related to the craft, a list of books for display or checkout, and any tips or advice for someone wanting to reproduce the program. Take this resource-sharing model a step further by boxing up leftover supplies along with written information and offering the entire box to other staff interested in doing a similar craft program.

When coordinating programming in an urban library system with multiple locations, there is sometimes an urge to make sure all programs offered have appeal to a broad audience. But not all programs need to follow the "anyone and everyone" rule to be successful. In fact, some of the most successful programs in urban areas have a very specific target audience. Focusing on one trend or topic of special interest to a particular segment of the teen population can actually result in a large-scale, heavily attended program. Librarians planning cooperatively in urban areas serve a large population of teens. Although a particular topic or subject may not appeal to every or even the majority of teen customers, the handful of teens from each neighborhood interested in a particular topic can form a virtual army of hard-core fans guaranteed to turn out for a particular program.

Make sure all staff are well informed about programs being offered throughout your library system and able to promote them in their outreach activities. When teen services staff do school visits, work at community festivals or events, or talk to community partners, they should be able to speak knowledgeably about programs being offered at nearby locations. Many teens in urban areas are fully capable of using public transportation and can attend a program in a nearby neighborhood if they know about the event in advance.

Systemwide Programs

Different from coordinating programming efforts across locations, the concept of systemwide programs refers to programs that are planned centrally and involve the same participation by teens at every library location. Systemwide programs include monthlong contests, such as poetry contests, photography contests, talent competitions, and summer reading programs. A particular presenter may also be scheduled to do the same program at several locations. Staff at potential locations should always have the chance to offer their opinions about the possible popularity of a presenter along with their input about the best dates and times for the program. Some systemwide programs involve partnering with a local fast-food restaurant or sports team to offer incentives for something as simple as any teen checking out a book during Teen Read Week receiving a gift certificate or coupon.

When considering incentives for systemwide events like a summer reading program or poetry contest, take into account whether teens in most neighborhoods will have an easy way to cash in their prizes, especially when it comes to fast-food certificates. Teens do not always have access to a restaurant outside of their community, and if the gift certificate or coupon they win is for a small amount, it is not worth the effort and expense to travel to a faraway restaurant. Offering actual physical prizes can help avoid this issue. Consider giving prizes that are both fun and useful. A book bag, calculator, ruler, or paperback book are all customizable items that can likely be purchased within the library's budget. Give teens in urban areas prizes that they then can actually use in everyday life.

Expected Results

Keep in mind what you hope to achieve with the programs you are planning and how you will measure whether your programming efforts have been successful. This includes both statistical results such as the numbers of programs offered and the numbers of teens attending programs as well as what positive impact your programming has had on both teens and the library. Libraries often utilize specific output measures when evaluating the success of programming. Outputs measure the "amount, the quality, or volume of use of a product or service" (Institute of Museum and Library Services, *NLG Project Planning*). Traditional output measures, which may include statistics on program attendance and the number of programs offered, can be a useful tool for evaluating the success of teen programming being offered on a systemwide scale by a library system. An example of a useful output measure is stating specifically how many teens are expected to attend programs over the course of a month or a year. When you are successful in achieving specific outputs, communicate this success across the organization. It is easy for staff at all levels to understand and appreciate when specific measurable outputs are achieved. Do not miss the opportunity to capitalize on these kinds of quantifiable successes.

The success of teen programs, however, should not be considered only by looking at output measurements. Although some teen programs may include an expectation that large numbers of teens will be involved or participate, achieving successful results for many teen programs is often not related to attendance numbers but to expected outcomes. Outcomes are gains or changes in an individual's knowledge, skills, attitudes, behaviors, status, or life condition (Institute of Museum and Library Services, *NLG Project Planning*). Both outputs and outcomes are indicators of success, but quantifiable output measures should not be overemphasized to the detriment of outcomes. This is a good thing to remember in urban areas where positive outcomes for teens are especially important. Keep in mind that outcomes and outputs are different and measure very different things. When discussing teen programming with staff and administrators, offer clear outcome-based evaluations of teen programs to be certain that the success is evaluated appropriately. Possible outcomes include:

- Increased awareness among teens of the library and its resources.
- More positive staff-teen interactions leading to a change in staff attitude.
- Expanding teens' concept of the library to include a place offering dynamic and engaging activities and supporting teens'

development of the Search Institute's 40 Developmental Assets, the essential building blocks of healthy communities.

The first question many new teen programmers ask is how many programs should the library offer? The answer to this question should be based on stated outcomes, input gathered directly from teens, and a determination of how the library's programs fit into the larger options for teens in the community. Setting a specific target, such as two programs per month or three programs per week, can be useful; however, programs and activities always need to fit into an overall plan. Doing programs simply to fit a predetermined schedule will also produce inflexibility that does not address the needs of teens in urban areas. Be sure to survey program options for teens across the community before setting your program schedule and expectations. In urban areas, this is especially important in order to avoid duplicating topics and overlapping dates and times. Once you have looked around your community; talked to teens, staff, and managers; and articulated your expected outcomes, it will be much easier to decide on the number of program you think is appropriate to offer teen customers.

TEEN ADVISORY GROUPS

Establishing a teen advisory group, or TAG, is a crucial step in developing or enhancing teen programming in urban libraries. This group can be used as a sounding board for ideas, can help you plan and present programs, and, if their advice and comments are acknowledged and followed when appropriate, can create a feeling of ownership of the library among teens. The experience of working as a teen advisory board member will help teens build assets that significantly contribute to healthy youth development. What could be better?

TAGs should have a mission or purpose statement, simple objectives, and goals and ideas for reaching these goals. Once teens have been recruited for a TAG, creating these necessary statements is the first order of business. This provides a clear focus for meetings and sets the tone for how a TAG meeting differs from a regular teen program.

Starting a traditional teen advisory group in many urban settings is not always as easy as it sounds. Efforts to recruit teens to attend an organized TAG often meet with lukewarm response. Involvement in a TAG requires consistent attendance at meetings, and although it is vital to communicate this information upfront, it may not be easy for teens to meet this consistency requirement. This does not necessarily mean teens are not interested in offering feedback or working cooperatively with library staff to improve library service to teens. It simply means that the traditional TAG format needs to be adapted. If teens respond positively to other interest-specific clubs or groups, like a weekly or monthly anime or gaming program, the teens attending these regular programs can act as an unofficial TAG. Set aside a few minutes at each meeting to talk to this group of engaged teens about library-related matters. You can also tie TAG meetings directly to other programs. If teen programs are regularly offered on the third Wednesday of every month at 7:00 P.M., a monthly TAG meeting can be held on the same day with a 6:30 P.M. start time. Teens may be particularly interested in one or the other of the two activities, but tying them together builds in a guaranteed audience.

Once you have decided that a TAG is a good addition to your library activities, think about your hoped-for outcomes. How would a TAG benefit both teens and the library? If a TAG is not working, are there other ways to work with teens to accomplish the same goals? Do not set up a TAG as an after-school activity to take care of perceived problems related to lots of teens hanging out at the library. A TAG that is started from a negative or deficient approach to teens has little chance of succeeding and can even cause more frustration for both teens and library staff.

If feedback about programming ideas is initially a primary goal for having a TAG, start the recruitment process by getting out from behind the circulation or reference desk whenever possible and talking to frequent teen customers. Posing specific questions to teens while they engage in their usual after-school activities allows teens to feel comfortable expressing their opinions. This interaction also helps staff gain a better understanding of what kinds of activities teens want at the library while avoiding the frustration of trying to make teens participate in an organized, structured TAG before an effective structure has been designed or desired outcomes have been established.

If teens are primarily interested in the technology offered by the library, tying TAG-like activities to technology events or volunteering opportunities for teens can be a successful way to establish an advisory group. A flyer calling for volunteers for a TAG may not catch the eye of a teen, but a flyer that emphasizes the role TAG members can play in providing computer and technology support might make a teen think about getting involved.

Another barrier faced by some teens in urban areas when it comes to joining a TAG is their responsibility to watch younger brothers or sisters. This can be a serious challenge for teen programming in urban areas in general but particularly difficult when asking teens to participate in something as focused as a TAG. One solution is to work with a children's librarian or a community group to offer a parallel program for people younger than 12 at the same time as your TAG meeting. Although library staff and community partners should never be placed in the role of ad hoc babysitters for the younger siblings of teens, cooperative programming is an option that allows a teen 30 minutes of relatively free time during which he or she can actively participate in a TAG meeting.

Once you have recruited teens for a TAG, actually having the meeting may suddenly seem a bit stressful. The World Café Process model in *Teens and Libraries: Getting It Right* (Walter and Meyers 2003) provides a great model for working with teens that can be easily adapted for any TAG meeting. Covering tables with paper and supplying teens with markers, crayons, and other craft supplies that they can casually use during meetings help teens stay focused. Doodling on the large sheets of paper with crayons or markers keeps teens' hands active while allowing them to stay on topic much longer than if they were just sitting in a room, talking, and listening but not engaging in any sort of physical outlet for their energy. This is especially important if a TAG meeting is scheduled right after school.

Because urban areas often have many branch libraries from the same library system located fairly close to one another, you may ask if every branch should form a TAG, if TAGs should be regional, or, for library systems with large central or main libraries, if the TAG group should be based at this central location. TAGs for each library or branch are ideal. Transportation is less of an issue for teens, and a local TAG offers teens the chance to develop a feeling of ownership for their neighborhood library. If your library does not have the staff capacity and resources to support branches at each location, regional TAGs or one TAG at a central location is a great place to start. Through these kinds of TAGs, teens can meet people from outside their school or neighborhood. Visiting other libraries also leads teens to new ideas and suggestions for their own neighborhood library.

If your library system does have multiple TAGS, either at each location or through the regional TAG model, a teen summit is one way to bring teens together to share ideas. If your library has only one TAG, a teen summit is still possible; many other teen-serving organizations in your community may have teen boards or volunteer groups. Connecting the library's TAG group or groups with other teen boards in the community brings diverse teens together and provides a chance for teens to engage in open dialogue with one another. A summit could feature a teen band or a number of bands, snacks, focused discussions about hot topics around the city, and a chance to meet city leaders. A library system can use a teen summit as a way to connect existing TAG groups or as a way to recruit teens for starting a TAG.

PROGRAM NUTS AND BOLTS
Registration

Will teens be required to sign up in advance to attend programs? In an urban area, this can be tricky. Because of transportation, babysitting, and other family responsibilities, teens cannot always guarantee they can come or stay for an event. One teen program attendee may at the last minute bring along four or five friends or two or three siblings. Can your programs accommodate these last-minute participants? If not, is there a way to change your programming so that advance registration is not necessary? Conversely, your troubles with programs may not be that too many teens show up at the last minute but that your attendance is too low. In these circumstances, registration lists are valuable for calling teens to remind them about an event and to confirm their attendance. If you use e-mail to communicate with teens, registration lists allow for teens to request that they receive regular e-mail notices about upcoming events. This kind of general e-mail list is a great way to build a base of possible program attendees. Registration in person or via e-mail is also a good way for librarians and staff to get to know teens' names, which can be helpful for a number of reasons. Remember that some teens are not comfortable with advance registration because last-minute changes in their schedules make it hard for them to guarantee they will be able to attend a program. Your best option may be to have programs with optional registration or advance registration requested. Make sure staff members are flexible and accommodating when registering teens, emphasizing that if a teen cannot make it or needs to bring along a friend or sibling at the last minute, it is not a problem.

Breaking the Ice

Programming in urban areas often means bringing together teens who do not know one another. To counter the possible negative effects of this, start your programs with a simple five-minute icebreaker whenever possible. Favorites include:

- Hold up a roll of toilet paper. Ask teens to take as many sheets as they want to from the roll. Once everyone has taken their sheets, ask each teen to share as many facts about themselves as they have toilet paper sheets. The same thing can be done using candy like M&Ms and Skittles.

- Give each teen a piece of paper and pencil. Tell them to write something about themselves on the paper and crumple it up. Teens then throw the paper up in the air. Each teen finds a piece of paper that is not their piece of paper, reads the fact, and guesses who wrote it.

- Find a copy of the board game Zobmondo, the lite version. This game is out of print, but copies are often available online through various sources. The Zobmondo cards that come with the game pose questions in a "would you rather" format in a number of categories offering, for example, a choice of two unappealing things to eat. The lite version works well with teens, and the questions are a lot fun. The questions can be asked of a group, and teens can answer as they feel comfortable or through a show of hands. This helps shy teens feel less put on the spot than many traditional icebreakers.

More Icebreaker Ideas

Kids Games. http://www.Gameskidsplay.net/. All kinds of games and game trivia.

Fun Team Building with Larry Lipman. http://funteambuilding.com/links. html. Team building activities and resources.

My Favorite Team Building Icebreaker: Find Ten Things in Common. http://humanresources.about.com/library/weekly/aa122001b.htm.

Warming Up Your Next Party with Ice Breakers. http://entertaining.about.com/library/weekly/aa032700b.htm. Breaking the ice.

Youthwork Links and Ideas. http://www.youthwork.com/ideas.html#activ. Great ideas and activities for groups.

Zobmondo.com. http://www.zobmondo.com/9_0.html#lite. Wacky party game that consists of conversation starters that are bizarre. Zobmondo Lite recommended for teens.

Refreshments

Snacks and refreshments are always appealing, and in urban environments they often disappear surprisingly quickly. Experiment to find the best way to incorporate refreshments into your programs, keeping in mind that in urban areas you will need to adapt the way you serve food to be sure it is playing a productive role in the activity from your perspective, too. Starting with refreshments may bring teens into a program, but are these teens staying for most or the entire program? If it is a free-form program that allows for quality participation at individual levels, this option may work. If the idea is to keep teens engaged in a group activity or to encourage teens already in the library to participate, offering refreshments in the middle or at the end of the program may be more appropriate. Also, consider what kinds of refreshments you would like to provide. Serve healthier choices when possible. For example, soda is a staple at many teen programs. Include diet soda and water as additional choices. You will be surprised by the number of teens who will drink bottled water as a first choice when it is made available. If you are providing chips and pretzels at a particular program, also give teens the choice of a bowl of apples, bananas, or other fruit (that is not too messy). One final consideration when planning for refreshments at programs is trying to determine how much food you will really need. Advance registration for teen programs is not always realistic, nor is it necessarily desirable to ask teens to sign up in advance. Two suggestions for coping with not knowing how many teens will actually show up at an event is to either wait until teens arrive to order food such as pizza instead of ordering in advance or to purchase refreshments with a longer shelf life that, if not used, can be saved for a program the following week or month.

Healthy, or Health*ier*, Food and Drinks for Teens

- Baked pretzels
- Peanut butter crackers
- Fruit roll-ups
- Trail mix
- Baked chips
- Bottled water
- Fruit
- Japanese sweets, cookies, and crackers
- Apples and caramel dip
- Light popcorn
- Diet soda
- Light lemonade
- Flavored bottled water
- Salsa and tortilla chips

(continued)

(*Continued*)

- Cereal and trail mixes (dump together several types of cereal, pretzels, nuts, M&Ms, raisins, little cheese crackers, and mix them all up; ladle into individual bowls or cups)
- Goldfish crackers
- Rice crackers
- Granola bars
- Veggies with dip
- Cider
- Juice pouches and boxes
- Chex mix

(Adapted from a compilation posted by Barrie Olmstead, ya-yaac listserv, March 30, 2007.)

Managing Distractions

Teens like to socialize during programs. Often, the chance to meet and talk to other teenagers is a primary reason a teen attends a library program. If you feel, however, that talking is negatively impacting your programs, you will need to adjust the kinds of programs you are offering. Chapter 3 includes training information on adolescent development. Review this information and evaluate your programs to make sure your behavior expectations are in line with teens' developmental needs.

Teens in urban areas are often in the role of babysitting or supervising younger siblings and family members. Some teens may have children of their own for whom they are caring. In these cases, they may want (or need) to bring younger children to a teen program. Chapter 7 provides ideas for partnering with community agencies to address this issue long term. For the short term, consider working with children's services staff to offer younger kids alternative programming during the same time you are offering teen programming. If staffing at your location is too tight for two staff members to be programming at the same time, consider working to develop safe, self-help-style crafts, such as creating fun bookmarks and picture frames using self-adhesive foam letters and shapes that younger kids can do in the public area while teens in a separate part of the library are engaged in a teen-specific programming activity.

Although some teens in urban areas frequently seem to have little parental supervision, other teens have parents or grandparents accustomed to staying with their teenager at all times. These parents or grandparents may want to stay with their teenager during a program. Be prepared to explain to parents that your program is a chance for teens to have a little time to be independent and hang out with their friends and peers. Graciously and thoroughly explain to parents exactly what is planned and what their teenager will be doing during the program. Be sure to answer completely any questions parents may have about the activities and how long the program will last.

Teens may want to come and go during programs. How you react to this may have a lot to do with the kind of program you are conducting. If leaving and returning does not distract other program attendees, ask yourself if there is really any problem with teens choosing to do this. Sometimes it can cause a problem in the rest of the library if teens continue to talk at the same level both inside and outside the programming space. Discuss the issue with your teens and clearly explain your expectations. If you are hosting a program that you feel will be negatively affected by teens' casual leaving and coming back, make it clear up front that teens will need to choose to stay or to leave. In this situation, include a break after 15 or 20 minutes. This will give teens the chance to return or not for the second half of the program.

Special Considerations

A few additional issues for which you should be prepared include how to respond to teens wanting to make more than one or two items during a craft project. For example, if you host a craft program involving making a tie-dye T-shirt or a beaded bracelet, many teens may want to make several of these items. If teens are enjoying your program, are engaged in the activity, and think the craft is cool enough that they want to give one to their sister, brother, girlfriend, or boyfriend, do your best to accommodate them. Explain that making more than one item usually depends on the amount of supplies, just to be sure teens understand that there may be limits at future programs. Include additional supplies into your program planning and budgets so that you can accommodate these kinds of requests from teens.

Some teens will not have a lot of experience attending organized programming activities. These teens may not fully understand that a program has a finite beginning and end. Make sure starting and ending times are included in promotional flyers and posters. Clearly explain this to teens briefly at the beginning of programs and ask if everyone has arranged for a ride home when the program ends. Offer them use of a telephone so that they can work on setting up transportation before the program is actually over.

EXAMPLE PROGRAMS

Each of the following ideas includes information on planning, structuring, promoting, determining needed materials, and evaluating the suggested program.

Program Idea 1: Teen Read Week Author Visit

A national literacy initiative aimed at teens, their parents, librarians, and educators, Teen Read Week is celebrated each year during the third week of October. Established in 1998 by the Young Adult Library Services Association, Teen Read Week is a great opportunity to raise awareness of teen services through creative programming offered at every library location.

Planning

1. Start 12 to 18 months in advance to find an author. Many popular authors are booked years in advance for Teen Read Week, so starting early is essential. Talk to teens, frontline staff, teachers, and school librarians about possible authors.

2. Plan on working a few hours each week in the early stages for securing feedback about author selection and working to arrange the visit. Many libraries in urban areas have an events coordinator who handles contracts and arrangements for visiting authors. If this is the case, be sure to communicate directly and frequently with this staff member to be sure arrangements have been finalized in a timely manner. Planning time = 15 hours.

3. As the event approaches, outreach and publicity will be essential, as will securing multiple copies of the author's books. Involve staff members from multiple locations in promoting the event by contacting schools and community partners to arrange outreach opportunities. Depending on staffing structures, one staff member or a small group may be responsible for handling publicity requests and press relations. Planning time = 30 hours.

4. Once the word is out about the upcoming author visits, ask schools to formally submit a request to attend the events. Consider using e-mail, fax, or even traditional snail mail when working with schools for this phase of the planning. Set a specific beginning and ending date for schools to submit requests to attend the visit and, if necessary, use a lottery system to determine which schools can attend. Although it is ideal to be able to accommodate all schools, sometimes space limitations make this impossible. It is

essential that any system determining who can and cannot attend be fair, understandable, and communicated in the same way to all schools. In urban areas, this can be particularly tricky, as libraries often serve multiple schools, multiple school systems, and various kinds of school structures, including homeschoolers, large public school systems, independent charter schools, private schools, and even virtual schools. Planning time = 30 hours.

Program

1. Decide if the audience will be school groups or teens coming to the library on their own. Or, alternately, work with the author to schedule one or two sessions during the school day aimed at class visits and an evening session designed for walk-in teen customers.

2. Determine a location for the actual presentation. Many large urban library systems have a central or main library with a developed teen center or space that is a natural place to hold visits. A heavily attended author visit is a great opportunity to introduce students to both the author and to the library's teen area. It is, however, worth considering combining a series of visits at a main library with a second day of visits at a smaller urban branch library. Some schools may be unable to secure bus transportation to a central library location but may be within walking distance of a small branch.

3. The library should also consider taking authors to the schools, rather than asking schools to visit the library. Many schools in urban areas do not have funding for bus transportation to the library for special events, no matter how great the author. Work with schools to determine what their transportation situation is and, when possible, be flexible about where the author presents.

4. Include a "lunch with the author" opportunity for a smaller group of teens. This group can be selected a number of ways. Hold a systemwide contest in which any teen submitting a very short book review of one of the visiting author's books is entered in a lottery. Or any teen checking out a teen book during a specific time period of a week or two can similarly be entered in a systemwide lottery.

5. Arrange for as many sessions as the author is willing to conduct on each day of the visit and try to group schools by age. If the author has work that is of interest to both middle and high school students, have one session focused on middle school and one on high school.

Promotion

1. Do booktalks of the author's books at as many schools as possible.

2. Design bookmarks listing the author's work with annotations included about each book and distribute at all library locations.

3. Utilize the library's teen Web presence to promote the author. Include traditional promotional material like bookmarks and information about the author with links to audio clips of author interviews and blogging opportunities for teens to discuss the author's work.

4. Involve community partners in promotional efforts whenever possible. Visit after-school centers and talk to teens informally about the upcoming event.

5. Work with the library's public relations department to ensure the event is publicized on the radio, TV, and in the newspaper.

6. If any branches maintain e-mail lists of teen volunteers or TAG members, send these teens information about the upcoming visit.

7. Create a display-ideas tip sheet or kit that can be used by multiple locations to create book displays of the author's work.

Materials

- Work with the library's collection development department to have multiple paperback copies of the author's books ordered and available well in advance of the visit.

- Work with school groups and the author's publisher to be sure students have the chance to order books in advance that can be autographed the day of the visit. Check with the author about the number of books he or she is willing to autograph. Some students in urban areas may not be able to purchase books but may still want an author's autograph. If the author is willing, produce a color flyer that can be autographed for students without extra money to purchase a book.

- Provide light refreshments, if desired, at any nonschool presentation.

- Provide box lunches for the small-group author lunch.

Evaluation

- On the day of the visit, hand out brief evaluations to students and teachers. Follow up with a more extensive e-mail evaluation designed for teachers and students attending the small lunch event.

- Share evaluations with teen services staff.
- Develop a summary and evaluation for upper-level administrative staff. Include quotes from teens attending the event.
- Send information via internal library communications that highlights the success of the author visit and includes information about the following year's Teen Read Week events.

Program Idea 2: Photography Contest
Planning

1. Start 6 to 12 months in advance. Communicate to all staff the specific dates during which the contest will take place. Having a monthlong contest is a great way to make sure individuals and schools have the opportunity to find out about the program and have time to submit quality work. Look for ways to gather teen input on ideas for a theme, including a survey or question on the library's teen Web page. Work with teen services staff to determine which locations might be interested in hosting a photography workshop. Planning time = 12 hours.

2. Locate a photographer or photography expert in the community to present a series of photography workshops at various locations during the month the contest is taking place. If your library system concentrates programming at a central location, hold the photography workshop at this location. Make sure the workshop is hands-on. Ask if the presenter can bring cameras with which teens can experiment. Manual cameras are a great addition, and many teens have never had the opportunity to hold or use one. Planning time = 15 hours.

3. Work to secure funds or donations for disposable cameras that can be given at the photography workshops. Searching online is a great way to find disposable cameras at reduced rates. Many may have recently expired film, and before passing on these cameras ask your photography expert their opinion about the film quality to find out if these reduced-price cameras are an option. Planning time = 10 hours.

4. Look for a film developer with multiple locations who is willing to donate coupons for free or reduced film-development costs. Planning time = 4 hours.

5. Hold a formal award ceremony for contest winners. Planning time = 4 hours.

6. Scan and mount photographs for display. Planning time = 4 to 8 hours, depending on the number of entries.

7. As the contest approaches, involve staff members from multiple locations in promoting the event at schools and community agencies. Two-sided flyers are a great option for promoting the contest. One side can be an eye-catching advertisement. The other side can serve as a quick application to be attached with each photograph entered. Planning time = 10 hours.

Program

1. Once the flyers have been distributed at libraries and in the community, ask TAG members to be contest judges or recruit regular teen customers to serve in this role. Make the judging a separate, unique part of the program. Set a specific date for the judging, during which all teen judges will work together as a team to determine a winner. Work with your photography expert to develop basic criteria to offer teen judges some background for making an informed decision. Offer snacks and refreshments to the judges as a thank-you for their hard work.

2. Select a winner and multiple honorable mention or runner-up awards. Depending on the number of entries, investigate the options for giving all participants a certificate or ribbon, using creative categories, such as "most colorful," "most thought-provoking," or "most creative." Set a date for an awards ceremony and formally invite winners and honorable mention recipients to attend with family and friends.

3. Ask teen judges to comment about each winning entry while they are doing their judging and use these teen quotes during the awards ceremony. Invite teen judges to the awards ceremony and formally recognize the important part they played in the program. Emphasize the "for teens, by teens" nature of the contest.

4. Get written permission from teens to scan photographs so that they can be displayed on the library's Web page. Create a slide show or PowerPoint presentation of the photographs that can be used during the awards ceremony.

5. Mount the photographs and put them on display. This display can be moved from branch to branch. Each photograph should have a label that includes the name and age of the teen who took the photograph.

Promotion

1. Develop a press kit if possible. Because this is a monthlong program and it should generate a lot of interest, it is worth the time to create a formal press release and supporting material. If possible, begin this process several months in advance, working with the library's public relations staff.

2. If the photography contest becomes an annual event, use previous winners' photographs in promotional material and quotes from previous winners in press release material.

3. Search the community for teen photography clubs. Recreation centers, art museums, churches, and schools are organizations that often sponsor photography clubs or classes. Contact advisors from local photography clubs and send information about the library's contest.

Materials

- Disposable cameras.
- Flyers, posters.
- Material for mounting photographs and creating labels.
- Refreshments for the judging session and awards ceremony.
- Ribbons, certificates for honorable mention and winning entries.
- Gift certificate to photography shop or, if possible, donated or partially donated digital camera for grand prizewinner.

Evaluation

- Hand out brief evaluations at awards ceremony and to teen judges.
- Share evaluations with teen services staff.
- Offer a summary and evaluation for upper-level administrative staff. Include photos and quotes from teens and their families participating in any or all aspects of the program.
- Send information via internal library communications that highlights the achievements of the teens.

Program Idea 3: Anime Club

Planning and Promotion

1. Anime clubs can easily be started within a month or two of initial planning.

2. Work with teens to determine what time is ideal for a one-hour program. Decide if you will offer the program on a weekly or monthly basis. Planning time = 2 hours.

3. Develop flyers and posters to promote the program. Put the flyers and posters near the library's collection of anime and manga. Planning time = 2 hours.

4. Determine what anime the library can show. Some libraries have a movie license from various major movie studios to show films. These licenses often do not cover anime, however, as the rights to most anime are not held by any major studio. Some companies that do hold the rights to anime offer anime clubs the option to sign up and receive monthly screeners that can be shown at the library. Usually these companies require anime club members to complete a short survey about each screener in order to stay in the club. Not all anime included on the screeners may be appropriate for a library teen anime club, so it is important to view everything before deciding what to show. Planning time = 2 hours.

Program

- Anime clubs often seem to run themselves. Librarians provide small-scale refreshments like soda, Pokey, water, and popcorn, and teen anime fans do the rest! Some clubs watch a series of anime episodes and have a brief discussion at the end of the meeting, whereas others watch each episode and then talk about it. Still others do very little formal discussion at all and just enjoy watching anime in one another's company.

- There is sometimes tension between teens who really want to watch the anime and teens who want to have the anime playing in the background while they talk, play or trade cards, discuss manga, or compare drawings of anime characters or collections of various anime-related paraphernalia. It is important to figure out how to resolve this tension. Your decision on how to handle this situation may depend on the space in which the club is being held. If the space is big enough, teens who want to talk and interact can be asked to hang out toward the back of the room, and serious anime watchers can sit near the front.

- Anime clubs can be enhanced by guest presenters or by opportunities for members to express their fandom. Consider having a Japanese language expert pay a visit. Invite teens to share their own manga before or after showing the anime. Invite members to come to a meeting dressed as their favorite anime character and set aside time for them to share details about their costume and character.

Materials

- Anime DVDs.
- DVD player.
- LCD projector that can hook into DVD player.
- Sound system.
- Screen or white wall.
- Using a television for an anime club can work, but an LCD projector and sound system make it a much better experience!

Evaluation

- Ask teens to fill out a survey after each anime club meeting.
- Measure the increase in attendance and watch for circulation increases in the library's manga collection. Both are indicators of increased teen interest.

Program Idea 4: Poetry Slam

Planning

1. Start 6 to 12 months in advance. Find a poet in the community or among library staff or older teen customers—one who has experience performing poetry and participating in slams—to serve an emcee for the event. Coffee shops that offer poetry readings are a great place to start a search for community poets. Local theaters and contemporary and performance art centers are also possible places to get a lead about a local poet. Planning time = 4 hours.

2. Make sure the slam emcee is enthusiastic about and able to work with teens. Discuss any concerns you might have about content during the initial stages of working with the emcee so that everyone is comfortable with the parameters for the slam. Planning time = 1 hour.

3. Decide if the slam will be held at one location or at multiple branches. If there will be multiple slams, decide if there will be a Grand Slam at which all participants are invited back to participate in a final slam as a large group. Planning time = 1 hour.

4. Work with the slam emcee to decide if the slam will be competitive or if the focus will be to simply offer teens a chance to

experiment with performance poetry, with no winner named. If judges are involved, recruit poets, teachers, or experienced teen poets to serve in this role. Planning time = 2 hours.

Promotion

1. Develop flyers and posters to distribute at the library and in the community. Distribute flyers to coffeehouses, theaters, school drama clubs, and art museums.

2. Include information about the origins of poetry slams on the library's Web site. Develop a booklist of poetry books with suggestions for performance poems.

3. Contact local radio stations. Investigate the options for having library staff, teens, or the slam emcee do a short radio performance promoting the slam.

Program

1. Set up slam workshops at the locations where the slams will be held. These workshops can be separate events from the slam or can take place immediately before the slams begin.

2. Offer guidelines for slam poets, making sure to explain the differences between a poetry reading and performance poetry.

3. Give each poet a time limit for his or her performance.

4. Explain to the audience the role they play in a slam. Encourage audience members to interact appropriately and help generate energy and excitement for performers.

5. Be sure formal recognition and appreciation of each poet's performance is expressed through clapping or whatever method is adopted by the audience. Instruct the audience that the comments must stay positive and lighthearted and that any suggestions for improvement are communicated in a positive, productive manner after the performance has ended.

Materials

- Small gifts and prizes for participants. Ideas include small, portable notebooks and pens that teens can easily keep with them at all times as a way to keep track of thoughts and ideas for poems and performances.
- Light refreshments.
- Thank-you gifts or notes for judges, if they are part of the slam.

- Microphone and sound system. Even if the crowd is not huge or a microphone is not necessary in order for the teen poet to be heard, these elements add a lot to the atmosphere and help create an official feel for the slam. Plus, teen performers may want to try their hand at slams in the community, and offering a similar experience at the library will help prepare them for these real-world experiences.

- Decorations as appropriate. Talk to teens about what would make the slam feel cool. A few lamps from home can be used instead of overhead lighting to create a more intimate, less intimidating atmosphere. Use butcher or other large pieces of paper to cover tables and give teens a place to write ideas for their own performance or comment about others' poems they liked or performers they admired. Play teen-requested music as the program begins, between performers, and during any performance breaks.

Evaluation

- Ask teens to fill out a quick evaluation form. If there is paper on the tables, ask them to answer a short series of questions by writing directly on this paper. This slight variation on evaluation forms might encourage teens who normally do not fill out evaluations to share their thoughts.

- Gather evaluation comments and create a summary to share with administrative staff and other departments and divisions of the library.

- Take photographs, making sure to have library-approved permission forms signed by teens and their parents so that you can reproduce these photos. Share the photos with other library staff and also with community newspapers.

Program Idea 5: Manga/Cartooning/ Drawing Sessions

Planning

1. Start 6 to 12 months in advance. Find out if a cartoonist, graphic novel artist or illustrator, or anyone associated with the process of creating manga, cartoons, or art for graphic novels lives in your area. If so, e-mail them and ask about the possibility of working with them. Many of these artists and illustrators are very busy, so be ready with information about specific dates, times, and presentation costs. Decide if you are willing to compromise. For example,

if you are hoping to run a three- or four-week course involving a weekly meeting, is it acceptable for the star artist to make an appearance at only the first or last session? Can a lesser-known artist teach the class, with the famous artist acting more as a hook or public relations angle for the event? Would you settle for an all-day Saturday workshop? Planning time = 15 hours.

2. Decide how often and where the classes will take place. Planning time = 1 hour.

3. Determine if there is a need to limit the number of participants and if sign-up is required. Although registration for programs in urban areas is often not ideal, in this case registration may be necessary to help accomplish desired outcomes. Planning time = 1 hour.

4. Work with library funds, community groups, or local businesses to secure art and drawing supplies for participating teens. This is an important element, both as an incentive in getting teens to sign up for the program and in supporting continued development of the skills acquired through the workshops. Planning time = 15 hours.

Promotion

1. If you are fortunate enough to be working with a well-known artist, ask to be listed on his or her Web site in any activity or events calendar.

2. Create a press kit and press release. Include quotes from the artist and details about any art supplies and materials teens will be given.

3. Distribute flyers to all library locations and in the community at art supply stores, bookstores that sell manga, comic book stores, art clubs, art museums, recreation centers, and schools.

4. Ask the artist presenting the class if he or she would be willing to install an exhibit of his or her work at a library location to promote the classes.

5. Investigate options for having teen artists' work displayed at the library or in the community at an art museum or art exhibition.

Program

1. Work with the artist to decide the appropriate length for each class.

2. Ask for a brief outline of what will be covered during each session. This will help ensure the artist has a plan and will also help staff promote the event and answer questions from curious parents and teens.

3. Build in a graduation or awards ceremony as part of the last session. Ask the artist if he or she is able to make a few positive comments about each teen and their work during this part of the session. Invite parents to attend.

Materials

Work with artist to develop a list of supplies. Make the list as specific as possible when approaching donors. Investigate grant opportunities. If you library has a development officer, this is an ideal project to take to them. Volunteer to help write a grant if one is available.

Evaluation

Teens should fill out pre- and postclass evaluations. This will help gauge the success of the program and provide invaluable feedback to funders and donors. These questionnaires should be identical and designed to determine how much knowledge teen participants gained through participation in the intensive workshops. Work with the artist to develop questions based on content that will be covered and skills that will be prioritized.

Program Idea 6: Applying and Paying for College

This is an excellent example of a program that can be created by one or two people and reproduced with virtually no additional planning by multiple staff members at multiple locations.

Planning

1. Start planning three months in advance. Partner with reference librarians who specialize in grants and scholarships when designing this program. Ask for lists of resources they often use to help prospective college students and their parents who are looking for college information. Arrange for a meeting room, set up for a computer and large screen. Planning time = 3 hours.

2. Create simple, teen-friendly handouts. Planning time = 3 hours.

Promotion

1. Distribute flyers in the library and the community.
2. Include information on the library's Web page about upcoming college-related programs.
3. Work with school counselors and teachers to promote the program.
4. Time the program for maximum benefit. Ask teens and their parents for recommendations on the best time to offer the program.
5. Promote the program as an event that teens can attend independently or with their parents.
6. If parents are interested in attending without their teen, encourage them to do so.

Program

1. Ask a college recruiter or guidance counselor to help present material and/or serve on a panel to answer questions from teens and their parents.
2. Present several Web sites with quality, up-to-date college information.
3. Discuss sources available at the library and from home about scholarship and loan information.
4. Ask a financial aid officer to be available to answer general questions.

Materials

Resource lists, material from guest presenters and panelists.

Evaluation

Use a basic evaluation form to gather audience feedback. Create a brief summary of improvement ideas based on feedback that can be used by the next staff member reproducing the program.

Program Idea 7: Get in Shape

Planning

1. Start 6 to 12 months in advance. Survey or ask teens what kind of exercise might interest them. Think outside the box when it

comes to exercise ideas. Including yoga and aerobics are fine, but these may already be available in your community. Many urban libraries have had success with exercise-related programs featuring step dancing, Balinese dancing, learning to dance like Napoleon Dynamite, and DDR (Dance Dance Revolution). Planning time = 8 hours.

2. Find a local fitness expert to present ideas for healthy living, including nutritional tips and exercise habits. Ask if they are willing or able to adapt their exercise ideas into an urban workout appropriate for teens with exercise ideas that can be done in the city free of charge. Planning time = 4 hours.

Promotion

Distribute flyers and posters in the library and throughout the community. Make sure flyers are available at free health care clinics, centers that serve teen parents, community recreation centers, and school weight rooms or training facilities.

Program

1. Work with the presenter to be sure there is enough room and any necessary equipment is available.

2. Determine how long each session will last and if sessions will be offered at more than one location.

3. If the program includes nutritional information and physical exercise, work with the presenter to be certain nutritional information is conveyed in a hands-on, dynamic way. If necessary, ask another expert from the community to present the nutritional information.

4. Consider making this a program series. Teens can come to all or one of the programs, and each program can be focused on a different aspect of healthy living.

5. Include healthy snacks. Offer participants the chance to make something as simple as a fruit smoothie with fresh strawberries, bananas, or blueberries. Make sure to have plenty of water on hand!

Materials

- Healthy snacks (such as those listed in the refreshments section of this chapter).

- Nutrition resource and booklists. Contact nonprofit organizations that may be willing to send information on healthy living and lifestyles free of charge.

Evaluation

Use pre- and posttests to determine if participants gained knowledge about exercise, healthy eating, and nutrition. This involves asking participants the same basic questions before and after the program and comparing results from the same individual to see if any knowledge or skills were gained. Privacy issues are easily avoided by simply numbering the tests.

Program Idea 8: Career and Job Planning

Planning

1. Start 6 to 12 months in advance. Recruit a presenter or group of panelists from human resources staff at the library and other community businesses and agencies. Ask these presenters to offer tips for effective résumé writing and interviewing. Ask for information that can be converted into print material for participants. Planning time = 8 hours.
2. Talk to teens about the kinds of careers they might be interested in learning about during a program. Recruit community members from various fields to talk about their careers and education. Planning time = 4 hours.
3. Include careers that have a variety of educational requirements, from high school only, to trade school, to four-year degrees, and beyond.
4. Make the program a half-day event and include presenters giving interviewing tips and a career panel, followed by a job fair.
5. Invite area businesses that hire teen employees to attend the job fair and encourage them to bring employment information and applications that can be filled out and returned by teens on the day of the event. Planning time = 8 hours.

Promotion

1. Distribute flyers and posters in the library and the community. Make sure flyers are available at other area job fairs, employment offices, schools, and local businesses that employ teen workers.
2. Create a press kit and press release.

3. Ask panelists and presenters for quotes and if they would be willing to be interviewed by radio or television reporters.

Program

1. All three elements—interviewing tips, career options, and a job fair—can be combined or offered at separate times. The advantage of combining the activities is that teens may have an easier time attending a one-time event at the library rather than trying to make it to multiple events.

2. Work with the presenter offering résumé and interviewing tips to make printed support material available. If time permits, ask the presenter if he or she would be willing to work one-on-one with teens after the program.

3. Give the career panel a set of prepared questions to help them develop their presentation. Make sure they discuss all of their education and job experiences.

4. Determine how many businesses are needed to make the job fair a success. Find a space that will support multiple booths or tables. Assign each business a table. Supply light refreshments to presenters and participants.

5. Make the job fair an annual event. Work with teens and businesses to find the best time to offer the program.

Evaluation

Ask for formal feedback from everyone involved. If possible, ask employers how many, if any, teens they recruited as a result of the library's job fair.

CONCLUSION

Always keep in mind that large urban areas are home to a great diversity of individuals and cultures. Whenever programs are planned, this diversity should be reflected in the kinds of programs, presenters, and program panelists. Although Black History Month and Hispanic Heritage Month are obvious tie-ins for specific culturally based programs, programs throughout the year should celebrate the diversity of large urban areas. Working in an urban area offers unique opportunities for teen programming. Be sure to use all of these resources to your advantage!

WORKS CITED

Institute of Museum and Library Services. *NLG Project Planning*. Accessed May 31, 2006, available at http://www.imls.gov/project%5Fplanning/module01/accessories/glossary.asp.

Synder, Howard N, and Melissa Sickmund. 1999. *Juvenile Offenders and Victims: 1999 National Reports*. Washington, DC: Office of Juvenile Justice and Delinquency Prevention.

Suellentrop, Tricia. 2006. "Letting Go." *School Library Journal* 52 (May): 39.

Walter, Virginia A., and Elaine Meyers. 2003. *Teens and Libraries: Getting It Right*. Chicago: American Library Association.

FURTHER READING

Chapman, Jan. 2003. "The Care and Feeding of a Teen Advisory Board." *Voice of Youth Advocates* 25 (6) (February): 449–50.

Chelton, Mary K., ed. 1997. *Excellence in Library Services to Young Adults: The Nation's Top Programs*. Chicago: American Library Association.

Chelton, Mary K., ed. 2000. *Excellence in Library Services to Young Adults: The Nation's Top Programs*. Chicago: American Library Association.

Chelton, Mary K., ed. 2004. *Excellence in Library Services to Young Adults: The Nation's Top Programs*. Chicago: American Library Association.

Ericson, Nels. 2001. The YMCA's Teen Action Agenda Fact Sheet. Washington, DC: U.S. Department of Justice, Office of Justice Programs, Office of Juvenile Justice and Delinquency Prevention. Accessed May 13, 2006, available at http://www.ncjrs.gov/pdffiles1/ojjdp/fs200114.pdf.

Gnehm, Kurstin Finch. 2002. *Youth Development and Public Libraries: Tools for Success*. Evanston, IL: Urban Libraries Council.

Holems, Fontayne, and Carol Baldwin. 1978. "Steps to Cooperative YA Programming." *School Library Journal* 24 (May): 28–31.

Honnold, RoseMary. 2002. *101 Teen Programs that Work*. New York: Neal-Schuman.

Honnold, RoseMary. 2005. *More Teen Programs that Work*. New York: Neal-Schuman.

Jones, Patrick, Michele Gorman, and Tricia Suellentrop. 2004. *Connecting Young Adults and Libraries*. New York: Neal-Schuman.

Langemack, Chapple. 2007. *The Author Event Primer: How to Plan, Execute and Enjoy Author Events*. Westport, CT: Libraries Unlimited.

McLaughlin, Milbrey W. 2000. *Community Counts: How Youth Organizations Matter for Youth Development*. Washington, DC: Public Education Network.

Mondowny, JoAnn G. 2001. *Hold Them in Your Heart: Successful Strategies for Library Services to At-Risk Teens*. New York: Neal-Schuman.

Search Institute. *40 Developmental Assets*. Accessed November 23, 2007, available at http://www.search-institute.org/assets/forty.html.

Snyder, Howard N., and Melissa Sickmund. 1999. *Juvenile Offenders and Victims: 1999 National Report*. Accessed June 2, 2006, available at http://www.ncjrs.gov/html/ojjdp/nationalreport99/toc.html.

Tuccillo, Diane. 2005. *Library Teen Advisory Groups.* Lanham, MD: VOYA Books

Wilson, Evie. 2003. "The Young Adult Advisory Board: How to Make It Work." *Voice of Youth Advocates* 25 (6) (February): 446–48.

Yohalem, Nicole, and Karen Pittman. 2003. "Public Libraries as Partners in Youth Development: Lessons and Voices from the Field." *The Forum for Youth Investment.* Accessed November 23, 2007, available at http://www.urbanlibraries.org/files/PLPYDreport_FINAL.pdf.

Youth Activism Project. Accessed April 26, 2006, available at http://www.youthactivism.com.

Zollo, Peter. 1999. *Wise Up to Teens: Insights into Marketing and Advertising to Teenagers.* Ithaca, NY: New Strategist.

7

◇ ◇ ◇

PARTNERSHIPS AND OUTREACH

If you want to expand service to teens in urban areas, there are three words you should remember: outreach, outreach, outreach. Outreach is to teen services what story times are to children's services: the building blocks on which other services develop. Outreach, whether it is done and whether it is done effectively, can make or break your attempts to serve teens. In many cases, outreach activities—in which you come in contact with many classrooms in a single visit—may make a bigger impact in terms of reaching teens and promoting their use of the library than in-house programs do. No investment in outreach services or viewing them as an if-time-permits element of service can double the effort needed to connect with teens. Fortunately, in urban areas, there are many organizations available and eager to work with the library on outreach activities. You simply cannot afford to ignore or miss these opportunities.

Ideally, libraries in urban areas are involved in community discussions about serving teenagers. Unfortunately, youth-serving organizations in urban areas do not always think of the library as a player in these important discussions. Outreach activities raise the library's profile not only among teens but also among these other organizations serving teens and lead to invitations for the library to become a more active contributor to community discussions. This is vital in urban areas because though there are more organizations dedicated to serving teens in urban communities than in rural or truly suburban communities, the greater number of organizations does not necessarily translate into a coordinated, effective, community-wide approach to serving teens. For example, it is not uncommon for a story to appear in the media focused on rowdy teens at a library serving an urban community. These stories indicate a need for a community-wide response. In such instances, it is not a library solution that will fix the situation; it is a community issue requiring a community solution, and the library must be at the table to discuss the options and clearly communicate what the library can (and cannot) contribute.

When librarians think of outreach, they naturally think of activities that involve delivering library services to teens not in the library. Oftentimes, these activities are developed as one-time or occasional visits to schools or community agencies whose ultimate goal is to bring teens into the library. For example, providing booktalks at a local school allows a librarian to introduce herself to numerous area teens, raise the profile of the library, promote new books and resources, and raise the odds that teens will, in turn, make a visit to the library (where they will frequently say "Hi" to the librarian who visited their school). Another example of a high-value outreach activity is conducting a book club or craft program at a local boys or girls club. Additionally, some urban public librarians working with teachers and school media specialists take their show on the road by leading or coleading discussions at after-school or lunchtime book clubs that actually take place at the school rather than at the library. Many teen services librarians find that visiting juvenile detention centers provides a new and valuable opportunity to deliver library services to a sometimes underserved but important community group.

A key type of outreach for serving urban areas, however, is building community *partnerships*. Partnerships are a type of community outreach that involves establishing long-term arrangements in which both the library and one or more community agencies offer resources or support for ongoing activities and programs. They tend to be more complicated, involve multiple staff from various agencies, and come in a variety of shapes and sizes. In fact, outreach *activities* may occur as part of larger *partnership efforts*. For example, consider an ongoing project that offers teens after-school tutoring at the library with tutors provided by another community organization; this is a partnership activity. In this endeavor, the library may be just one of a number of organizations involved, and the project will likely include working with various staff from several organizations for things like public relations support. Each organization, including the library, pools its resources and works together toward a collaborative goal—a tremendous opportunity and a sterling example of how libraries in urban areas can take outreach to the next level.

Clearly, there are many unique factors that affect partnerships in urban library settings. Suggestions for making these factors work for, rather than against, libraries are offered in this chapter, as are examples of outstanding services for teens in urban areas developed through effective outreach and partnerships. If you are looking to lay the foundation for expanding teen services beyond the library's four walls, you will find tips on how to start this important and sometimes overwhelming task. If you already have established partnership activities, you will gain a fresh perspective and find ways to initiate new, expanded outreach options or revitalize existing partnerships with community agencies.

WHY DEVELOP PARTNERSHIPS?

You have just opened your new teen area. Your shelves are full of the newest, hottest paperbacks. You have a bank of computers arranged to encourage teens to surf the Net or work on their homework. The only problem is that when you look out, there is not a teen in sight. Or maybe you are in an urban library with plenty of teens hanging out in your teen area. So many, in fact, that it is becoming difficult to manage teen behavior, especially during the busy after-school hours. You or your staff may ask, "Why would we develop partnerships to bring even *more* teens into the library? What's the point of reaching out to teens *outside* of the library walls when the teens *inside* the library are hard enough to handle?"

If either of these situations sounds familiar, ask yourself these important questions to see if developing partnerships can work for you:

- If you are *not* getting teens into your library, are there schools or churches where you can advertise your resources?
- If the crowd of teens you are getting is coming from a nearby school, are you communicating with the school to explore opportunities for collaboration in handling teens' needs?
- Are you working with community recreation sites or boys and girls clubs to find out how to strategically share resources to best address the needs of teens in your community? (Remember, other community agencies may be experiencing the same issues and looking for a partner to help *them* out as well.)
- Are there grants, corporate sponsors, and other special funding opportunities available that can help open the lines of communication with other teen-serving community agencies?

- If you are having disciplinary problems, have you established good relationships with your community police officer so that you can easily ask for his or her help?

Libraries are a welcoming, relatively safe place for teens, and with their history of being "intentionally safe and supportive environments that are rich in developmental nutrients" (Yohalem and Pittman 2003, 2), libraries are often among the first in the community to realize that young people do not have the options they need to productively and positively fill their out-of-school hours. Libraries are excellent places for teens to hang out, work on homework, find books to read and anime to watch, and develop their personalities in a stimulating and nurturing environment. Remember, however, that there are limits on what services your library can provide. That is why you must work to communicate the needs of the teens you are seeing every day to others in the community. Although your neighborhood recreation center may also be very aware of these needs, there may be other important community agencies that are not. Teens like using the library after school but may also be looking for a place to go play basketball or football, and the library cannot offer teens the same kind of options and activities that a community basketball court or swimming pool can. Is there a way for the library to take a leadership role in crafting a community-wide response for addressing teens' needs? In *New Directions for Library Service to Young Adults,* Patrick Jones explains, "There is a strong correlation between quality library service and a higher success rate when libraries partner with other agencies" (Jones 2002, 27). Jones goes on to discuss the National Research Council's 2001 *Community Programs to Promote Youth Development* report, which concludes that teens in communities offering a variety of programs and activities "experience less risk and demonstrate higher rates of positive youth development" (Jones 2002, 27).

Urban settings offer a wide variety of rich opportunities for community partnerships with an array of different types of organizations. Librarians looking for ways to extend service to teens beyond the four walls of the library will not have to look very far to find potential partners and promising venues for these opportunities. This is especially true if you are hoping to reach out to a specific subset of teens. Urban areas support organizations with a more narrow focus than rural or truly suburban areas. For example, an urban area may have a group or organization dedicated to helping new immigrants find services and ease their transition to living in a U.S. city. This kind of organization, which likely would not exist in a small town or sparsely populated rural area, is just the kind of unique partner that can be a significant help for a librarian looking to expand service to immigrant teens. Clearly, with so many community agencies and organizations serving young people and working to make a positive impact on teens' lives, a motivated teen librarian has many options for connecting with worthwhile partners. These connections lead to sharing information and developing outstanding outreach and community partnerships, all designed to work and advocate for teens.

Establishing and maintaining partnerships and outreach activities is often time consuming and complicated, however. This can be especially true when working with large organizations, like many found in urban areas, that have distinct corporate cultures, multiple layers of management and oversight, and priorities that are not always clear. But with planning and perseverance, the results of collaborative efforts can be truly rewarding.

Effective partnerships help ensure the smartest and most efficient use of community resources. When community agencies serving the same target audience do not talk to one another, programs and activities are often duplicated. In urban areas, where there are usually numerous and diverse agencies, this can mean a lot of duplication! Instead of teens being able to choose between a variety of different programs, the same options may end up being offered, just at different locations.

Think for a minute about some of the major agencies focused on serving teens in your community. How much do you know about them? Do you know what kind of programs, volunteer options, and activities they offer? Librarians sometimes develop a habit of planning in a bubble and then wondering why teens are not taking advantage of the great programs and opportunities being offered at the library. In fact, another community agency may have a similar and long-established program, so that need is already being filled. Partnerships lead to information sharing, which helps agencies avoid offering overlapping programs or overprogramming to a particular topic. If agencies work cooperatively, resources can be redirected and used strategically to develop a variety of unique programs and services for teens.

Librarians in urban areas know there is a strong need for positive programming and activities for teens, but they are also painfully aware of the limited resources available to create and maintain these programs. Many organizations operating in urban communities have broad missions but limited resources. Unfortunately, urban libraries often fall into this category. It is hard for libraries and community organizations to fully realize their goals of offering teens high-quality options for programs and activities when they act independently. But when these agencies join forces, the pool of resources is expanded, and more resources create more possibilities. A collaborative approach produces a comprehensive community network of service to teens.

PARTNERSHIP TYPES

The term *partnership* is used frequently by libraries. Librarians searching for funds to establish or maintain teen programs often hear the recommendation, "Why don't you find a partner to work with on that project/ grant/etc.?" When teens are needed for library focus groups or a volunteer project, the idea of finding a community partner to make this happen is often suggested. But librarians hoping to incorporate partnerships into teen services need to fully understand and explore the various *kinds* of partnerships before embarking on a collaborative project.

Not all partnerships are the same, and different situations call for different kinds of collaboration. In *Connecting Young Adults and Libraries*, Patrick Jones and his coauthors define three levels of partnerships: communicative, cooperative, and collaborative (Jones, Gorman, and Suellentrop 2004). This framework is an excellent starting point for considering partnerships in urban areas. All three types of partnerships are important for libraries, and urban environments provide a wealth of opportunities for creating all three. All three types, when developed effectively, can provide valuable opportunities for supporting teen services.

Communicative Partnerships

Consider a communicative partnership, especially if your library is just beginning the process of establishing teen services. Communicative partnerships are the most basic and familiar type of partnership. These involve partners simply agreeing to share or communicate information with each other and with their respective customers or target audience. Many libraries serving urban areas have a long tradition of maintaining these types of partnerships and communicating with community partners in informal ways. Examples of this kind of partnership include a library distributing information about summer jobs for a local organization working to recruit teen employees, and the organization reciprocates by posting posters advertising summer library programs on a bulletin board or handing out flyers at a job fair for teenagers. These interactions between the library and other organizations frequently evolve naturally in urban areas, where many youth-serving agencies operate in close proximity.

An agency benefits when information about its mission and activities are advertised and talked about at many locations in the community. Because the benefits of communicative partnerships are usually clear, it does not take much to convince target partners to agree to such an arrangement. Additionally, this type of partnership does not require reworking or re-creating your mission or goals and can be established by frontline staff. It does not require the involvement of higher-level managers and administrators, making these types of partnerships relatively easy to set up once an appropriate contact is made from each organization.

An important step to making sure that partnerships revolving around basic information sharing remain productive and effective is to formalize them. All organizations and individuals involved should understand from the beginning that information-sharing situations are true partnerships and should treat them accordingly. Simply because they are a natural fit and do not require a lot of labor to establish does not mean that these partnerships should be taken for granted or not monitored.

One way to be certain this happens is for the library to assign a specific contact person to each agency or school with whom a communicative partnership exists. If you inherit a long-standing information-sharing arrangement, you have a perfect opportunity to reevaluate and reassess the structure and effectiveness of the partnership. Are the goals and outcomes of the partnership clear? Are they being achieved? Are there opportunities for greater resource sharing or moving toward a higher-level partnership (such as the cooperative or collaborative partnership types discussed later in this chapter)? Be sure library staff members serving as contacts have introduced themselves to staff at the partnering agency. If possible, the outgoing librarian should introduce the incoming librarian to the contact. Library staff serving as agency contacts should also understand their responsibility for proactively seeking and sharing information and following up with each agency when necessary.

Checklist for Library Staff Members Serving as Contacts for Communicative/Information-Sharing Partners

Name of organization.
Location.
Name of contact person from organization.
E-mail/phone/address.

(*continued*)

(*Continued*)

> Library's role as a partner. When has information been exchanged in the
> last year?
> > Specific kind of information (e.g., number of flyers distributed or received)
> > Benefits for the library resulting from this information sharing.

Some examples of a communicative partnership in action include:

- Dropping off flyers about a library program at a local recreation center.
- Distributing information about the summer reading program to schools.
- Asking local community agencies to post information about upcoming library events or new services on the teen section of their Web page.

Cooperative Partnerships

Once your library has developed a network of communicative partners with whom you share information, you can begin identifying possible cooperative partners. Cooperating with another agency involves more than exchanging flyers or raising awareness about your organizations' respective missions. Cooperation involves partners working together and supporting each other's events and services by *sharing resources*. In a communicative partnership, you distribute flyers for another agency's upcoming event. In a cooperative partnership, you recruit volunteers from your library's teen volunteer program to help staff your partner's event.

Cooperation clearly requires making formal arrangements with partners. This agreement can be focused on a one-time or an annual event. It is vital to ensure that the cooperation is equitable. Many organizations in urban areas have limited resources and staff. Although most community agencies have no intention of taking advantage of the library's willingness to partner, if formal arrangements are not in place, the cooperation can sometimes become one-sided. Examples of cooperative partnerships include:

- A local museum is hosting a craft day for younger children. The library's teen advisory board volunteers to assist with crafts. The museum receives additional volunteers, and the library has an opportunity to enhance and expand the experience of teen advisory board members.

- A library is hosting an anime club. A local recreation center arranges to transport a group of teens from the recreation center to the library. The library has a chance to work with teens who might not otherwise have been able to come to the library because of transportation issues. In turn, recreation center staff are able to offer their teens an exciting, organized activity without investing additional staff resources from their organization. If the recreation center cannot provide transportation for teens to come to a program at the library, the library may consider sending staff off-site to present the program at the recreation center.

- A local hospital receives a grant to offer stress management training for teens. The hospital works with the library to set up multiple trainings at several library locations. The hospital, with only one location, benefits from using the library as an outlet for a grant-funded program. The library is able to offer quality programming from a qualified trainer without incurring any programming costs.

Collaborative Partnerships

To realize the full power of your community partnerships, you must collaborate effectively. Although communicative and cooperative relationships do not necessarily require large amounts of staff time, funding, or commitment, achieving a collaborative level of partnership in urban settings can be labor-intensive project. Activities accomplished through communicative and cooperative partnerships such as advertising activities and promoting the library's resources by sending flyers to community agencies (communicative) or staffing a booth with teen volunteers at a fair or event hosted by another community agency (cooperative) are important elements of serving teens, but in urban areas, when it comes to supporting healthy youth development, "programs alone aren't enough" (Yohalem and Pittman 2003, 10). In collaborative partnerships, all partners work together to create an entirely new set of goals for the partnership. These kinds of partnerships are the most likely to create a sustainable, community-wide environment that is conducive to teens achieving healthy youth development. There are a wide variety of excellent resources detailing the specific steps for developing collaborative partnerships. Many are listed in the further reading section of this chapter. If you are working to create collaborative partnerships, review this information, keeping in mind the following factors that can be particularly important for librarians working in large urban areas:

- Bring in the right people. When building a collaborative partner-ship with organizations in urban areas, it is important to get all of the necessary stakeholders involved from the start, from front-line staff to high-level administrators. In communicative and cooperative levels of partnership, it is often appropriate for front-line staff to establish and formalize partnership arrangements. It would seem strange to contact an administrator and discuss the outcomes and goals of dropping off a flyer at a local business! But because true collaboration involves creating new goals for the entire organization, it is essential that these partnerships are established with the full knowledge and input from the library at all levels. Frontline staff may still represent the library in these partnerships, but key decision makers must be informed of the details.

- Consider, whenever possible, utilizing a staff team to represent the library in the partnership being developed. Include experts in teen services, frontline staff, and coordinators. Again, make sure to include an administrative or management sponsor or contact. This administrative contact, who may not regularly attend meetings or work directly on creating the partnership, is vital to the success of the project and should always be kept well informed. Develop a formal process for sharing information with this sponsor and always keep them in the loop.

- Review your library's mission and the missions of all potential partners. Do the missions indicate a similar perspective on healthy youth development? Libraries are not the only organizations in large urban areas that sometimes face pressure to deal with the so-called teen problem. If the potential partner appears to be approaching a collaboration from a different perspective, pay attention. It may be necessary to spend time educating partners about an asset-based approach to healthy youth development before proceeding with any project.

- Make sure partners are, in turn, engaging the appropriate staff within their organization. If the library has done its part in bring-ing higher-level managers and administrators to the table, but potential partners do not seem to be doing the same, this can be a warning sign of problems to come. It is the responsibility of all partners to make sure their organization is fully informed and completely supportive of collaborative partnerships. If this does not seem to be the case, diplomatically ask about the situation. If not reassured by the answer, ask your administrative sponsor to discreetly inquire with their administrative counterparts working for the potential partner.

- Understand the organizational structure of potential partners. Many layers of staff frequently work on a potential partnership project. Take time to learn names and titles and be sure to understand what each person's position is within the partnering organization. This is particularly valuable if working with partners that have high staff turnover. Understanding a partner's structure helps keep the process moving forward even if the personnel involved changes.

- Do not be afraid to let other organizations take the lead. Some potential partners may have special project manager positions or other staffing structures conducive to focusing on a specific partnership project, for example a grant project. Many librarians serving teens in urban areas have many duties and are stretched thin. If a potential partner proposes that they take the lead in overseeing the project, seriously consider the benefits of their offer.

- If the partnership involves a grant, know how your library's finances work or talk to someone in your organization who does know. Address these questions early in the process, even if the financial piece is not actually developed until much later in the project. The way money is distributed can affect the structure for administering the grant. If a potential partnership does involve a grant (or involves applying for a grant in the future) and you are not a grant writer, admit it. If your library has a grant specialist on staff, make sure he or she is fully informed about the partnership endeavor and comfortable with any role to be played in the grant process. If your library does not have a grant writer on staff but one of the potential partners does, discuss in detail the role of a grant writer in collaborative projects.

- Do not skip the evaluation element. Most libraries in urban areas do regular evaluation of programs and services. Many employ general evaluation methods that provide a broad overview of customer reaction or community impact. Other community partners may be interested in more specific evaluations. Because libraries have strong policies and values regarding customer privacy, evaluation methods used by other partners need to be adapted for the library setting. It is important to educate partners about issues related to evaluating and tracking individual teen customers. Confirm that general evaluation measures will satisfy the needs of all partners involved.

POSSIBLE PARTNERS

Church and religious organizations. This option is particularly important for libraries in communities serving a large number of African American teens to consider, as church plays a central role in many African American communities (Walker and Manjarrez 2003).

Organizations serving recent immigrants. As the number of immigrants continues to swell in the United States, neighborhoods and communities in urban areas continue to see a rise in recent immigrant populations. Organizations serving this growing group are often eager to partner with the library and offer a great opportunity to reach a wide, diverse, and increasing audience.

Parks and recreation departments. As noted in a policy commentary by the Forum for Youth Investment, parks and recreation departments are a key provider of services to young people in the United States (Forum for Youth Investment 2005). Parks are a regular part of most urban landscapes, but their reach is sometimes underappreciated. Librarians should keep in mind that "a rough estimate suggests that there is a city owned park or playground within one mile of most urban neighborhoods" when searching for community partners (Forum for Youth Investment 2005, 2).

Sports teams. Many professional athletes have foundations looking for a worthy cause. Why not suggest the library? Urban areas are also often the home of semiprofessional or amateur league teams willing to embrace partnerships that raise their profile and project a positive image.

Juvenile detention centers. Urban areas are usually home to one or more detention facilities. Some are large group homes, whereas others target smaller groups of serious or violent offenders. The average stay at some facilities may be as short as 48 hours. Others may have residents who stay much longer—up to a year or more. Many of the teens in these facilities are also frequent visitors to area libraries. Outreaching to teens while they are at the detention centers offers a new way for librarians to connect with some of the most at-risk teens they serve. Find a contact at a local detention center and explore the options for working together. Offer to provide collections of books as a first step (with an understanding of leniency when it comes to fines and lost items) and see what possibilities exist for building a long-lasting partnership.

Also Try

- Arts programs.
- Bookstores.

- Boys and girls clubs.
- Businesses.
- Creative writing programs.
- Drug treatment facilities.
- Fairs.
- Festivals.
- Government agencies.
- Homeschool associations.
- Hospitals.
- Health departments.
- Museums of all types.
- Newspapers.
- Nutrition councils.
- Other libraries.
- Public broadcasting stations.
- Radio stations.
- Theater groups.
- TV stations.
- Universities.
- YMCA/YWCA.
- Zoos.

PARTNERSHIP CHALLENGES

Partnerships can help organizations and communities realize outcomes and achieve goals that they could never have accomplished individually; however, building and maintaining partnerships can involve challenging situations. The following examples of partnership problems typify these challenges and offer suggestions on how to overcome them.

Partnership Challenge 1: What Do You Do?

You are a teen librarian working in one of several midsize branch libraries for a multibranch library system with centralized collection development. Your branch is located in a diverse, urban neighborhood. In the last few

(continued)

(Continued)

years, the neighborhood has become the home of many new immigrants whose native language is not English. The library does not have much material for non-English-speaking customers, but when you have inquired about purchasing more material, you have been told there simply is not enough money in the collection development budget.

A few weeks before school is scheduled to start, you receive a call from the principal at a middle school less than a mile away. You have worked with the principal on minor projects in the past, such as promoting the teen summer reading program, and it has always gone well. The principal is working on a grant proposal for funds that will support services to the large number of new immigrant students entering her school in the fall. She has heard that the library could use more English as a second language material for teens. If the library agrees to be a partner in the grant, she would be happy to include in the grant proposal a request for several thousand dollars that the library could use to purchase this much-needed material. The grant application is due in a week, and she needs your answer in the next two days. She assures you that the only obligation on the library's part is to house the grant material and make sure it is available to middle school students. What do you do?

Possible Responses

Thank the principal for the call. No matter what the ultimate outcome, it is an accomplishment that a busy principal at an urban middle school thought of the library for such a project.

Ask if it is possible for you to have a copy of the grant proposal that day. Volunteer to pick up the proposal at the school if necessary.

Ask if there are any other partners involved.

Consider you library's corporate culture, keeping in mind that even if your library is very serious about empowering all staff to make decisions, agreeing without more details is probably not a good idea.

Talk to your branch manager. If he or she is not available or seems less sure of what to do than you do, ask to elevate the question to the next level of administration. Before doing so, however, be sure to have a copy of the grant and a list of all partners involved. Administrators are busy people and, just like the rest of us, do not like to hear, "I need the answer today or tomorrow." The more information you can provide immediately, the better.

If a manager or administrator says no, respect that answer. Make it a point to sincerely thank him or her for taking the time to consider the project on such short notice.

If you do not receive an official response in the necessary time frame, weigh the potential risks and benefits of moving forward. For example, if the grant is $200 and you anticipate significant issues in dealing with a collection development department or policy problems related to where the material will be housed, this grant may not be worth the effort. On the other hand, if the grant provides $2,000, it may be worth the risks to move forward without specific approval.

Partnership Challenge 2: What Do You Do?

You work in a small library branch that is part of a 12-branch library system. All branches are located in urban areas or inner-ring suburbs. Because it is sometimes difficult to generate teen interest in organized programming, your branch has a long-standing arrangement with the parks department, which has a recreation center in your neighborhood, to transport teens from their day camp to the library for programs during summer. The relationship has always been a positive one, and in recent years the library branch has scheduled programs with the recreation center teens in mind, as they are a reliable and enthusiastic audience. The process has been formalized with library staff working in advance with parks department staff to finalize scheduling and transportation issues. On the rare occasions when transportation does not go as planned, a teen services staff member from the library has gone to the recreation center to present programs.

This year, the parks department youth coordinator is the same person you have always worked with, but there has been significant turnover at the recreation center site. The frontline staff at the recreation center has started bringing younger children to the scheduled teen programs on a regular basis. Several eight-year-olds showed up for the most recent program, along with the usual dozen or so teenagers. The planned programs involve a variety of activities developmentally appropriate for teens but not for younger children, including complicated crafts, booktalks, and anime films rated as appropriate for a teen audience. What do you do?

Possible Responses

Work with your children's services librarian or other willing staff to create separate activities for the younger children who are coming with the recreation center group.

If staffing is tight or no staff is willing or able to help develop separate children's activities, rework your plan and include several independent activities for younger children. Make clear your expectation that recreation center staff help younger kids with these additional activities.

This is a cooperative partnership with a long history of success and effort on the part of both organizations, so the first rule should be to tread softly. Issues come up in all partnerships, and dealing with them diplomatically is essential.

Talk to the recreation center staff. Although you have worked with the parks department youth coordinator for many years and trust that he or she understands the arrangement, there is no guarantee that the details were clearly communicated to frontline staff.

Keep in mind that staff members at recreation centers often have limited experience in working with teens or overseeing youth activities. Ask if they are aware that the library offers a variety of programs for all ages. Look over a schedule of library events together and ask if it is possible for younger

(continued)

(Continued)

children to come to activities and programs designed specifically for people in their age range.

Talk to the parks department youth coordinator. Start by graciously thanking the parks department for their support and complimenting the teens on their participation in the library's programs. Make sure to discuss the issue of younger kids coming to the program in light of the effect the younger kids are having on teens' activities, not in terms of impact on you or your planning. Be sure to keep the conversation from heading in the direction of blaming any recreation center staff for poor judgment.

If the issue is still not resolved to your satisfaction, realize that the model you have had in the past needs to change, at least for one summer.

Look to the teens to help. Do your best to maintain some element of teen-only activities to the program but also enlist teens to help the younger kids with several specific activities. Institute a book buddies program (similar to the program discussed in chapter 2) as part of the programs, in which teens pair up with a younger child at the end of each session and read to them for 10 minutes.

At the end of summer, evaluate what worked and what did not. If some of the newly designed elements were successful, incorporate them into the planning for the following year. If the teens responded positively to their role as helpers, you may be surprised to find yourself asking the recreation center to bring younger kids along next summer.

Partnership Challenge 3: What Do You Do?

A short-term drug treatment facility for teen girls has heard about your work with the local detention center. A teacher from the facility asks you to work with their teens once a week on "something library related." You suggest booktalks and prepare a 45-minute presentation. When you arrive, you are shuttled into a dining area where 15 girls age 13 to 17 are just starting their snack. The teacher introduces you and then bows out of the room, leaving you with the girls and one bored-looking adult room monitor. You proceed with your presentation, noting that a few of the girls finish eating and sleep through the rest of your talk.

After an hour, the teacher does not reappear, and you explain to the room monitor that you have completed your presentation. She tells you that she thought you were going to be with the girls for two hours but calls the teacher for you. The teacher returns and, while escorting you out, asks if you would be willing to come back "every week for an hour or two." This exceeds the time you are available to be away from your library. The teacher also hints that, now that the library is turning into such a great partner, the board of the facility would love to discuss plans for setting up a library in the drug treatment center.

Possible Responses

Experiences like this one are understandably frustrating. The most important thing to do is take a deep breath and realistically assess the situation, keeping in mind the risks and benefits to proceeding with any kind of partnership.

Admit that you may not have taken the necessary steps to building a quality partnership when arranging the visit. Acknowledge that you bear some responsibility for the way things turned out. An exciting opportunity to reach teens who clearly could benefit from the positive influence of the library and a caring teen librarian may seems so ideal you want to jump right in and worry about the details later. But doing your homework is just as important here as in the development of any other possible partnership situation.

When approached with such a proposal, ask if it is possible to meet in advance and tour (or at least see the inside of) the facility. Remember, if you have not been approached by organizations serving confined teen populations like detention centers, alternative schools, or drug treatment facilities, being proactive and seeking out opportunities to work with teens in these situations is an essential part of teen services for libraries in urban settings.

Ask if the teens you will be working with have done any reading as a group. If not, ask what the academic or educational expectations for the teens are while they are at the facility.

Clearly explain how long you will be working with the teens, how frequently you can visit, and what kind of assistance or monitoring you will expect from facility staff during your visit. Nonprofit groups are often desperate for support, so be careful not to encourage false expectations.

Ask if there are other projects the facility has ever thought about working on with the library. Hopefully, this kind of open-ended question will prompt your contact to discuss larger projects the are considering, such as creating a library at the facility.

Let your manager and, if appropriate, an administrative contact know that you have started working with a facility serving confined teen populations. Keep them abreast of your progress. This will help lay the foundation for any future large-scale projects, like on-site deposit collection or a library.

Have realistic expectations. Do not expect 15 smiling faces cheering to see the librarian when you show up. Teens in detention facilities, drug treatment centers, or alternative boarding schools are dealing with a lot. Many will be happy to see you, even if they are not effusive. Once you have established regular outreach to such facilities as part of a cooperative or collaborative partnership, you will be surprised by the number of teens in the library that you recognize from your visits and who appreciatively acknowledge you.

Assess how your organization might benefit from such a partnership in relation to the costs before making a commitment.

Partnership Challenge 4: What Do You Do?

Your small urban library branch is located right next to a middle school. Every day at 3:00 p.m. the library is inundated with teenagers. Your staff is frustrated by having 50 to 75 teens running around in the library for several hours every weekday afternoon. You are taking steps to educate the staff

(continued)

(*Continued*)

about teen behavior and effective ways to manage issues related to serving large numbers of teens, but you are searching for additional steps to take in helping create an environment that works for the teens, other library customers, and the staff. What do you do?

Possible Responses

There are many factors involved in this kind of familiar situation, but one that is sometimes overlooked is the possibility of pulling in partners or the role of outreach. Start by making sure the library has an active outreach relationship with the school in question. Although it may seem counterintuitive to prioritize outreach when teens are already coming to the library in droves, remember that there are many reasons for outreach. Convincing teens to come to the library is only one of these reasons. Outreach can help you build a relationship with teens in a less stressful environment than the busy after-school hours at the library. If they know you from school, teens may be more cooperative and willing to function as partners in creating a productive library environment outside of school.

Talk to the school administration or teachers. Ask them what programming or activities might tie in with school projects or curriculum. At very least, make them aware that many of the school's students frequent the library. Possible partnerships with the school may not be immediately apparent, but the first step is to get on their radar. This will help ensure the library is part of any grant or community initiative involving service to the students.

If you have on-site security, work closely with this security staff to develop strategies for managing the after-school hours. Review specific suggestions for working with security staff offered in chapter 2.

Keep managers and administrators informed about the situation. If you talk to school officials or teachers, make sure library decision makers are aware of steps you have taken to make the situation a win-win one for everyone.

Remember to keep the goal of healthy youth development at the top of everyone's list when developing strategies.

Work with the teens. Develop relationships with any willing teens and use these teens as active partners in managing the situation. Ask for their suggestions and implement any that you can. Review the steps for setting up a teen advisory group offered in chapter 6 and work to establish some form as an advisory group to help guide you and your staff through the situation.

Questions to Ask when Developing Partnerships

- Why are you partnering with this community institution?
- What are the potential benefits for partnering?

- Do you already share overlapping markets with these potential partners?
- How is the audience your partner is likely to reach different from the audience you are already reaching?
- Does the partner's mission align with the library's mission?
- What will the final product look like?
- What are your partner's assets?
- What are your partner's liabilities?
- What resources will each partner bring to the table?
- How do these resources complement one another?
- Are there any historical tensions between your organizations?
- What are the political connections of each?
- What is the common goal?
- How is the partnership increasing the strength of each institution's teen programs?
- How is the partnership contributing to the safety net for youth in the community?
- What are the specific benefits for the library?
- How will the partnership be financially supported?
- How do the corporate cultures of each partner compare?
- Are there any political pressures affecting the partnership?
- Who will make decisions?
- Have the key responsibilities been assigned? These responsibilities may include outreach/marketing, recruitment, programming, evaluation, facilities, technical support, hosting of digital content, content creation, and overall project management.
- Have all library staff likely to be affected by the grant been brought into the discussions?
- Have you taken the library's partnership temperature for serving teens? That is, how does the library rate in key partnership areas: available resources, staff support, accessibility, responsiveness?
- Does the partnering agency already offer programs specifically designed for teens?

WORKING WITH SCHOOLS

No library service to teens in urban areas is complete without a concerted effort to reach out to and build effective partnerships with schools. However, building these partnerships is often easier said than done. Most urban areas have multiple school districts, including public schools, private schools, charter schools, and an array of alternative schools. Often, these school districts have different schedules, different rules, and different ways of operating.

One key component for developing partnerships with schools in this complex environment is having a plan, always keeping in mind the key question, "How does this benefit the school?" If the benefits to the school in any partnership or outreach proposal cannot be explained clearly and understandably in just a few words, busy teachers and administrators are not likely to be interested.

Start by developing a list of all schools in your area. Assign the maintenance of this list to a specific staff member or, in a multibranch system, to a specific department or division. In urban environments, the location and age range of students served by individual schools changes, often on a yearly basis. Keeping the list complete and updated must be a priority. Post the list on an intranet or collaborative Web site and allow authorized staff to update the list whenever they become aware of a change.

Make sure all staff are aware of existing services offered to middle and high school teachers. Promote and highlight special teacher services such as teachers' cards with special privileges (e.g., no or reduced late fees) and collections of books teachers can order for their classrooms. Be as flexible as possible in offering these services, particularly in gathering sets of books. It would be helpful if teachers gave ample notice to librarians about their upcoming needs, but they often do not. Librarians must do their best to accommodate teachers' busy schedules. Although it is difficult to deal with a teacher who continually makes last-minute requests, if you are to be successful in partnering with schools, you must consistently send the message that librarians are indeed partners in supporting teachers' needs.

Concentrate on a few schools or school districts at a time. Although all schools should be made aware of services, librarians do not have time every year to visit every school. Develop a long-term plan that rotates priority from school to school every year.

If at first you do not succeed, try, try again. Some districts are bottom up, others top down. The same approach may not work everywhere. At some schools, the principal makes all the decisions. You may even be offered a chance to speak in front of a school board. At other schools, teachers and school media specialists are the best contacts. Be persistent and keep track of what works with each school or school district. If the current principal or a particular teacher is not interested in partnering, try again after that person moves on to another position.

Avoid frustration. If you have given it your best shot with a school or school district and your persistence has not paid off, move on to another school. In urban areas, there are plenty of schools in need of your service. Often, once one school begins to see the benefits of working with the library, other schools become convinced that partnering with the library is worth the time and effort.

EXAMPLES OF SUCCESSFUL PARTNERSHIPS

Here is a selective list of successful partnerships developed by libraries in urban areas. Some of these examples may no longer be active or may have changed in other ways, but all demonstrate the significant impact that well-planned and innovative partnerships can have for libraries in urban environments. Many of these partnerships are nationally recognized, award-winning projects; they offer ideas for design, funding, and nontraditional potential partners.

AFTER-SCHOOL PROGRAM: AFTER SCHOOL IS COOL

Description: At-risk teens are offered activities and homework help by teen program assistants during the after-school hours.

Partners: Denver Public Library, Robert R. McCormick Tribune Foundation, Denver Post.

Source: Urban Libraries Council, *Highsmith Award of Excellence*.

ASPIRE: AFTER-SCHOOL PROGRAMS INSPIRE READING ENRICHMENT

Description: Homework-help program geared toward at-risk students in grades 5 through 9.

Partners: Houston Public Library; various private corporations and foundations provide funding.

Source: Chelton 2000.

BILLBOARD AD CONTEST

Description: Library-card campaign featuring competition for middle and high school students to design a billboard.

Partners: Boston Public Library, Boston Public School System.
Source: Chelton 1994.

BITS AND BYTES TECH TEAM ASSISTANT PROGRAM

Description: Teens are employed as technology trainers, offering help to other customers at library branches.
Partners: Free Library of Philadelphia, William Penn Foundation (funding through a Model Urban Library Services for Children grant).
Source: Chelton 2000; Urban Libraries Council, *Highsmith Award of Excellence.*

BORN TO READ

Description: Designed to help the city's large number of teen mothers support the early development of their infant children.
Partners: San Antonio Public Library, Metropolitan Health District Women, Infants, and Children (program sites), Texas State Library (funding), U.S. Department of Education (funding), the Edge Partnership (public relations).
Source: San Antonio Public Library, *Born to Read.*

BUILDING BLOCKS TO LITERACY: AN INTERGENERATION LITERACY PROGRAM FOR TEEN PARENTS AND THEIR BABIES

Description: Designed to help teen parents teach their young children early literacy skills.
Partners: Dekalb County (Georgia) Public Library.
Source: Chelton 1994.

CHANGING LIVES THROUGH LITERATURE

Description: An alternative-sentencing literature discussion program for teens. The program brings together teen probationers, their probation officers, and one judge for librarian-facilitated discussions about fiction.
Partners: Johnson County (Kansas) Library, Johnson County Corrections Department, Johnson County District Court, Johnson County Community College.
Source: Institute of Museum and Library Services 2005.

GIRL CULTURE PHOTO EXHIBIT

Description: Photo exhibit dealing with female body image housed at Trinity Episcopal Cathedral; accompanying programming and discussions held at various locations, including libraries.

Partners: Trinity Episcopal Cathedral, Junior League of Cleveland, YWCA of Greater Cleveland, Cuyahoga County (Ohio) Public Library, Case Western Reserve, and others.

Source: Partnerships Advocating for Teens Committee 2006.

GREAT TRANSITIONS: STRUGGLE, CHANGE, ACHIEVE

Description: Offers incarcerated teenagers, age 12 to 17, access to library resources and services.

Partners: Hennepin County (Minnesota) Library, Hennepin County Home School, Minneapolis Public Library, Hennepin County Juvenile Probation.

Source: Chelton 2000.

HOMEWORK CENTERS

Description: Homework centers in all branches, the central library, and area satellite sites specializing in helping young people complete homework assignments.

Partners: Program offered at the San Diego Public Library, recreation centers, YMCAs, Girls and Boys Clubs, area housing complexes.

Source: Chelton 1994.

HOMEWORK HELP

Description: Sites in branch libraries, schools, parks and recreation facilities, public housing complexes, and a variety of other community centers where tutors help students with homework, preparing for tests, and improving reading, math, and study skills.

Partners: Tucson-Pima (Arizona) Public Library, various city organizations, and members of the city manager's task force for youth, teachers, college students.

Source: Public Libraries as Partners in Youth Development 1999; Urban Libraries Council, *Highsmith Award of Excellence.*

HOMEWORKNYC.ORG

Description: Collaborative Web site offering links to resources and providing students the opportunity to connect with a librarian by phone, e-mail, or chat in a variety of languages.

Partners: Brooklyn Public Library, New York Public Library, Queens Library, New York City Department of Education, the Wallace Foundation (funding through a leadership grant).

Source: *School Library Journal's Extra Helpings* (Lau Whelan 2006).

LEAP AHEAD

Description: Outreach program designed to offer traditional library services and programs to teens who spend part or all of their adolescence in residential institutions.

Partners: Cuyahoga County (Ohio) Public Library.

Source: Chelton 1994.

MATH PEERS TUTORING

Description: After-school program for middle and high school students that utilizes peer tutors for one-on-one help with math in a relaxed atmosphere.

Partners: Brooklyn (New York) Public Library, Brooklyn area high schools.

Source: Public Libraries as Partners in Youth Development 1999; Urban Libraries Council, *Highsmith Award of Excellence.*

PASS!: PARTNERS FOR ACHIEVING
SCHOOL SUCCESS

Description: Paid older teen mentors work with elementary-age students and younger middle schoolers to provide homework help and assistance in independent reading and studying skills.

Partners: Oakland (California) Public Library, local school district, community-based youth employment agency, area teenagers, Oakland Public Library Foundation (funding).

Source: Chelton 2000.

POETRY IN THE BRANCHES

Description: Poetry workshops and programs for teens age 12 to 18.

Partners: New York Public Library, Poets House, area poetry presenters.

Source: Chelton 1997.

POWER LIBRARY: BRANCH LIBRARY iN THE CLUB

Description: Encourages club members and their families to read a story together and to record the experience. Parents or grandparents retell the story in Spanish or Navajo.

Partners: The Farmington (New Mexico) Public Library, Boys and Girls Club of Farmington, Mayor's Teen Advisory Council, Farmington *Daily Times,* San Juan County Partnership for Mothers Against Drunk Driving, Head Start Center at San Juan College, Shiprock Medical Center/San Juan Regional Medical Center for a Books for Babies project.

Source: Library of Congress 2004.

PROJECT HORIZON

Description: Deposit collections provided for homeless families at area shelters.

Partners: DeKalb (Georgia) Public Library, funded through Department of Education (McKinney Homeless Assistance Act), coalition of shelters and organizations.

Source: Urban Libraries Council, *Highsmith Award of Excellence.*

RAP: READ ALOUD PROGRAM

Description: Male high school students serve as read-aloud partners for elementary school boys.

Partners: Chicago Public Library, DuSable High School, Chicago Children's Museum.

Source: Chelton 1994.

THE RED CARD: LIBRARY CARD SIGN-UP CAMPAIGN

Description: Comprehensive library card campaign using a wildlife theme targeted to all students and resulting in record numbers of new card registrations for kids and teenagers.

Partners: Public Library of Cincinnati (Ohio) and Hamilton County, Cincinnati Zoo and Botanical Garden, area schools.

Source: John Cotton Dana Library Public Relations Awards.

SOCIAL WORKER AT TEEN CENTRAL

Description: Caseworker was provided to Teen Central to help teens who needed assistance with issues beyond the scope of library resources or staff.

Partners: Phoenix (Arizona) Public Library, City of Phoenix Human Services Department.

Source: Kendall 2003.

TAP: TEEN AGENCY PROGRAM

Description: Teens painted a public transportation bus to advertise the library, promote reading, and raise awareness of the variety of ethnic groups using libraries.

Partners: Albany Park and Douglass Branches (Chicago Public Library), two area high schools, Chicago Police Department, Chicago Transit Authority, Chicago Public Art Group.

Source: Chelton 1997.

TEEN ENRICHMENT INITIATIVE

Description: Funded through a Juvenile Justice grant, the Laurelton branch of the Queens Borough (New York) Public Library focused on giving teens life skills, including tips for interviewing and basic computer skills. On-site youth counselor created programs, while mentoring them, that engage young adults, and a contracted social worker was on-site part-time to handle referrals as needed.

Partners: Queens Borough Public Library, Queens District Attorney's Office's Second Chance.

Source: *School Library Journal*, Ishizuka 2003.

TEEN PARENT PROJECT

Description: Workshops were created and presented that focused on helping new teen parents learn the value of reading, the library, and other life skills. Offered at the library and other community sites, including a shelter for runaways.

Partners: Fresno County (California) Public Library, University Medical Center, Fresno Unified School District Parent and Child Education Program (PACE).

Source: Vaillancourt 2004.

TIM O'BRIEN'S *The Things They Carried*

Description: Prior to live performances of Tim O'Brien's novel, adapted for the stage by the American Place Theater's Literature to Life program, libraries hosted the author at several locations and held many book discussions.

Partners: Cuyahoga County (Ohio) Public Library, Cleveland Public Library, Playhouse Square Foundation, American Place Theater's Literature to Life program.

Source: Partnerships Advocating for Teens Committee. 2006.

YOUTH CONNECTION

Description: Offers resources on teen crisis topics, including enhanced collections in these areas, programming at schools and libraries on selected topics, and kits to be used by families and community groups serving teens.

Partners: Toledo-Lucas County (Ohio) Public Library, Health Department, Alcohol and Drug Rehabilitation, area churches, Planned Parenthood, United Way.

Source: Chelton 1997.

WORKS CITED

Chelton, Mary K. 1994. *Excellence in Library Services to Young Adults: The Nation's Top Programs, 1st Edition.* Chicago: American Library Association

Chelton, Mary K. 1997. *Excellence in Library Services to Young Adults: The Nation's Top Programs, 2nd Edition.* Chicago: American Library Association.

Chelton, Mary K. 2000. *Excellence in Library Services to Young Adults: The Nation's Top Programs, 3rd Edition*. Chicago: American Library Association.

Forum for Youth Investment. 2005. *When School Is Out, Museums, Parks and Libraries Are In: Out-of-School Time Policy Commentary* (9).

Institute of Museum and Library Services. 2005. *NLG Project Planning: A Tutorial*. Accessed May 15, 2006, available at http://www.imls.gov/project%5Fplanning/.

Ishizuka, Kathy. 2003. "NY Library Gives Teens a Second Chance." *School Library Journal* 9 (November). Accessed August 30, 2007, available at http://www.schoollibraryjournal.com/article/CA332681.html.

John Cotton Dana Library Public Relations Award. Accessed August 30, 2007, available at http://www.worldmusicians.com/jcdawards/jcdwin2006.htm.

Jones, Patrick. 2002. *New Directions for Library Service to Young Adults*. Chicago: American Library Association.

Jones, Patrick, Michele Gorman, and Tricia Suellentrop. 2004. *Connecting Young Adults and Libraries*. New York: Neal-Schuman.

Kendall, Karl. 2003. "Teen Central: Safe Structured, and Teen-Friendly." *Voice of Youth Advocates* 26 (5) (December): 380–81.

Lau Whelan, Debra. 2006. "HomeworkNYC.org Offers Kids a Helping Hand." *School Library Journal's Extra Helpings* (January 18). Accessed August 25, 2006, available at http://www.schoollibraryjournal.com/article/CA6299958.html.

Library of Congress. 2004. "12 Family Literacy Projects Receive Support from the Center for the Book at the Library of Congress," press release, July 6. Accessed July 31, 2006, available at http://www.loc.gov/today/pr/2004/04-129.html.

Partnerships Advocating for Teens Committee. 2006. "Power Partnerships…Some Examples." Young Adult Library Services Association handout, American Library Association annual conference, New Orleans, LA, June.

"Public Libraries as Partners in Youth Development." 1999. *Wallace Foundation Report*. Alexandria, VA: DeWitt-Wallace Reader's Digest Fund.

San Antonio Public Library. *Born to Read: A Guide for Teen Mothers*. Accessed August 30, 2007, available at http://www.sat.lib.tx.us/html/bornto.htm.

Urban Libraries Council. *Highsmith Award of Excellence*. Accessed May 6, 2006, available at http://www.urbanlibraries.org/highsmithaward.html.

Vaillancourt, Renee. 2004. *Excellence in Library Services to Young Adults: The Nation's Top Programs, 4th Edition*. Chicago: American Library Association.

Walker, Chris, and Carlos A. Manjarrez. 2003. *Partnerships for Free Choice Learning: Public Libraries, Museums and Public Broadcasters Working Together*. Chicago: The Urban Institute & Urban Libraries Council.

Yohalem, Nicole, and Karen Pittman. 2003. "Public Libraries as Partners in Youth Development: Lessons and Voices from the Field." *The Forum for Youth Investment*. Accessed November 23, 2007, available at http://www.urbanlibraries.org/files/PLPYDreport_FINAL.pdf.

FURTHER READING

California State Library. 2001. *Joint Ventures: The Promise, Power, and Performance of Partnering.* Accessed June 3, 2006, available at http://www.library.ca.gov/assets/acrobat/JointVentures.pdf.

Crowther, Janet L., and Barry Trott. 2004. *Partnering with Purpose: A Guide to Strategic Partnership Development for Libraries and Other Organizations.* Westport, CT: Libraries Unlimited.

Institute for Museum and Library Services. (no date) *Perspectives on Outcome Based Evaluation for Libraries and Museums.* Washington, DC: Institute of Museum and Library Services. Accessed November 24, 2007, available at http://www.imls.gov/pdf/pubobe.pdf.

Jones, Jami. 2005. "Power of Partnerships." *School Library Journal* 51 (May): 33.

Kohm, Amelia, and Sunil Garg. 1998. *Exploring the Scope of Primary Supports in an Urban Area.* Chicago: Chapin Hall Center for Children at the University of Chicago.

Madenski, Melissa. 2001. "Books Behind Bars." *School Library Journal* 47 (July): 40–42.

"Partners in Anticrime." 2005 *Library Journal, Movers & Shakers 2005* 130 (March 15). Accessed July 13, 2006, available at http://www.libraryjournal.com/article/CA510771.html.

Walters, Virginia, and Elaine Meyers. 2003. *Teens and Libraries: Getting It Right.* Chicago: American Library Association.

CONCLUSION

During summer 1999 while working as a youth services librarian for the Kansas City (Missouri) Public Library, I was fortunate enough to attend the Library Leadership Institute at Snowbird (Utah). I met many excellent librarians there, including Jane Chamberlain, who was at the time working at the Bloomington Public Library in Illinois. Sitting next to Jane at dinner one evening, I began to tell her about an idea I had for an elaborate teen program. I also launched into an extensive discussion of all the reasons I could not possibly make the program a reality. Midway through my explanation, Jane held up her hand and said, "You know, if you wait until everything is perfect to do this, trust me, you will never get it done. Nothing is ever perfect. If you want to do it and you think it is important, figure out a way to do it and get it done."

I have held on to Jane's words of wisdom for nearly a decade and still use them as inspiration more than I would care to admit when working to enhance and expand public library service to teens in urban areas. Librarians and library staff members who care about our community's young people cannot wait to push for more services to teens until budgets have increased, staff positions are readily available, and everything is perfect. Budgets will always be tight. Additional staff will continue to be scarce or nonexistent. As a librarian or library staff member serving teens in an urban area, you have a tremendous opportunity to be a positive influence in a teenager's life. I hope this resource guide has given you a foundation for understanding the needs of teen library customers in urban areas and ideas for how to effectively address those needs. Now it is up to you to translate your new knowledge into action and results for the important teen customers you serve. Or, as Jane told me, "figure out a way to do it and get it done."

APPENDIX: TEEN SERVICES IN URBAN LIBRARIES SURVEY

How many branches are in your library system? How many do you consider urban?

What is the range of sizes of your urban locations? What is the range of sizes of your nonurban locations?

Do you have staff in your urban locations who have a specific portion of their job duties dedicated to serving teens? If so, at how many urban locations do you have these staff? Does their job title specifically include teen services? Are these staff members required to have an MLS?

If not, you do not have dedicated teen services staff that delivers teen services (children's librarian, youth services librarian, branch managers, or someone else)?

At how many of your urban locations are teen programs regularly offered? At those locations, how many per month?

Do your urban locations have designated teen spaces? Is it a separate space? Relative to the overall size of each location, how large is teen space? Do these spaces include more than just shelving for books? If so, what else is offered?

Do you offer staff training on serving teens? If so, to whom is this training offered and is it required or optional?

What types of materials are typically contained in your teen collections? Are there types of materials included in your urban locations that are not typically found at your nonurban locations (e.g., manga, CDs, DVDs, magazines)?

What kind of technology is available to teens in your urban locations?

Do you often partner with community agencies when offering programs and services at your urban locations? If so, with what types of agencies do you frequently partner?

Are visits to schools or other community locations a regular part of your teen services in urban areas?

Do you have teen volunteers at your urban locations?

Would you be willing to provide tours of teen spaces at your urban locations and describe the service you provide to teens? If so, please include your name, location, and contact information.

This survey was informally distributed to several libraries assumed to be serving teens in urban areas. Sixteen responses were received.

INDEX

About the Author

 PAULA BREHM-HEEGER has worked in public libraries of all sizes in a variety of cities and states for more than fifteen years and has also served as President of the Young Adult Library Services Association. A frequent presenter and speaker at library conferences, Brehm-Heeger never misses a chance to advocate on behalf of young adults and to speak out about the need to provide outstanding library service to all teens.